The Genesis of Artistic Creativity

Asperger's Syndrome and the Arts

Michael Fitzgerald

Jessica Kingsley Publishers.
London and Philadelphia

First published in 2005
by Jessica Kingsley Publishers
116 Pentonville Road
London N1 9JB, UK
and
400 Market Street, Suite 400
Philadelphia, PA 19106, USA

www.jkp.com

Library of Congress Cataloging in Publication Data

Fitzgerald, Michael, 1946-
    The genesis of artistic creativity : Asperger's syndrome and the arts / Michael Fitzgerald.
        p. cm.
    Includes bibliographical references and index.
    ISBN-13: 978-1-84310-334-9 (pbk.)
    ISBN-10: 1-84310-334-6 (pbk.)
    1. Asperger's syndrome. 2. Autism. 3. Artists—Psychology. 4. Authors—Psychology. 5.
Philosophers—Psychology. 6. Creation (Literary, artistic, etc.)—Psychological aspects. 7.
Creative ability—Psychological aspects. 8. Genius and mental illness. 9. Art and mental
illness. I. Title.
    RC533.A88F55 2005
    616.85'8832—dc22

                                                                            2005001022

British Library Cataloguing in Publication Data
A CIP catalogue record for this book is available from the British Library

ISBN 978 1 84310 334 9

Printed and Bound in Great Britain by
Athenaeum Press, Gateshead, Tyne and Wear

Contents

Acknowledgements

I am particularly grateful to Mr Brendan O'Brien for his editorial work on this book. Ms Ellen Cranley was extremely patient and helpful (as always) in typing repeated drafts. I had useful discussions with David Berman, Viktoria Lyons, Antoinette Walker, Mark Bellgrove, Michael Gill, Maria Lawlor, Jerry Harper, Ioan James and Muhammad Arshad. I am grateful to Mr Pat Matthews (President of the World Autism Association), the Irish Society for Autism, and many parents of children with autism as well as persons with autism/Asperger's syndrome who have educated me for the past 30 years.

The librarians at Trinity College Dublin, particularly Ms Virginia McLoughlin and Mr Joe O'Brien, were most helpful. I am also grateful to the library of the Royal College of Surgeons in Ireland. I would like to thank Ms Frances Brennan and the staff at the Ballyfermot Child and Family Centre, and Mr Michael Walsh of the Northern Area Health Board. I am grateful to Jessica Kingsley for commissioning this book. I would like to thank my wife Frances and three sons Owen, Mark and Robert for their support during the writing of this book and for giving me the time to write it.

The author and publisher gratefully acknowledge the permission granted to reproduce the copyright material in this book.

Extracts in Chapter 2 from *Hans Christian Anderson: The Life of a Storyteller* by Jackie Wullschlager (Allen Lane The Penguin Press). Copyright © Jackie Wullschlager, 2000. Used by permission of The Penguin Group (UK).

Extracts in Chapter 2 from *Hans Christian Anderson: The Life of a Storyteller* by Jackie Wullschlager. Copyright © 2000 by Jackie Wullschlager. Used by permission of Alfred A. Knopf, a division of Random House, Inc.

Extracts in Chapter 4 from *Lewis Carroll: A Biography* by Morton N. Cohen. Copyright © Morton N. Cohen 1995. Used by permission of Macmillan, London, UK and A P Watt Ltd on behalf of Morton N. Cohen.

Extracts in Chapter 7 from *Orwell* by Jeffrey Meyers, edited by AVL. Copyright © 2000 by Jeffrey Meyers. Used by permission of W. W. Norton & Company, Inc.

Extracts in Chapter 8 from *Bruce Chatwin: A Biography* by Nicholas Shakespeare, published by Jonathan Cape. Reprinted by permission of The Random House Group Ltd.

Extracts in Chapter 8 from *Bruce Chatwin: A Biography* by Nicholas Shakespeare. Copyright © Nicholas Shakespeare 1999. Used by permission of Gillon Aitken Associates.

INTRODUCTION

Asperger's Syndrome and Artistic Creativity

AUTISM WAS FIRST described by Leo Kanner in 1943. Kanner noted the profound withdrawal from contact with people, an obsessive desire for the preservation of sameness, a skilful relation to objects, the retention of an intelligent and pensive physiognomy, and either mutism or the kind of language that does not seem intended to serve the purpose of interpersonal communication. (Kanner 1943)

In 1943 Hans Asperger independently described a condition similar to that which Kanner described (Asperger 1944). Kanner wrote of 'autistic disturbances of affective contact'; Asperger wrote of 'autistic psychopathy'. The terms 'high-functioning autism' (HFA) and 'Asperger's syndrome' are mainly used interchangeably in this book, though differences are pointed out where relevant. Both are on the autistic spectrum; indeed, it is possible to be diagnosed with autism at one point in one's life and with Asperger's syndrome at another.

When first put forward, the idea of an association between autism and *artistic* creativity may seem a contradiction in terms. In autism and Asperger's syndrome (which is at the high-functioning end of the autistic spectrum), creativity is usually associated with mathematics, physics and engineering, rather than the various branches of the arts. To explain this apparent contradiction is not an easy task; indeed, at this stage the association cannot be explained fully. Nonetheless, it is possible to make a start.

To begin with, certain aspects of Asperger's syndrome – e.g. 'workaholism' and an extraordinary capacity for persistence – can accompany many forms of creativity. Persons with Asperger's syndrome live very much in their intellects, and certain forms of creativity benefit greatly from intellectual interests: for example, George Orwell's novels are tremendously focused on intellectual issues. The 'Asperger' ability to focus narrowly on a topic and resist distraction is enormously important.

Hans Asperger had noted a disturbance in social relationships: 'the fundamental disorder of autistic individuals is the limitation of their social relationships'. In addition he identified communication difficulties, with 'abnormalities in the language of autistic individuals'. He also identified narrow interests and repetitive activities – 'special interests', 'abnormal fixations' and 'stereotypic movements'. He noted associated food fads and unusual reactions to sensory sensations, for example tactile and sound, as well as problems with attention. He was particularly taken with autistic intelligence, but nevertheless stated that the people in question had 'all levels of ability from the highly original genius…to the…mentally retarded individual'.

Lorna Wing (1981) renamed autistic psychopathy 'Asperger's syndrome', and emphasized the following issues in people displaying this syndrome:

- a lack of normal interest and pleasure in people around them

- a reduction in the quality and quantity of babbling [in infants]

- a significant reduction in shared interests

- a significant reduction in the wish to communicate verbally or non-verbally

- a delay in speech acquisition, and impoverishment of content

- no imaginative play, or imaginative play confined to one or two rigid patterns.

Asperger noted that, unlike other children who struggled to progress from mechanical learning to original thought, the children he was describing were capable only of forming their own strategies. They could not, or did not, follow those used by their teachers. The originality of the people concerned is what this book is about.

In 1962 van Krevelen and Kuipers discussed Asperger's autistic psychopathology and emphasized the 'personal unapproachability' and the inability 'to distinguish between dream and reality'. They pointed out that 'the eye roams, evades and is turned inwards. The speech is stilted, it is not addressed to the person but into the empty space…it sounds false owing to exaggerated inflection'. They identified a lack of 'child-likeness…being old-fashioned in word and gesture'.

Persons with Asperger's syndrome show signs of an original intelligence. They also develop their own methods. When they are gifted – and this is not infrequently the case – they are often characterized by specific interests. Their schoolmates' play does not appeal to them. They are tied to solitary pursuits. Accordingly, they read much, anything they can lay hands on; they often develop a veritable mania for reading (van Krevelen and Kuipers 1962).

Tantam (1991) talks about 'people with Asperger's syndrome who make up stories, imaginary words or imaginary play comparisons', and states that when people with Asperger's syndrome 'act a part on the stage, they have difficulty in infusing it with a character other than their own'. A number of people in this book illustrate this point. Lorna Wing points out that 'recognising patterns within this bewildering complexity is akin to classifying clouds'.

A number of authors have subsequently suggested diagnostic criteria, but the six proposed by Gillberg (1991) are among the most useful descriptions of Asperger's syndrome that I have found:

- social impairments

- narrow interests

- repetitive routines

- speech and language problems

- non-verbal communication problems

- motor clumsiness.

I will use these criteria throughout this book to assess whether the various creative people under discussion may have had Asperger's syndrome. I will also refer to the American Psychiatric Association's criteria for 'Asperger's disorder' published in the *Diagnostic and Statistical Manual of Mental Disorders* (DSM-IV: APA 1994). The main DSM-IV criteria are:

- impairment in social interaction

- restricted, repetitive patterns of behaviour, interests and activities

- resulting clinically significant impairment in social, occupational or other functioning.

DSM-IV diagnosis does not require any significant delay in language skills or cognitive development, nor any lack of childhood curiosity about the environment. Motor clumsiness is an associated feature that is often observed.

According to Iles (1906), an inventor

> must have more than the patience of Job, more than the perseverance of the beaver, more than the industry of the bee. He must work hard, and be content to work for months at a time without making any progress. He must be content to travel over the same field again and again and indefatigably.

This is equally relevant to artistic creativity.

Creative artists must have extraordinary levels of energy and motivation, and a tremendous capacity for observation and concentration (thus Mozart could concentrate on his ideas in circumstances that others would have found distracting). They must have a vast curiosity and be driven to understand the world in an artistic way, and also to rebel and go against the orthodox artistic mode of expression of their time. Indeed, they are often contemptuous of the artistic mode of expression of their day. Their contemporaries often perceive them to be arrogant, egocentric and narcissistic. This applies to many of the artists described in this book. It is not true to state that persons with Asperger's syndrome have no imagination: indeed, they have vast imagination of the autistic type. They are very commonly discontented and conflicted.

Anthony Storr (1988) made a very important link between discontent and imagination: '...man's extraordinary success as a species springs from his discontent, which compels him to employ his imagination...discontent, therefore, may be considered adaptive because it encourages the use of the imagination, and thus spurs men on to further conquests' (and, one could add, to artistic mastery of their environment). Storr also points out that

> if, unlike Freud, we assume that an inner imaginative world is part of man's biological endowment, and that man's success as a species has depended upon it, we can see that we should not merely strive to replace fantasy by reason, as Freud would have us do. Instead, we should use our capacity for fantasy to build bridges between the inner world of the imagination and the external world.

This is precisely what the great artist with Asperger's syndrome achieves. In the past, psychoanalysts have attempted to understand the individuals in this book via classical psychoanalysis, with minimal success. Classical psychoanalysis does not explain a developmental disorder such as Asperger's syndrome, where hereditary factors play the major part.

Steptoe (1998) notes that, while Freudian thought has reinforced the notion that artistic expression is a product of unrealized psychic conflict, and of dark forces that defy logical analysis,

> [m]odern creativity researchers have described the artistic personality as hypersensitive, aggressive, autonomous, and independent, preoccupied with work to the exclusion of social activity, intolerant of order and seeking novelty and change, suffused with intense but chaotic emotions, and opposed to the conventional and banal.

The idea of all artistic expression being explained by 'unrealised psychic conflict' is grossly reductionistic; it trivializes creativity and explains only a very minor proportion of artistic expression.

Persons with Asperger's syndrome have problems with autobiographical memory; they also have difficulty in understanding themselves and others. Nevertheless, the high intellectual level of philosophers with Asperger's syndrome allows them to produce what they see as a kind of detached philosophy independent of their personal socio-emotional history. Though, of course, this is impossible to achieve fully. The problems that philosophers with Asperger's syndrome (e.g. Wittgenstein, Kant, Spinoza and William Quine) experienced with autobiographical memory appear to have helped them in terms of recognition by other philosophers.

The psychopathology of genius

The *Oxford English Dictionary* defines genius as 'native intellectual power of an exalted type, such as is attributed to those who are esteemed greatest in any department of art, speculation or practice; instinctive and extraordinary capacity for imaginative creation, original thought, inventions, or discovery. Often contrasted with talent.' It also states that talent is 'frequently, skill cultivated by effort, as opposed to genius'. Clearly, talent and genius are two different things.

According to Gregory (1987),

> it is necessary to consider the idea that genius and madness are closely allied. It is not true, of course, that great poets, painters, scientists, and mathematicians are mad; far from it. On the other hand, it may well be that they work as intensely and imaginatively as they do in order to remain sane; but they have access to aspects of the mind's functioning from which those who live more staid and conventional lives are excluded, and that it is this access which gives their work both its flair and its sense of risk.

Seneca stated that 'no great genius has ever existed without some touch of madness'. Shakespeare wrote in *A Midsummer Night's Dream* that 'the lunatic, the lover, and the poet/Are of imagination all compact'. Similarly, John Dryden wrote that 'Great Wits are sure to Madness near alli'd/And thin Partitions do their Bounds divide'. When the question was raised as to why there is no tradition of happy genius in Western culture, the philosopher Raymond Klibansky replied: 'Could a happy man have written *Hamlet?*' (Murray 1989).

Simonton (1994) asks whether psychopathology is the cost of greatness, and suggests that, for certain kinds of greatness, a form of psychopathology (e.g. Asperger's syndrome, as addressed in this book) is very helpful. Sigmund Freud stated that an artist is not far removed from neurosis. Indeed, as Gregory notes above, it may not be that the activity of geniuses drives them mad, but that they carry out this activity in order to remain sane. Persons with Asperger's syndrome are more likely to become suicidally depressed when they have a creative work block.

Temple Grandin (1995) has stated that 'it is likely that genius is an abnormality'. However, Grandin believes that autistic intelligence is necessary in order to add diversity and creativity to the world: 'It is possible that persons with bits of these traits are more creative, are possibly even geniuses... If science eliminated these genes, maybe the whole world would be taken over by accountants.'

Persons with Asperger's syndrome and genius are very often concerned about immortality, or about dying before they have achieved their potential. This gives their creative work a sense of urgency. Grandin (1995) remarks:

> I have read that libraries are where immortality lies... I don't want my thoughts to die with me... I want to have done something... I am not interested in power, or piles of money. I want to leave something behind. I want to make a positive contribution – know that my life has meaning. Right now, I am talking about things that are the very core of my existence.

Howe (1999) points out that for Immanuel Kant 'genius was an incommunicable gift that cannot be taught or handed on, but is mysteriously imparted to certain artists by nature, and dies with the person'. I would contend that it might be passed on in part, but rarely in full.

The mystery of creativity and the awesome nature of genius remain to be fully explained.

Autistic intelligence: Genes versus environment

Howard Gardner (1997) proposed the following 'initial list' of intelligences: linguistic and logical; spatial; musical; bodily kinaesthetic; and two forms of personal intelligence – one oriented towards the understanding of other persons, the other towards an understanding of self. This contribution had enormous impact, because people had become aware of the gross limitations of standard IQ testing. As we shall see in this book, 'autistic intelligence' can be linguistic, spatial, musical or logical. Oliver Sacks (1995) notes that Gardner 'postulates a multitude of separate and separable intelligences – visual, musical, lexical etc. – all of them autonomous and independent, with their own powers of apprehending regularities and structures in each cognitive domain, their own "rules", and probably their own verbal bases'.

Hans Asperger (1944) wrote about 'autistic intelligence' and saw it as a sort of intelligence hardly touched by tradition and culture – 'unconventional, unorthodox, strangely "pure" and original, akin to the intelligence of true creativity'. Such pure intelligence can be found in the descriptions of many of the people studied in this book. It is an intelligence that often does not show itself in school: indeed, W.B. Yeats, Ludwig Wittgenstein and George Orwell, all of whom had Asperger's syndrome, did poorly academically at school. Furthermore, Gregory (1987) states that:

> it has been found, time and again, that those who display great originality as adults were often like Charles Darwin only mediocre as students. British scientists who become Fellows of the Royal Society show roughly the same distribution of good, mediocre, and poor degree results as those who go into research but achieve little. The same holds for intelligence test scores: above a surprisingly low level, there is little or no relationship between IQ and achievement in any sphere of adult endeavour yet studied. As a result, we would expect future Nobel Prize winners to show roughly the same distribution of IQ scores as their fellow students at university. In the American context, the budding scientist of high renown seems typically to be a B+ student: one who works hard when a topic captures his (or her) imagination, but otherwise does the bare minimum. Science springs to life for such individuals when they discover that instead of assimilating knowledge created by others, they can create knowledge for themselves – and are hooked from that moment onwards.

Nevertheless, creative genius probably requires an IQ of 120 or more on standardized tests. Cox (1926), in a discussion of psychometry and historiometry, investigated the intelligence of historical characters 'by the application to historical data of the criteria of standardized measures of the mental ability of children'. Estimated IQs of persons with Asperger's syndrome include Thomas Jefferson 145, Immanuel Kant 135, Michelangelo 145, Mozart 150, Spinoza 130, Jonathan Swift 125, Hans Christian Andersen 115. Clearly all these figures are very approximate. Nevertheless, reliability coefficients of the data are available, and there were a number of raters.

In my book *Autism and Creativity* (2004) I noted that the innate aetiology of the artistic genius of persons with Asperger's cannot be explained by their IQ. It may be associated with the package of genes that are associated with Asperger's syndrome. This is something that we are a long way from elucidating fully. We do not know how a 'package' of genes expresses itself through a work of artistic genius. Certainly the environment plays a very minor role.

Murray (1989) notes that

> we attribute the extraordinary quality of, for example, Mozart's music to the genius of its creator because we recognise that such works are not simply the product of learning, technique, or sheer hard work…no amount of analysis has yet been able to explain the capacities of those rare and gifted individuals who can produce creative work of lasting quality and value.

I agree with Cox (1926) that 'heredity sets limits' to achievement. Nonetheless, it is unusual to find more than one genius in a family. This is probably because the configuration of genes required to produce a genius comes together extremely rarely. Of course, siblings share only 50 per cent of their genes. Cox points out that

> it was known to the author of the greatest ideal republic that the ablest citizens in the state are the sons and daughters of the ablest parents. Plato was further aware that the transmission of physical and mental characteristics by heredity would not ensure the full realization of their possibilities in the individual.

I would agree with this, i.e. that nature is insufficient on its own without some nurture. Gardner (1997) states that

> the suggestive evidence for the brain basis of giftedness, as well as the evidence for a genetic component to IQ, makes it increasingly likely that all forms of giftedness have some biological basis. It is highly improbable that any amount of deliberate practice by ordinary people could bring them up to the level reached so quickly by a child prodigy or savant. Also with respect to the origins of giftedness, the common sense view turns out to be less of a myth than the psychologists' view.

I fully agree with this. Gardner goes on:

> Some traits that do not run in families may still be genetically transmit-
> ted according to a principle called emergenesis by which traits are
> passed on by a package of genes, but only if the entire package is trans-
> mitted. Part of the package does not result in part of the trait. The claim
> runs counter to standard models of behavioural genetics, according to
> which genetic traits must, by definition, run in families. According to
> the standard model, the concordance rate in non-identical pairs should
> be half that of identical pairs. However, some traits simply do not fit this
> model... The question is no longer whether genetic or environment
> factors determine behaviour, but how they interact. It is extremely
> unlikely that there is such a thing as a 'poetry gene' or a 'music gene',
> since complex human behaviours typically have a polygenic basis.

Lykken *et al.* (1992) describe the concept of emergenesis, an extreme form of
epitasis, in which a unique combination of genes may lead to qualitative shifts
in capacity or ability. I believe that

> genetic factors are likely to contribute not only to specific abilities, but
> also to traits such as persistence, the capacity to concentrate for
> extended periods, and curiosity about certain types of stimulation.
> These properties may in turn affect the individual's response to educa-
> tional stimulation and tuition. The result is a complex interplay
> between inherited traits and environmental factors, in which genetics
> may underpin exposure to nurturing social and physical appearance.
> (Fitzgerald 2004)

Lykken (1998) asks why, if the genius of certain men was prefigured in their
genes, it never manifested elsewhere in their lineage – 'the answer is, I think,
that genius consists of unique configurations of attributes that cannot be
transmitted in half helpings'. Feats of genius early in life would suggest
genetic factors. Lykken also states that

> most traits that are of psychological interest are metrical traits rather
> than binary characteristics, and vary continuously from person to
> person. They are similar to stature in being polygenic traits, which
> means they are determined by the combined activity of many polymor-
> phic genes. Stature is determined by the additive action of many differ-
> ent polymorphic genes.

A famous American racehorse, Secretariat, sired only one other top-class racehorse – Risen Star – out of over 400 foals. 'Although emergenic traits do not
"run in families", they are more likely to reappear in a carrier family than in a

random lineage. No doubt Risen Star's dam contributed key elements of the emergenic configuration' (Lykken 1998). An important example of such an emergenic class includes those people we call geniuses.

Gagne (1998) points out that 'the genotype imposes definite limits on the maximum attainable level of cognitive development', and that with prodigies, the

> ease of learning is the hallmark of natural abilities. It produces speed of learning which gives rise to precocious achievements. Prodigies are the tip of the iceberg, the most striking embodiment of giftedness, but below them are thousands of others who, even if less extremely gifted, show enough advance over their peers to be judged 'innately talented'.

Heller and Ziegler (1998) state that 'conservative figures in the field of behaviour genetics estimate the amount of variance explained by individual differences in personality and cognition to be about 50%'. Lykken (1998) notes that 'about half of the variance in measures of creativity has been shown by the Minnesota studies to derive from genetic variation'. Genius has higher genetic loading.

Plomin (1998) points out that genetic factors contribute significantly to cognitive abilities, and that

> genetics does not mean innate. Innate implies hard-wired, fixed action patterns of a species that are impervious to experience. Genetic influence on abilities and other complex traits does not denote the hard-wired deterministic effect of a single gene but rather probabilistic propensities of many genes in multiple-gene systems.

According to Simonton (1998),

> the most eminent and prolific composers – in terms of both annual rates and lifetime output – required less musical and compositional experience before they began to make lasting contributions to the classical repertoire. Thus, this study [Simonton 1991] seems to suggest that some musical talent can lead quickly to world-class levels of compositional expertise.

Howe (1999) also makes an extremely important point, which is much put forward by those who propound the environmental view of genius, i.e. that 'geniuses began their lives made from much the same basic materials as all the rest of us'. This book attempts to show that this view is absurd. The major reason why they are geniuses is that they began with *different* basic materials to the rest of us, i.e. the configuration of their genes was different.

Psychologists put enormous emphasis on the idea of ten years of training and 10,000 hours of practice. The vast majority of children in the world, if they were given four times this input, would not turn into a Mozart or produce works of similar standard to those of Mozart. Mozart's stimulatory musical family environment did not produce his genius but only introduced him to music. His sister was in the same stimulated family home but produced nothing like Wolfgang did. The combination of genes in his make-up was the important factor.

Howe (1999) claims that 'sophisticated inborn capabilities simply cannot exist'. In this book I have set out to show precisely the opposite – that inborn capabilities, indeed, are the key to understanding a genius such as either of the Yeats brothers or Mozart.

John Stuart Mill was a genius. Howe points out that

> Mill…was very conscious of the fact that the intellectual qualities he possessed had to a large extent been deliberately instilled in him by his father. 'Manufactured' was his own choice of word for this state of affairs…there is no other genius for whom the term 'manufactured' is quite as fitting as it is for Mill.

I don't agree that this is so, because his father was also a prodigy. Again the genes were highly significant.

'American cultural anthropology declared war on the idea that differences in culture derived from differences in innate capacity', and Alfred Kroeber asserted that 'heredity cannot be allowed to have acted any part in history' (Deglar 1991). Margaret Mead (1949) explicitly asserted the radical environ-mentalist philosophy when she stated that 'learned behaviours have replaced the biologically given ones'. She believed that cultural stereotypes, rather than innate genetic factors, play an important role. We now know that Mead's Samoan research was superficial and that her conclusions were based largely on innocent deceptions practised upon her by her young female Samoan informants (Freeman 1983).

Behaviourists tended to be radical 'environmentalists'. For example, John Broadus Watson, the founder of the behaviourism movement, wrote:

> …give a dozen healthy infants, well formed, and my own specified world to bring them up in and I will guarantee to take any one at random and train him to become any type of specialist I might select – doctor, lawyer, artist, merchant chief, and yes even beggar man and thief, regardless of his talents, penchants, tendencies, abilities, voca-tions, and the race of his ancestors. (Watson 1924)

This is simply absurd environmentalism.

Even more anti-individualistic is the Confucian view that all can be skilled, and that differences in skill reflect only effort and moral commitment, not any special talents. This is also absurd. St Francis Xavier (1506–52) declared 'give me the children until they are seven and anyone may have them afterwards' (Radford 1990). He was also incorrect (even though early care and education are important), as genetic factors play a greater role as a child gets older.

High-ability parents may pass on high abilities genetically and create enriched environments simply because they themselves have high ability. As Scar and McCartney (1983) have pointed out, the environment is not necessarily what acts on the child; rather, the child's genetic traits may lead the child to select certain kinds of environments.

Stanley (1993) notes that 'it seems that extensive early "practice" in psychology is not the mode even for the most renowned figures in the field'.

Savantism and creativity

As defined in the literature, autistic savants have learning disability (mental retardation). In contrast, this book focuses on high-functioning creative artists: Asperger savants with above-average intelligence levels. The phrase 'Asperger savant' needs explanation: it refers to persons with high-functioning autism or Asperger's syndrome who produce work of genius.

Sacks (1995) notes that savant abilities differ from ordinary abilities 'only by being isolated and heightened in degree'. He points out that savant gifts appear 'fully fledged from the start', and that savant talents 'have a more autonomous, even automatic quality than normal ones'.

Howard Gardner (1993), in discussing the savant issue in persons with mental retardation, states that

> we behold the unique sparing of one particular human ability against a background of mediocre or highly retarded human performances in other domains... The existence of these populations allows us to observe the human intelligence in relative – even splendid – isolation.

According to Christopher Gillberg (2002), savant skills

> are relatively more common in autism spectrum disorders including Asperger's syndrome. The term is now used for special talents at a very high level of functioning, much above that which would be expected on the basis of a person's IQ.

I call these persons 'Asperger savants'. In this book, the term denotes superior functioning in artistic domains in persons with Asperger's syndrome and average or above-average IQ.

Hermelin (2001) points out that '1 per 200 of those within the autistic spectrum can justifiably be regarded as having genuine talent'. Barlow (1952) states that out of every 1000 children born, 50 are bright, 20 are brilliant and one only is a prodigy. The prevalence of 'Asperger savantism' is unknown.

Hermelin also notes that 'while talent usually manifests itself as a specific, quasi-modular entity, intelligence is understood to be a general capacity to deal effectively with all kinds of mental problems', and distinguishes between intelligence and cognition. Intelligence refers to a 'stable mental capacity', while cognition 'is seen as an active process through which knowledge is acquired'. Leon Miller (author of *Musical Savants*) noted that 'the degree of excellence shown by an individual in his particular [savant] domain was independent of his level of intelligence' (cited in Hermelin 2001).

Nettlebeck (quoted in Frith 1989) wrote about 'savant skills – rhyme without reason', i.e. that 'savant skills demonstrate the brain's capacity to develop new cognitive modules in certain domains that create a hotline to knowledge stored in long-term memory, and operate independently of information-processing capacity'. Frith concludes that 'a detail focused cognitive style may be the basis for many of the characteristics of autistic intelligence'. This is a so-called weak central coherence style of cognitive functioning. According to Prior and Ozonoff (1998), it leaves affected persons 'prone to "modular" (non-coherent) abilities'.

We have to ask whether there is a link between autistic savants (low IQ) and Asperger savants (high IQ). Does the 'modular' view of the mind provide a link? Are modules of the brain, for talent of genius proportions, linked biologically and genetically? The answer is yes.

According to Fodor (author of *The Modularity of Mind*), as described by Hermelin (2001),

> modules draw their specific information from different senses, such as sight, hearing, touch, etc. These sensory-based systems are modular as they are each domain specific, fast, self-contained and encapsulated. The modules do not share their information with each other but pass it on to a central system. The central system also forms concepts, enables also abstract thought...

It is interesting to note here that Asperger described his patients as 'abstract thinkers'.

The best explanation of savant talent has been put forward by O'Connor and Hermelin (1987). They point out that

> a specific gift for art, music…tends to be self-contained, as are Fodor's modules, but it also includes its own aspects of central processing. We could thus regard savant ability as 'quasi-modular', i.e. being circumscribed by, but not restricted to, sensory perceptual processing.

Focusing on their savant activities, a person with autism/Asperger's syndrome can then avoid a confusing, chaotic socio-emotional world.

Hermelin (2001) notes that some psychologists investigating 'creativity' have suggested that 'field independence' and 'diverse thinking' (i.e. forming unusual and unexpected associations) show the working of an original mind. This is what the individuals described in this book demonstrate. Hermelin asks whether such a tendency of 'field independence' in autistic perception and thought could help to account for the fact that most savants are autistic. I believe the answer is yes.

Sir Michael Rutter, in the foreword to Hermelin (2001), points out that 'the underlying feature is that the savants use the strategy of taking a mental path from single units to a subsequent higher order extraction of overarching patterns and structures'. He goes on to state that these strategies 'do not lead on to artistic…innovations'. This book shows that the opposite is the truth in the case of Asperger's syndrome and high IQ.

Hermelin (2001) notes that it may be the initial focus on details and segments that leads to the development of integrated pictures, music or poetry, and savant ability. Pring, Hermelin and Hearey (1995) note savants' superiority in block design (a method of measuring spatial skills), which 'suggests that they have a special ability to segment a holistic stimulus into its component parts'. This, they argue, can be especially significant in drawing and painting and is an ability that appears to be independent of general intelligence in artistically talented people. A parallel argument can be made with regard to musical ability and the facility with pitch discrimination (subcomponents of music) within a musical 'Gestalt'. Hermelin's group have linked such abilities to Frith's (1989) 'central coherence theory', in which the core deficit in autism is seen as a failure to derive coherence (meaningful wholes) from the information one may apprehend, leaving one prone to 'modular (non-coherent) abilities'.

Mottron and Burack (2001) state that the 'notion that an unusual interest in certain types of objects may lead to long-term behavioural and neurological changes is consistent with Schultz et al.'s (2000) finding that persons with autism exhibit a developmental displacement of their processing zone towards an "object" region'.

In relation to the writings of great Asperger savants, Hermelin quotes W.B. Yeats's statement that a 'poem, just like a picture or piece of music, assumes an autonomous existence, representing its own self-contained truths'. Hermelin (2001) also notes that frequently 'savants have no relevant environmental experiences available to them, and their talent often becomes apparent quite suddenly at a young age'. Therefore innate factors are critical.

O'Connor and Hermelin (1987) feel that savants' ability is 'relatively independent of general mental development. It seems that the artist may have a richer and more acceptable store of visual images or forms, a picture lexicon.'

It is not surprising that poets with Asperger's syndrome will often write about the areas of their greatest difficulty – personal relationships. In T.S. Eliot, notwithstanding 'the three voices of poetry', the autistic voice or the 'one-person dialogue' is predominant. Asperger poets of genius are more likely to do what Walt Whitman described as laying 'end to end words, never seen in each other's company before'. They are also quite well able to use simile and metaphor, and are not tied to simple concrete language expressions. Poets with Asperger's syndrome are probably using their poetry as 'a means of self-expression rather than communication', in Hermelin's words.

Hermelin also states that a 'requirement for true creative ability, which is certainly missing in savants, is a search for new forms of expression that characterise the history of Western art'. This certainly does not apply to Asperger savants described in this book. Asperger savants are highly revolutionary and innovative in their artistic production and, indeed, can lead their fields.

Shattock and Savery (1997) suggest the importance of 'inability to forget' and an inability to filter out irrelevant material. According to Stella Waterhouse (2000), Wilson (1989) explains these talents by linking them to 'a sixth or "super" sense (which some people would term the unconscious)'. Wilson suggests that 'there can be no doubting that, deprived of one or more of its five monitors of the external world, the inner entity we are calling the super self has no shortage of compensating heightened sensory resources to call upon. It is equally clear that…it often does so in ways the normal consciousness finds difficult if not impossible to comprehend' (1989).

As quoted by Waterhouse (2000), Donna Williams, in her 1998 book *Autism and Sensing*, proposes 'that in the early stages of development we have a system of "sensing" which is gradually lost by most people as they go on to develop another system: that of interpretations'. Persons with autism retain this ability. Certainly, as we have seen, a child-like immaturity of personality is a characteristic of persons with Asperger's syndrome and autism. There is some similarity between Wilson's and Williams's views.

Waterhouse also quotes Rita Carter: 'Photographic memory is commonly found among young children although as the brain grows and the neurons are pruned such skills are generally lost.' It is believed that there is incomplete pruning of skills in autism spectrum disorders. This indeed is a promising hypothesis to explain autistic savantism at the neuronal brain level.

Mottron and Burack (2001) note the suggestion of Miller *et al.* (1998) that savant phenomena can develop in persons with fronto-temporal dementia because 'selective degeneration of the anterior temporal and orbital frontal cortex decreases inhibition of the more posteriorly located visual systems involved with perception, thereby enhancing these particularly artistic interests and abilities'. There are frontal lobe abnormalities in persons with autism.

Mottron and Burack (2001) developed a model of 'enhanced perceptual functioning':

> Superior performance among persons with autism involves low level processing (the functions of the perceptual brain areas, the sites of this lower level processing, are the most localised and circumscribed in the brain), and examples of enhanced behaviour can be found in most perceptual domain-specific systems, such as spatial perception. Typically, only one peak on special ability is found in any individual, which is consistent with the notion of a 'blind' process that involves only one area of 'over-functioning' and the resultant areas of enhancement.

Mottron and Burack also point out that enhanced performance goes with the

> notion of brain plasticity through which competing cognitive functions may evolve when one is impaired or eliminated. This entails the integration of neuronal bases and the training and eventual over-training of skills that leads to enhanced performance on cognitive tasks. Enhanced performance represents an extensive course of development and brain reorganisation rather than the simple unfolding of 'sleeping modules' that remain inactive among typically developing persons.

This book suggests that the 'unfolding of sleeping modules' is far more important than Mottron and Burack suggest.

A theme runs through discussions on savantism of weakness in one area of the brain and strength in another. It's almost as if an individual must have a flaw in order to be a savant. One is reminded of the poet Dryden's couplet, mentioned above: 'Great Wits are sure to Madness near alli'd/And thin

Partitions do their Bounds divide'. Mottron and Burack also note 'enhanced auditory perception…among persons with congenital visual impairment, for whom detection of auditory features compensates for impairment in vision'. In terms of savants they suggest that

> special abilities are evidence for a layer in cognition that is the site of low-level visual and auditory perception and that seems to be the location of considerable cognitive activity among persons with autism. The domains of enhanced functioning among persons with savant abilities and those with autism are, therefore, similar with regard to type and level of processing. Even if some areas of special abilities involve operations that are not solely perceptual (e.g. drawing or computation) and include several modalities, they are all pertinent to either perception of physical properties of stimuli (e.g. pitch processing) or simple operations (e.g. associating, combining, matching) on long-lasting tracks of perceptual aspects of visual or auditory stimuli. (Mottron and Burack 2001)

The difficulty of persons with autism spectrum disorder in attention shifting may also enhance performance and increase focus on a task.

'Diagnosing the dead': A legitimate activity?

Some people are critical of the linking of Asperger's syndrome and persons of genius, and indeed of the diagnosis of individuals that are no longer alive. Clearly such diagnosis is not possible unless detailed information, documented during their lifetimes, is available from autobiographical, biographical and other sources. A great deal of such information is available for all the persons with Asperger's syndrome described in this book.

The style of the book is in the tradition of major international academic experts on psychiatry/psychology who have written using this methodology and in this manner. It is particularly influenced by the international autism researcher Uta Frith, and her book with Houston called *Autism in History* (Frith and Houston 2000). Some of the most respected scientific researchers in the field of autism have used this approach: Sula Wolff in *Loners: The Life Path of Unusual Children* (1995); Christopher Gillberg and Mary Coleman commenting on historical figures in *The Biological Basis of Autism* (2000); Simon Baron-Cohen in *The Essential Difference* (2003). Indeed, Francesca Happé makes reference to this body of work in her book *Autism* (1994). Tony Attwood (1991) cites Einstein as having 'elements indicative of Asperger's syndrome'. Lorna Wing (1996) discusses the 'Wild Boy of Aveyron' and states that 'reading the account now, it is possible to see that Victor behaved like a child with autism'.

I agree with Frith and Houston (2000) that it is possible to come to a conclusion as to whether or not a person has autism 'by examining…evidence with the hindsight of current knowledge'. It is clear that this 'psycho-historical' approach has major currency among distinguished writers on autism.

PART I

Asperger's Syndrome
and Writers

I T IS POSSIBLE to have major problems in reciprocal social relationships and be a literary genius. Persons with literary genius and Asperger's syndrome are often quite interested in social relationships (this will come as a surprise to many readers). Although they lack know-how in making relationships, this does not inhibit their observation of them or their capacity to write about them in the form of novels, fairy stories or other imaginative literary forms. Pinker makes the important point that 'narrative fiction engages [an] ability to explore hypothetical worlds, whether for edification – expanding the number of scenarios whose outcome can be predicted – or for pleasure – vicariously experiencing love, adulation, exploration, or victory. Hence Horace's definition of the purpose of literature as to instruct and delight' (Pinker 2002).

Van Krevelen and Kuipers (1962) point out that persons with Asperger's syndrome (formerly known as autistic psychopathy) show 'signs of original intelligence' and are often 'naturalists'; they are 'tied to solitary pursuits' and have 'a veritable mania for reading'.

Digby Tantam (1991) was correct when he wrote about 'people with Asperger's syndrome who [can] make up stories, imaginary words or imaginary play comparisons'. The literary figures described in the following chapters illustrate this. Asperger (1974) noticed that children with autistic psychopathy developed 'highly grammatical speech and they may be uncommonly apt at using experiences coined spontaneously'. This can be helpful in the production of some literary works.

Persons with Asperger's syndrome show more originality of thought than persons with high-functioning autism. There is no doubt that in a literary sense there is something distinctive and unusual in their literary works. They produce a kind of autistic/Asperger-type written language and dialogue. Their writing is often tailored more to the writer than to the reader: they don't always help the reader with information so that he or she can follow the topic. They often express themselves excessively briefly. They can put huge effort into finding the right word or phrase, and can be obsessed with linguistic precision. This can lead them to making up new words. Sometimes their writing can have a 'robotic' flavour, as if produced by a computer. These writers often demonstrate a sense of identity diffusion associated with their 'autistic brains', which leads to narrative problems. There is a diffuse sense of self and problems with reflective capacity, which can make the works difficult to understand.

Such writers have huge problems in what Jean Quigley (2000) calls 'self-construction'. Paradoxically, these massive struggles can help them in their creative literary works. They have to construct deliberately what comes automatically for neurotypicals (non-autistic people). A great deal of literary writing is about 'different selves', and people who have a problem with their sense of self are often the best at writing about it. This can lead to literary success.

Persons with Asperger's syndrome often have an idiosyncratic perspective on the world that readers find very novel and illuminating, as it is different from that of neurotypicals. In addition, the tendency for high verbal IQ in persons with Asperger's syndrome would favour literary talents.

ONE

Jonathan Swift
(1667–1745)

JONATHAN SWIFT WAS a major literary figure who also had major political impact as a propagandist, polemicist and pamphleteer. His major work was *Gulliver's Travels*. He was Dean of St Patrick's Cathedral in Dublin, but did not achieve church preferment because of severe impairment in social relations. He meets the American Psychiatric Association's DSM-IV criteria for Asperger's disorder (APA 1994). Unless otherwise indicated, the biographical details and quoted extracts in this chapter come from Glendinning (1998).

Life history

Jonathan Swift was born a Protestant of English parentage in Dublin, Ireland, on 30 November 1667. His mother, Abigail, was from a Leicester family but was born in Ireland – her marriage certificate describes her as a spinster of the city of Dublin. She married a man called Swift who had recently emigrated to Ireland, and who died before Jonathan was born. Abigail Swift left Jonathan and his elder sister, Jane, to be raised by uncles and aunts. Jonathan's childhood was 'ruled by uncles'. He later claimed that he could read any chapter in the Bible by the time he was three years old.

At the age of six he was sent to Kilkenny Grammar School as a boarder – a sojourn that he later recalled unhappily. He never referred to his boyhood without resentment. In 1682 he entered Trinity College Dublin, where he was a troublesome and rebellious student. In 1687 he was questioned by the Trinity authorities for neglect of duties and for 'frequenting the town' and 'causing tumults'. He was about to take his master's degree in 1689 when the

Irish 'Troubles' supervened; he went to Leicester to see his mother, whom he hadn't seen since he was a tiny child.

In England, Swift found a position as secretary to the former diplomat Sir William Temple, and later worked as a political speechwriter. Next he took holy orders in Ireland and became a priest in a 'dead-end parish in Kilroot in the North of Ireland'. Finally he became Dean of St Patrick's in Dublin, a Protestant cathedral where he worked for the rest of his life.

In the late 1730s his temper, his memory and his reason deteriorated. In 1742 he was found to be of unsound mind. He willed his money to the foundation of a hospital in Dublin for 'idiots and lunatics', and died in 1745.

Indicators of Asperger's syndrome

Social behaviour

Glendinning describes Swift as 'not always "nice" in our sense of lovable and pleasant. He is a disturbing person. He provokes admiration and fear and pity.'

It is likely that Swift never married: he stated that he had never seen a woman for whose sake he would part with the middle of his bed, and always defended himself against emotional dependency. His relationships with women, whom he teased with an aggressive kind of flirtatiousness, bordered on cruelty. Vanessa (Hester Vanhomrigh), who loved him, 'suffered from this cold, inexpressive anger'. Laetitia Pilkington, who stood up to him, suffered from his 'sadistic silliness'. She said that what gave the Dean pleasure was to instruct women, and that he was 'a very rough sort of tutor for one of my years and sex; for whenever I made use of an inelegant phrase, I was sure of a deadly pinch, and frequently received chastisement before I knew my crime' (Elias 1997). She received 'blue and black flowers of bruises' from him, and he sometimes lost his temper and beat her for trivial reasons. He could be quite crude about women, particularly after childbirth, when he described one as 'the ugliest sight I have ever seen, pale, dead, old and yellow, for want of her paint. She turned my stomach.'

He knew Vanessa, one of the two most important women in his life, for 12 years in total but could not respond to her. Vanessa, who was in love with Swift, wrote to him of her suffering, and of the 'killing, killing, killing words' that he addressed to her. Swift led a double life with Stella (Esther Johnson), the other major woman in his life, whom he shared friends with and had dinner with on almost daily visits. He basically wove Vanessa into his Dublin life on a normal social level, while keeping her apart from Stella. He wrote to Vanessa that all women apart from her were beasts in petticoats. He was very upset when Vanessa paid him a visit in Ireland unannounced. Clearly this level of intimacy threatened him.

His secret relationship with the passionate Vanessa caused him anxiety. There is speculation, but no evidence, that he secretly married Stella in 1716. Swift did not want to be near Stella when she died.

As a young man, Swift resolved 'not to be fond of children, or let them come near me hardly'. In the words of William Temple's nephew, Jack Temple, his 'bitterness, satire, moroseness' made him 'insufferable both to equals and inferiors, and unsafe for his superiors to countenance'. He had endless quarrels with Archbishop William King, his superior in Dublin, who regarded him as unpredictable. He was a very prickly character.

Swift wanted to make his mark in the world. He longed for the world's rewards but could not respect the world's rules. He was 'out of tune' with people. He probably had a fear of being an outsider in London, and wanted to be 'in the swim in the great world'.

He published the *Temple Memoirs* against the wishes of Sir William Temple's sister, Martha Giffard, and her hostility to him was conveyed to influential acquaintances, which did him lasting harm. In the process he made an enemy of the Duchess of Somerset (a friend of Giffard and of Queen Anne), who described him as 'a man of no principle either of honour or religion' (Longe 1911). He could not see the consequences of his actions and showed a gross lack of empathy. He damaged himself very severely many times in this fashion. Verbally, he was too vicious for people. Clearly he was alienating people in power, and it is hardly surprising that he did not make progress in his career – after becoming Dean of St Patrick's it was clear that he was not going to get anything better because of his tactlessness and insensitivity. He showed 'a perverse kind of folly'. His general lack of tact was also seen in his lampooning of Sir Robert Walpole, the Prime Minister, which of course made an enemy of Walpole.

Swift had no notion of curbing his behaviour, his expressions or his opinions. He insulted the friends he wished to attract (especially if they were women); with his enemies no holds were barred. He attacked *ad hominem*, and *ad feminam*, shamelessly. He had an 'aspiration to be in the world but not of it'.

Narrow interests and obsessiveness

Swift was intensively involved in writing and physical exercise. His letter-writing sounds obsessional – he wrote to Stella almost daily. Intimacy at a distance was safe.

Routines and control

Glendinning notes that Swift was preoccupied with 'cleanliness and its opposite, filth…especially in connection with women'. His personal cleanliness was well known, and extreme by the standards of the time. He was hypersensitive to smells and hated human waste products, yet his writing was often scatological.

Swift had an obsession with physical exercise. He seldom walked less than four miles a day, and sometimes eight or ten. In the Deanery at St Patrick's he would run up and down flights of stairs for exercise; while he was William Temple's secretary he had exercised by running up and down a hill.

He very much liked lists, and kept detailed accounts of everything he spent (this is a common feature of people with high-functioning autism). He took an obsessional interest in the construction of his garden. He read prayers to his whole household 'at a fixed hour every night, in his own bed'.

Swift was 'a conscientious and authoritarian Dean, involving himself deeply in every detail of the Cathedral's ritual and routine'. In company he was 'always taking his watch out of his fob-pocket to look at it, and to check its time-keeping against others – never entirely at ease in the unmeasured moment'.

For Swift, 'No one must ever have power over him – the power to melt his self-possession, the power to hurt.' According to Glendinning, he was 'an emotional bully, through a mixture of deflected desire, and contempt, and self-contempt'. With Vanessa, Swift was the teacher and she was the pupil, and he wanted 'submission' and sometimes 'abasement' from her. Lord Orrery wrote that Swift had a command 'over all his females', that 'seraglio of very virtuous women who attended him for morning till night, with an obedience, and awe, and an assiduity, that are seldom paid to the richest, or the most powerful lovers'. It was the 'despotic power' that he exercised over his circle, said Orrery, that permitted him to give free reign to 'passions that ought to have been kept under proper restraint'. He always had a 'circle' that he dominated and sometimes bullied.

Speech, language and humour

There is no definite evidence of speech and language problems in Swift. In St Patrick's Cathedral he read the prayers in a 'voice sharp, and high-toned, rather than harmonious'.

Glendinning points out that 'Swift's wit is often shocking. It has a lash. He challenges the hypocrisies and received opinions which enable people to rub along together. He rarely indicates with any reliability what he might consider "the truth" on any issue. In his polemical prose, you cannot always wholly count out, or count in, any expressed value or opinion.' Swift was 'verbally ingenious and agile. He had a great liking for codes, riddles and puns.' Clearly Swift was highly capable of humour.

He was very preoccupied with language, and, according to Glendinning, 'deplored what he saw as a slovenly falling-off from proper standards in the speech of his contemporaries'. Indeed, he wrote a proposal for 'Correcting, Improving and Ascertaining the English Tongue'.

Appearance and demeanour

Swift seldom smiled, and almost never laughed. He had, wrote Lord Orrery, 'a natural severity of face, which even his smiles could scarce soften, or his upmost gaiety render placid and serene', and 'when he was angry, this natural severity became frightening, it is scarce possible to imagine looks, or features, that carried in them more terror and austerity'.

Daniel Button, the proprietor of Button's Coffee House in London, observed that over several successive days 'a strange clergyman [Swift] came in', obviously unacquainted with anyone there. He would put his hat down on a table, 'and walk backward and forward at a good pace for half an hour or an hour, without speaking to any mortal'. Then he picked up his hat, paid for his coffee and left without having said a word to anyone. The writer Addison and his friends amused themselves by watching him, and nicknamed him 'the mad parson'.

SWIFT MEETS FOUR out of the six Gillberg (1991) criteria for Asperger's syndrome, but there is uncertainty about speech and language problems and no information on motor problems. Nevertheless, he does meet the DSM-IV criteria, which do not require any clinically significant delay in language development or any motor problems. He also suffered from depression, which is quite common in persons with Asperger's disorder. He dealt with the depression by being very active, by intensive work, writing and physical exercise. No doubt this will not be the last word on the psychopathology of this 'inexhaustibly intriguing figure'.

TWO

Hans Christian Andersen
(1805–75)

T HE DANISH AUTHOR Hans Christian Andersen has a secure place among the world's great storytellers. Although he wrote many plays, poems, travel books and novels, his lasting fame has been as a writer for children.

Andersen's life – particularly in his social relations – was somewhat unhappy. After his death, Edvard Collin wrote that 'I cannot deviate from the opinion that the best service to Andersen is done by showing the world how diseased a mind he had, so that it is clear to everyone, that everything repulsive, everything that the world was scandalized by, was caused by this mind' (Collin 1882). It seems that Collin was referring to autism without realizing it – this is a harsh and unsympathetic portrait of a person with autism. The present chapter presents the evidence that Andersen was indeed autistic – specifically, that he had an autism spectrum disorder (Asperger's syndrome). Unless otherwise indicated,

© Lebrecht Music & Arts Photo Library

the biographical details and quoted extracts in this chapter come from
Wullschlager (2000).

Life history

Andersen was born on 2 April 1805 in a deprived part of Odense. His father
was a shoemaker. His parents got married just before his birth. His mother,
Ann Marie Andersdatter, has been described as 'a practical, robust, energetic
woman'. She was rather superstitious, and 'stuck pieces of St John's wort into
the clefts between the beams on the ceiling, and from their growth judged
whether people would live long or die soon'. Her conversation was full of
trolls and ghosts. Both parents were dreamy and unpractical. The father
apparently showed evidence of pride and impulsiveness. He died when Hans
was 23 years old, and was buried in a pauper's grave.

Hans's paternal grandfather, Anders Hansen Traes, was also a shoemaker.
Andersen remembered him sitting 'carving strange figures out of wood – men
with beasts' heads and beasts with wings' (Andersen 1855/1975). In later life
this man 'wandered into the woods and came back covered in garlands of
flowers and twigs, singing at the top of his voice and pursued through the
streets by shrieking children'. We also learn that Andersen's 'mad grandfather
lived alone, hoarding coins which had not been valid since the national bank-
ruptcy of 1813'. Did he have Asperger's syndrome as well?

Andersen himself stated that 'from as early as I can remember, reading was
my soul and my most loved pastime…my father enjoyed reading very much
and so had some books, which I swallowed. I never played with other boys, I
was always alone' (Collin 1945–8). Andersen remembered walking in the
forest with his father and noted that he did not talk much, but would sit
silently, sunk in deep thought. The father was a loner who indulged a great
deal in reading. Andersen also stated that:

> At home I had playthings enough, which my father made for me. My
> greatest delight was in making clothes for my dolls, or in stretching out
> one of my mother's aprons between the wall and two sticks before a
> currant-bush which I had planted in the yard, and thus to gaze in
> between the sun-illumined leaves. I was a singularly dreamy child, and
> so constantly went about with my eyes shut…to give the impression of
> having weak sight. (Andersen 1855/1975)

Given that this was a childhood typical of a person with Asperger's syndrome,
it is hardly surprising that 'there are no accounts in his autobiographies of the

ordinary pleasures and mishaps of childhood, of skating or playing ball or tree-climbing'. He showed other features of Asperger's syndrome in being clumsy, hopeless at physical activities, over-sensitive and proud.

Not surprisingly, he was 'hit' at school, and bullied, teased, and beaten by other children in the neighbourhood. A biographer has pointed out that a child so fixed in character could not be taught. He showed evidence of poor concentration and had very poor spelling ability – this is not uncommonly associated with autistic spectrum disorders (ASD). He told a girl that he was a changeling; she said 'he's mad, just like his grandfather'. (William Butler Yeats, discussed in Chapter 5, wrote a poem about a changeling.)

At about the age of 11, Andersen, who had been listening to a story of predestination, suddenly

> was firmly and resolutely determined to drown myself. I ran to where the water was deepest, and then a new thought passed through my soul. 'It is the devil who wishes to have power over me'. I uttered a loud cry, and running away from the place as if I were pursued, fell weeping into my mother's arms, but neither she nor anyone else could wring from me what was wrong with me. (Andersen 1855/1975)

He then went to work in a cloth mill. The other workers noticed his ambiguous identity, and stripped him to see if he was a girl: 'I cried and screamed. The other journeymen thought it was very amusing, and held me fast by my arms and legs. I screamed aloud, and was as much ashamed as a girl; and then darting from them, rushed home to my mother' (Andersen 1855/1975).

Andersen felt different from everyone around him as he grew up. He was taken to the theatre and became absolutely fascinated by it; he later stated that

> from the day I saw the first play my whole soul was on fire with this art. I still recall how I could sit for days all alone before the mirror, an apron around my shoulders instead of a knight's cloak, acting out Das Donauweibchen [the little lady of the Danube] in German though I barely knew five German words. I soon learned entire Danish plays by heart. (Collin 1945–8)

Persons with ASD are often transfixed in expression. Here Andersen was showing evidence of repetitive play as well as very significant memory feats. It was this interest in the arts that saved him from suicide in later life.

He went to Copenhagen as a naïve boy of 14. In an autistic fashion, 'he was oblivious to the sense of menace, and his accounts of his response do not mention those aspects which struck other contemporary commentators – the poverty, the stench, the rubbish floating down the canals'.

Andersen found school difficult because of his dreamy and restless temperament. He had a kind of autistic restlessness. He suffered severe criticism for his academic work, and it is hardly surprising he was in despair. Professor Guldberg said to him: 'Nothing good can come of you now! You are no good any more! God is angry, you must die!' (Topsøe-Jensen 1962). Nevertheless, he had extraordinary persistence (a kind of autistic persistence) and talent, which saved him. He was still in the classroom at 17 and was therefore out of place.

In grammar school he was six years older than his classmates, and was again severely mistreated and humiliated. He had great problems with grammar and spelling. The principal of the school, Meisling, absolutely terrified him: he 'unleashed on him a battery of ridicule and contempt, calling him nicknames such as "Shakespeare with the vamp's eye" (Topsøe-Jensen 1962). Meisling told him, 'You're a stupid boy, who will never be any good and when you start to stand on your own two feet you can write a lot of nonsense, but no one will ever read what you write, and it will be sold as pulp. Don't start crying, you overgrown boy!' (Topsøe-Jensen 1962). He received the typical treatment of boys with Asperger's syndrome. Meisling also exploited him by using him as a babysitter. Not surprisingly, he was soon discouraged and entered the vicious cycle of lost confidence, academic failure, boredom and depression. Again, this is typically what happens to boys with Asperger's syndrome. In 1824 he was unsuccessful at his examinations.

Andersen's experience at school, and at the hands of Meisling, left him with symptoms of post-traumatic stress disorder. 'Until he died he dreamed about Meisling, associating him forever with the social humiliation of his early years. The recurring dreams suggest how deep the social scars went, and how vital a role they played in his psychological makeup.' Persons with Asperger's syndrome are particularly vulnerable to long-term post-traumatic stress reactions, because they are less able than other children to deal with bullying from teachers and pupils.

Annie Wood, writing anonymously in *The Spectator* in 1875, gives a brilliant description of a person with Asperger's syndrome and the importance of their being in control. She writes that Andersen, an acquaintance of hers, was

> a child, according to the ideal of childhood; keenly sensitive, entirely egoistical, innocently vain, the centre of life, interest, concern and meaning to himself, perfectly unconscious that there existed another

standard, an outer circle, taking it for granted that everywhere he was to be the first and all…he had no notion of time and as pertinaciously required everyone to be at his beck and call as any curled darling in the nursery who is at once the plague and joy of his household. (quoted in Bredsdorff 1954)

Later, having failed in his efforts to work in the theatre and to become a singer, Andersen became a writer. He published poems, novels, and books on his travels through Europe, Asia and Africa but gained fame by writing over 150 children's stories, including 'The Ugly Duckling', 'The Steadfast Tin Soldier', 'The Emperor's New Clothes', 'The Snow Queen', 'The Little Mermaid', 'The Little Matchgirl', 'The Red Shoes' and 'The Tinderbox'. He died of carcinoma of the liver on 4 August 1875.

Interests/work

Andersen was a voracious reader and a compulsive autobiographer, like W.B. Yeats. Wullschlager (2000) points out: 'His best-known self-portraits, inventive, harsh, spiritually true, are in his fairytales. He is the triumphant Ugly Duckling and the loyal Little Mermaid, the steadfast Tin Soldier and the king-loving Nightingale, the demonic Shadow, the depressive Fir Tree, the forlorn Little Matchgirl.' Andersen himself wrote that 'Every character is taken from life…not one of them is invented. I know and have known them all' (Larsen 1941–6).

Clearly Andersen had a great capacity for imagination (it is not true to say that persons with Asperger's syndrome have no imagination). Was it an autistic imagination, like that of W.B. Yeats? In fact, his novel *O.T.* may have failed because it was too concrete and lacked imagination – it has been described as 'flat and schematic'. Andersen was extremely visual, and very sensitive to landscape. In his extensive travels in Europe, he got enormous satisfaction from the physical environment.

According to Wullschlager, Andersen showed that 'writing for children and literary and imaginative talent could go together. He introduced the idea of fantasy in children's stories, preparing the climate for Lewis Carroll in the 1860s.' The fantasy element included speaking toys and animals. Andersen's characters were often outsiders – for example, the little boy who sees that the emperor is wearing no clothes. Persons with Asperger's syndrome are less focused on context and on the social environment, and therefore can see more clearly than other people in certain situations. His tale 'The Steadfast Tin Soldier', according to Wullschlager, is an ironic self-portrait, the odd man out in a box of tin soldiers...each soldier was the living image of the next, except for one who was a little bit different. He had only one leg, as he was the last to be made and there hadn't been enough tin to go around. But he stood just as firmly on his one leg as the others did on two, and he was the one that was to stand out from the rest.

The person with autism also lacks something, i.e. the capacity for relating in a non-autistic way. The little tin soldier, like a person with Asperger's syndrome, had problems communicating and could not shout when he was thrown in the fire. Wullschlager sees this story as having a strong autistic character and as mirroring Stephen Spielberg's film *AI*.

Like many persons with Asperger's syndrome, Andersen was hypersensitive – like the princess in 'The Princess and the Pea', who can feel a pea through many mattresses. There is an autistic directness about his fairytales.

Persons with high-functioning autism have the capacity to break through in highly innovative ways – they are often the most innovative people on earth. Andersen was critical of academic life; he wrote about meeting a professor 'who said nothing in seven languages'. Andersen's fairytales operated to their own script, which allowed them to break free from the cultural traditions in which they existed. Nevertheless, he was very uncertain about his creative ability.

Like many people with Asperger's syndrome (as shown by the high numbers in secure prison hospitals), Andersen had considerable rage against society. There is much aggression in his stories. Wullschlager (2000) points out that 'they are shot through with violence, death, and the folk tale's inexorable sense of fate. Death plays a central role in three of the four stories in his first volume, and is present in the majority of his tales.' Lewis Carroll (see Chapter 4) also expressed violence in his stories. For Andersen it appears as 'Cut your head off!' ('The Tinderbox') and for Carroll, in *Alice's Adventures in Wonderland*, as 'Off with her head!' Both Carroll and Andersen wrote imaginative and anarchic stories. In the fairytales, Andersen vicariously exacted revenge on the people who upset him in early life.

In another tale, 'The Wild Swans', the princes and their sister struggle for years to escape from a spell by which their wicked stepmother has turned them into swans. This is a kind of 'autistic spell'. (It is interesting that W.B. Yeats also wrote about swans.) The swans, like Andersen, were cut off. They also represented his autism. At other times he wrote about storks, which, according to Wullschlager, symbolized his 'gaucheness and singularity and love of chatter'. 'The Ugly Duckling' may represent Andersen with his Asperger's syndrome: he wishes that he could look in the water and become a swan or something different, i.e. a non-autistic person.

Indicators of Asperger's syndrome

Social behaviour

Andersen wrote a poem about the wandering Jew Ahasuerus, and clearly identified with this man. He was self-obsessed and an archetypal social outsider, sexually uncertain and lonely. In his letters, Andersen wrote endlessly about his loneliness. An acquaintance wrote that he 'seemed to me to live in a world peculiarly his own, all his ideas, thoughts and actions differing from those around him' (Annie Wood, quoted in Bredsdorff 1954). He lived half his life as a kind of autistic wanderer through Europe. According to Wullschlager, 'Andersen's heroes and heroines are portraits of himself as an eccentric – the gawky duck, the brilliant nightingale, the dizzy top – and each goes through life alone'.

The outsider theme is again evident in the tale of 'The Little Matchgirl'. In this story the girl is looking through the window at a rich person's dinner-table while she freezes. One could see the little matchgirl as representing Andersen, with his Asperger's syndrome, cut off from communication. Another angle, noted by Wullschlager, is that 'with the ruthless selfishness of the dedicated artist, Andersen took what he needed from people and ignored the rest'. A central characteristic of many great artists is the ability to use people creatively for their own purposes.

Many people with Asperger's syndrome have a great need to be cared for and looked after in a sympathetic way: Andersen 'was always productive being pampered at the manor houses of the nobility'. When male Asperger's subjects marry, the wife often takes a mothering role and deals with all practical domestic matters. Andersen had few possessions. At 60, he still had no furniture: he simply packed his bag when going on a journey. Like many people with autism, he was better able to relate to people younger than himself.

Around the age of 25 Andersen was experiencing the 'continuing loneliness of the rootless young man in the city uncertain how to make emotional connections, and aware of an attraction to certain male friends which none reciprocated with equal intensity'. Here he is showing the social relationship difficulties of autism.

He had great difficulty in getting on the same wavelength as other people. Wullschlager points out that 'many were alienated by the shrill exuberance with which Andersen claimed attention'. Edvard Collin warned him about his vanity and his ludicrous behaviour in public. Andersen had a difficult relationship with Collin: 'Each time [Collin] wanted to establish landmarks of intimacy, Andersen lost his nerve. He found that he had to leave Copenhagen to try to conquer Edvard by written rather than spoken words.' While Andersen yearned for intimacy, he also feared it: he wrote in his diary 'alone I shall always be'. Not surprisingly, his sexual outlet was masturbation.

It appears, according to Wullschlager, that 'The Little Mermaid' symbolizes Andersen – she is fascinated by the people who live in the countryside, and falls in love with a prince, who thinks of her 'as a sexless creature, a sort of mute page'. The prince marries somebody else. The history of Andersen's relationships is one of unrequited love. Possibly this was his most successful fairytale because it described so accurately the position of a person with autism cut off from the non-autistic human world. Persons of genius with autism may seek immortality more through their work than through the production of children. The mermaid was an autistic mermaid.

Jenny Lind, the famous Swedish singer, was very similar in personality to Andersen: both realized that genius had more to do with nature than with nurture. Andersen fell in love with Lind immediately, and thought of marriage within days. Again the love was not reciprocated.

Andersen's lack of empathy in social relationships was seen in his handling of the powerful Danish playwright and critic Johan Ludwig Heiberg and his wife, the actress Johanne Luise Heiberg. After she refused the title role in Andersen's play *The Moorish Maid*, he wrote a bitter preface to the play which made lifelong enemies of the Heibergs and made Andersen a laughing stock. This is similar to the behaviour of Jonathan Swift. According to Wullschlager, in relation to the theatre Andersen 'remained emotionally an adolescent'. Because of his Asperger's syndrome he was emotionally arrested throughout his life; he could be cranky and easily upset.

Another example of Andersen's difficulties with social relationships and his lack of empathy was the fact that he stayed much too long with Charles Dickens and his family. Kate Dickens said that 'he was a bony bore, and stayed on and on' (Storey 1939). After he left, Dickens wrote 'Hans Andersen slept in this room for five weeks – which seemed to the family AGES!' (Storey 1939). This is reminiscent of what Keynes said about Ludwig Wittgenstein (who also had Asperger's syndrome: see Fitzgerald 2004): that he wasn't sure if he could bear to have him in his house for a week. It also reminds one of the *modus operandi* of the mathematician Paul Erdös, who would show up on the doorstep of a fellow mathematician, declare that 'my brain is open', work with his host until he was bored or the host was exhausted, and then move on. Erdös had so few clothes that his hosts had to wash his socks and underwear several times a week (Hoffman 1998).

Andersen was never fully successful in personal relationships. This caused him enormous torment. He really couldn't understand the sensibilities of people with non-autistic personalities. On one occasion Christian Voigt wrote in great detail about relationships, and made a tremendous effort to explain relationships, and his relationship to Andersen. But they never seemed to be getting through to each other: it was almost as if they were passing each other in the night. This inability to make contact with a man made him lonelier than ever. His inability to communicate with Edvard Collin, and his sense of rejection by Collin, upset him for many years.

He had the sense of being strange, so characteristic of persons with autism. On 26 August 1832 he wrote to Ludvig Müller, a young theology student with whom he had fallen in love:

> I am a strange being, my feelings run off with me too quickly and I only make myself unhappy. How empty it was at home in my little room last night! I went in to look at your bed, walked around alone, fell into a miserable mood and hardly slept at all – Oh, do come, come my dear, dear Ludvig, and I will – I will not be loving to you at all, that is what you like best! Then you will come, won't you – Of all people I know I am most fond of Edvard and you, if you find this strange, then remember, as you say, I am an original.

Wullschlager also shows Andersen's difficulties in relating to Edvard Collin socially. A letter that he wrote was 'the convoluted, clumsy attempt of someone grappling to express emotions he cannot control'. He was utterly desperate for friendship but didn't know how to relate in an appropriate social fashion. At the same time he had low self-esteem and was very dependent on the admiration of others.

When Andersen was 17 he introduced himself to Admiral Wulff as follows: 'You have translated Shakespeare; I admire him greatly, but I have also written a tragedy; shall I read it to you?' (Andersen 1855/1975). Nobody but a person with Asperger's syndrome could start a conversation like this.

The philologist and librarian Just Matthias Thiele contributed to a fund set up to help the young Andersen, who called to thank him. Thiele (1873) wrote that Andersen asked, 'May I have the honour to express my feelings for the theatre in a poem I have written myself?' Then, according to Thiele:

In my astonishment I did not even start to move before he was in the middle of the declamation, and when he ended with another reference, there followed immediately the execution of a scene from *Hagbarth and Signe* [Oehlenschläger's tragedy], a scene in which he played all the roles. I sat dumbfounded and waited for the entr'acte which might give me an opportunity for a question and answer. But in vain: the performance brought me from one scene in a tragedy to another in a comedy, and when he finally reached the epilogue that he also had written himself, he ended with several theatrical bows, grasped his cap lying as a gaping spectator by the door, and – off he was down the stairs!

This is the classic presentation of a person with Asperger's syndrome.

There is an autistic tone to his comparison of himself to Moses, who stands 'on the mountain gazing in to the Promised Land which I shall never reach'.

Narrow interests and obsessiveness

In 1825 he began a diary and was a compulsive writer. He once stated that he wrote 'because I have to, I can't help it'.

He was quite obsessive in writing 'The Little Mermaid', and changed it many times. It appears that he merged with his characters ('I suffer with my characters, I share their moods whether good or bad'): this is easier to do for a person with little sense of himself. One wonders whether the six mermaids at the bottom of the sea in 'The Little Mermaid' had autistic voices – 'they had lovely voices, more beautiful than human beings'.

According to Wullschlager, Andersen was 'manically driven to journey to far-flung places – by restlessness, curiosity, the need to forget himself in new and undiscovered settings, the thrill of being recognized, the desire to spread his name' – and to get away from critics at home. He showed by the extent of his travels that he was a man of courage – courage is a very common feature of persons with ASD.

He was extremely perfectionistic. His autistic compulsiveness was shown in the way that he repeatedly told his life story. He also had the autistic persistence that often leads to success in highly talented persons. One of his rituals was to go to the theatre every night.

In 1827 he became obsessed with the Collin family; he held an autistic-like obsession with them for the rest of his life.

Because of the way he was, life had to be lived within a narrow autistic frame. He wrote to Otto Müller, a brother of Ludvig, as follows: 'It is all new to you, one thing follows another, but *I* sit within the narrow ramparts, in the same old narrow circumstances, talk and listen and talk and so on and so forth, the familiar life da capo and always da capo'. Otto Müller later wrote to Andersen hoping that he had become less egotistic and less obstinate.

When he was a child, his mother noticed his fastidiousness in cutting clothes for his puppets. This appears to have been a rather autistic kind of activity, not unlike the paper cut-outs that he later indulged in, particularly at parties. According to Annie Wood, he cut paper figures 'so absurd in their expression and attitudes that roars of laughter always follow their appearance on the table'.

Routines and control

Andersen expected people to be at his beck and call. He could be controlling and ritualistic, for example in playing the game of lottery, which most people found irksome.

Speech, language and humour

Persons with Asperger's syndrome can grow and develop, and in later life Andersen developed a capacity for humour.

Around the age of 11 it was brought to his attention that he had 'a remarkably beautiful and high soprano voice' (Andersen 1855/1975). He wrote later that 'the strange characteristics of my entire nature compared with those of other children of my social class, my love of reading, and my wonderful voice all drew people's attention to me' (Topsøe-Jensen 1962). His voice in adulthood was described as deep, clear, mellow and musical.

He was fascinated with language and interested in slang words.

Naïvety and childishness

Andersen was often described as innocent, naïve and child-like. At the age of 14 he showed his naïvety by visiting the ballerina Madame Schall, hoping that she would support him in his efforts to be a dancer: 'I placed my shoes in a corner and danced wearing only socks on my feet'. According to Wullschlager, Madame Schall 'thought him a lunatic, and had him instantly removed from her house'. He later demonstrated naïvety by showing others letters about a homoerotic attachment.

Andersen wrote that 'I certainly feel that I am child-like, for just a smile or a sympathetic word makes me overjoyed instantly, while a cold face can cause profound unhappiness in my soul' (letter to Jonas Collin, 19 June 1825).

Demeanour and non-verbal communication

Andersen showed unusual non-verbal behaviour. A travelling companion, William Bloch, described him as

> strange and bizarre in his movements and carriage. His arms and legs were long and thin and out of all proportion, his hands were broad and flat, and his feet of such gigantic dimensions that it seemed reasonable that no one would ever have thought of stealing his boots. His nose was in the so-called Roman style, but so disproportionately large that it seemed to dominate his whole face. After one had left him it was definitely his nose that one remembered most clearly, whereas his eyes, which were small and pale and well-hidden in their sockets behind a couple of huge eyelids half covering them, did not leave any impression... On the other hand there was both soul and beauty in his tall, open forehead and round his unusually well-shaped mouth. (Bloch 1975)

One is reminded of Abraham Lincoln, who was supposed to have Marfan's syndrome.

An impression of Andersen's appearance and general demeanour can be discerned from the terms used to describe him at various times: loose-limbed, lanky, awkward, gauche, ridiculous, peculiar, strange, ungainly, slouching, disconcerting, surprising, incongruous, a dandy, foppish, timid, vain, clumsy, exhibitionist, gawping, ugly, ghostly, languid.

Heinrich Heine wrote that 'he looked like a tailor. He is a lean man with a hollow lantern-jawed face, and in his outward appearance he betrays a servile lack of self-confidence which is appreciated by dukes and princes' (Heine 1955).

Wullschlager comments on Andersen's 'physical unease with himself'. Annie Wood noticed that after telling a story he would make an 'awkward bow' and then 'with a light wave of his hand, retire to the corner, and shut his eyes and rest'.

Narcissism

He showed his narcissism by producing autobiographies about every ten years from 1832. He was troubled by this side of his character, and wrote of 'my nasty vanity'. Nonetheless, as is common with persons with Asperger's syndrome, his self-esteem was fragile and easily crushed by people around him. He was too uncertain of himself to become absorbed in anyone else. The swans in 'The Wild Swans' represented his narcissistic side – what Wullschlager calls 'symbols of mystery and grandeur'.

Andersen adored recognition and appreciation, writing in his diary in 1825 that he was contented 'only when admired by everybody, even the most insignificant person who will not do so can make me miserable'. His greed for recognition was enormous. He wrote to Edvard Collin: 'Oh Edvard! My soul yearns to be recognized like a thirsty man for water!'

Wullschlager has noted that he had 'a manic sense of self-grandiose ideas about fortune and nobility, interleaved with a fear of madness and rejection'. This kind of grandiosity is not uncommon in persons with Asperger's syndrome. He could express his narcissistic fantasies indirectly through the fairytales in the triumphs that he created in them. As Wullschlager points out, the fairytales allowed Andersen to write as he was and felt – not only as the social outsider but as the forbidden lover.

It appears to me that persons with Asperger's syndrome are not uncommonly misdiagnosed as having a narcissistic personality disorder. One wonders whether some of them would fit into Sigmund Freud's narcissistic neurosis. Even when Andersen was writing well, he feared that his writing would deteriorate.

Mood states

Throughout his life Andersen suffered from considerable depression. Aged 20, he wrote in his diary that 'my powerful fantasy will drive me into the insane asylum, my violent temperament will make a suicide of me! Before, the two of these together would have made me a great writer.' Soon after, he wrote: 'Depression, a nasty downpour, grey and autumn-like outside, foggy and raw, as in my soul; God, I wish I were dead!' In the following years he often repeated that he wished he was dead and that life held no joy for him. It is clear that while it is not uncommon for people with Asperger's syndrome to attempt or succeed at suicide, what kept Andersen alive was his literary ability.

He showed typically autistic varities of rage, anxiety, imagination and hypochondria – he wrote often of morbid feelings, of his spirit being demon-ridden, of his foul moods, and so on. He also showed hypochondria and miscellaneous deep-seated fears, such as a fear of dogs, a fear of fire and a fear of being buried alive (which he shared with Alfred Nobel, Frédéric

Chopin and Artur Schopenhauer). A few days before his death, he asked a friend to cut his veins when he died.

Andersen wrote in a letter in 1832: 'I am a peculiar being!... I can never enjoy the present, my life is in the past and in the future, and there is in reality too little for a *real* man. I have been in bad, very bad spirits.' His description of himself as peculiar is classically autistic. Depression is also a very common co-morbidity of persons with autism. The sense of not existing in the present suggests a lack of a core self rooted in the present.

Identity diffusion

Persons with Asperger's syndrome probably have a child's perspective, and because of their major difficulties with a sense of identity and a sense of self have enormous problems in their search for a sense of meaning to their life. Wullschlager describes Andersen as 'a self-publicist so skilful that he barely knew where the persona ended and the real self began'.

Andersen's sexual identity problems, sexual ambiguity and sense of strangeness are seen in his fairytales. His tale 'Only a Fiddler', according to Wullschlager, 'deals with characters trying to escape their background and finding themselves rootless in an alien, fast-changing world. Most lost is Naomi, whose sexual identity is consistently confused. In one episode she dresses up "in her male attire, which was so becoming to her, and with the little moustache on her beautiful upper lip".' This story reminds one of a person with autism.

All his life, Andersen had homoerotic longings and obsessions with individual men. His homosexual desires were tremendously excited by 'throbbing male dancers' in Turkey; 'a highly charged erotic sensibility...was always his response to hot countries'. He also had desires for women, but probably less intense than his desires for men. In Italy he was aware of strong heterosexual attraction, writing in his diary:

> My blood is churning. Huge sensuality and struggle with myself... I am still innocent, but my blood is burning. In my dreams, I am boiling inside. The south will have its way! I am half sick. Happy is the man who is married... Oh if only I were bound by strong bonds!

This sexual ambiguity is possibly a characteristic of Asperger's syndrome. He had tremendous fear of intimacy. In Rome, according to Wullschlager, other artists 'picked up on Andersen's erotic fervour and talked about his innocence, about seducing him. They planned to take him to a brothel, they teased him mercilessly.' This experience is again typical of a young man with Asperger's syndrome, and is painful.

His identity diffusion, or his penchant for an 'alter ego', can be seen in the fact that many of his stories started with objects – soldiers, snowmen, spinning tops, darning needles, etc. Andersen himself wrote in a letter: 'I have heaps of material, more than for any other kind of writing; it often seems to me as if every hoarding, every little flower is saying to me, "look at me, just for a moment, and then my story will go right into you".'

Even at an early stage his identity diffusion was clear, and was seen partly in his effeminacy and love of dressing up. One might say that he operated through a false self and had very little sense of a real self or core self.

Andersen's wish was to be fully human, and this is seen in a quotation from his story 'The Shadow': 'I looked where no one could see, and I saw what no one else saw; what no one was meant to see! When all's said and done, it's a mean world. I never want to be human, but for the fact that it's the thing to be.' It would appear then that he was ambivalent about changing his personality: it is interesting that persons with high-functioning autism can often see things that other people can't see because of their central coherence deficit, and, like Andersen, they don't want a complete personality change. Manley Hopkins (father of Gerard) wrote in *The Times* (26 December 1848) that the whole of Andersen's autobiography, *True Story of My Life* (1874), was a pretence. Maybe the issue is more autism than pretence.

According to Wullschlager, 'The Shadow', a 'tale of a man without a shadow, and a shadow who becomes a man without a soul, is a psychological horror story which works on many levels. A scholar, a good but ineffective man from the north, loses his shadow in a Naples heatwave.' This sounds like Andersen, and may be a description of how it is to live in the world with Asperger's syndrome. There is again the sense of the phantom self. Wullschlager notes that in his autobiography Andersen ends up as 'little more than a puppet shaking hands with the high and mighty'. This is a classic autistic autobiography. Wullschlager also describes 'The Shadow' as

> a terrifying story of the loss of self-identity. It recalls the hollow feelings Andersen complained about in letters written in his twenties, and it suggests that, as he pandered to kings, princes and an international audience, he knew that he remained lonely and loveless. He feared the void in himself while acknowledging that it was a crucial part of his creativity.

This is a reference to the phantom or 'autistic' self of the person with autism.

Andersen also showed a lack of identity in 1855 when he wrote to Edvard Collin: 'I am like water, everything moves me, everything is reflected in me, I suppose this is part of my nature as a poet, and often I enjoy this and receive blessings from it, but often it also torments me'. Here he was describing himself as an invisible man or ghost. According to Wullschlager, 'he may have recognized that his attraction to both men and women was part of his floating identity as a writer'. His Asperger's syndrome gave his character a sense of fixity but also gave him 'feelings of emptiness, of a hollow self-identity'. Here again we see the lack of a core self – the phantom self, the identity diffusion. In *The Book of My Life* (1832) this lack of self-identity is clearly seen when he writes: 'I cannot recall my own features, although God knows I look at myself in the mirror often enough.' His compulsive autobiographical writings were really a search for himself. Wullschlager remarks on 'the faceless image in his autobiography, and the problems he had meeting others in a relationship, because his idea of himself was so uncertain'.

The critic George Brandes pointed out that Andersen's novels failed because of a lack of

> the cool, calm power of observation of the man of the world…his men are not manly enough, his women not sufficiently feminine … I know no poet whose mind is more devoid of sexual distinctions, whose talent is less of a nature to betray a defined sex, than Andersen's. Therefore his strength lies in portraying children, in whom the conscious sense of sex is not yet prominent. The whole secret lies in the fact that he is exclusively what he is – not a champion, as many of our great writers have been, not a thinker, not a standard-bearer, but simply a poet. A poet is a man who is at the same time a woman. (Brandes 1886)

Mary Russell Mitford, the novelist, wrote in a letter that Andersen was

> essentially a toad-eater, a hanger-on in great houses, like the led captains of former days, a man who values his acquaintances for their rank and their riches and their importance in the world…who uses fame merely as a key to open drawing-room doors, a ladder to climb to high places.

This is a perfect description of a man without an authentic self, or with a false self. It was impossible for Hans to be any different.

FROM THE EVIDENCE presented above, it seems very likely that Andersen did in fact have Asperger's syndrome.

THREE

Herman Melville
(1819–91)

T HE AMERICAN NOVELIST Herman Melville was born in New York on 1 August 1819. His father died when he was 12 years old, and he had a succession of jobs through his teenage years – clerk, teacher, farmhand. In 1839 he went to sea, and subsequently made numerous Atlantic and South Sea voyages, the latter providing colourful material for several successful novels.

In 1847 Melville married Elizabeth Shaw, daughter of the chief justice of Massachusetts; they would have four children. In 1850 the couple settled on a farm in Pittsfield, Massachusetts. Nathaniel Hawthorne was a neighbour, and became a friend to Melville – *Moby-Dick* is dedicated to him. This book, Melville's masterpiece, was published in 1851 but did not replicate the success of his earlier works. Disappointed and struggling financially, he worked as a New York customs agent, and died of heart failure on 28 September 1891. His genius was only recognized long after his death; he is now one of America's canonical writers.

Melville has been described as a marvellous enigma and an ungraspable phantom. Robertson-Lorant (1998) notes that no American writer has been more puzzled over. The purpose of this chapter is to demonstrate that his enigmatic nature can be ascribed at least in part to Asperger's syndrome. All of the biographical details and quoted extracts in this chapter come from Robertson-Lorant (1998).

Family background

Herman Melville was born into an established merchant family. His grandfathers, Thomas Melville of Boston and Peter Gansevoort of Albany, were heroes of the American Revolution. It is interesting that the former was an eccentric character who wore the 'small clothes' of the revolutionary era long after they were out of fashion. Ludwig Wittgenstein, who had Asperger's syndrome, wore his military uniform long after the First World War (Fitzgerald 2004).

Herman's father was Allan Melville, an importer, who 'cut a dashing figure on the dance floor' and had 'elegant manners and suave solicitude'. Allan got involved in naïve and silly investments, and was full of fantasies of financial success. His lack of judgement in borrowing money had catastrophic financial consequences. Indeed, he may have had Asperger's syndrome as well. There was also an eccentric uncle who served as an acting American consul in France.

Herman's mother, Maria Gansevoort, 'had been raised to conform to the highest standard of Dutch womanhood – a standard based less on either intelligence or beauty than on piety, moral rectitude, and family pride'. She suffered recurring bouts of depression.

Childhood and education

After weaning, Herman was as 'rugged as a bear'. He was slow to talk, even slower to read, 'docile' and 'somewhat slow in comprehension'. Being slow to talk is often a feature of Asperger's syndrome, notwithstanding the inaccurate description of persons with Asperger's syndrome in the American Psychiatric Association's DSM-IV (APA 1994).

At the age of six, 'Herman, who by nature was a day-dreamer and a poet, resented the school's rigid and unimaginative daily drill, but he feared humiliation more'. His ability to 'blend into the woodwork' probably helped him (as it later helped him to escape the lash on the ships he sailed on, where there was much flogging).

He was 'a shy, sensitive lad' who 'liked to spend Sunday afternoons browsing through the two large portfolios of French prints his father kept in the library; one of them showed whaleboats in pursuit of a whale'.

At nine years of age he was 'still struggling to master cursive script'. He 'often had trouble sorting out his thoughts and feelings, and he liked being alone'. These are classic features of persons with Asperger's syndrome.

When Herman went to school he did 'not appear so fond of his books as to injure his health'. His favourite pastime was 'teasing his older brother'. Nevertheless, he made great progress in talking.

At the time of his father's death in 1832, Herman was described as innocent, amiable and shy. He was sent to work clerking in a bank.

Indicators of Asperger's syndrome

Social behaviour

For Melville, human beings were 'inconsistent, ever-changing, constantly evolving, and ultimately unknowable creatures; what is any novelist or biographer but a trickster and confidence man?' He was 'a rover' who yearned for 'an intimacy he could neither define nor sustain'. He could be insensitive to those around him: he often frightened his grandchildren, and 'subjected his wife and children to hurtful remarks and emotional neglect'.

He had severe outbursts of temper, and could be aloof, cantankerous and reclusive. He liked people who would talk about his own intellectual interests. He showed autistic novelty-seeking.

In the house he was unpredictable, and had a habit 'of nervously interfering in domestic matters whenever his writing was not going well'. He badgered Elizabeth about his morning coffee, 'often changing his preferences from day to day but not telling her until she had prepared it'. He bullied her, the children and the servants. Nevertheless, he depended on her management skills.

He had very severe marital problems, and Elizabeth considered leaving him. 'Like many creative, controlling, egocentric men, Melville was unpredictable and inconsistent with his children.'

Robertson-Lorant notes that in his treatment of his son Malcolm there was 'no room for human frailty or error'. He tended to take 'the stern, admonitory tone that Victorian fathers were expected to have with their sons, forgetting that boys, too, need love and nurturing in order to grow'.

He was sometimes 'emotionally withholding and tyrannical'. 'Prone to baffling contradictions and dramatic mood swings, he could be sociable and high-spirited in public, then moody and irascible at home.' He drank heavily for many years.

Speech, language and humour

Melville loved 'the sounds of words'. He had 'clinical diction and a neutral tone as well as tight-lipped stoicism'. When he gave talks 'they went on too long and had a tepid but polite reception'. His lectures were described as dull, subdued, singsong, monotonous and solemn. He had no 'ability for communicating passion for his subject to large audiences'.

His books, for example *Mardi*, were full of erudite allusions but there were reckless violations of narrative convention and bursts of melodramatic language. There are parallels with the 'autistic narrative' of Lewis Carroll – as noted in Chapter 4, Carroll's work has been described as 'anti-meaning' and having no moral (Cohen 1995). People with Asperger's syndrome are often atheoretical , and the incomprehensibility of their world may be reflected in their writings.

Non-verbal communication

He had 'a characteristic gravity and reserve of manner'. Sophie Hawthorne (wife of Nathaniel) said:

> He has very keen perceptive power, but what astonishes me is, that his eyes are not large and deep – He seems to see everything very accurately, and how he can do so with his small eyes, I cannot tell. They are not keen eyes, either, but quite undistinguished in any way. His nose is straight and rather handsome, his mouth expressive of sensibility and emotion – He is tall and erect with an air free, brave, and manly. When conversing he is full of gesture and force and loses himself in his subject – There is no grace nor polish – once in a while, his animation gives place to a singularly quiet expression out of those eyes to which I have objected – an indrawn, dim look, but which at the same time makes you feel that he is at that instant taking deepest note of what is before him – It is a strange, lazy glance, but with a power in it quite unique – It does not seem to penetrate through you, but to take you into himself.

Narrow interests and obsessiveness

Melville read voraciously. He became obsessed with becoming a writer, and with discovering the 'Truth'. He was an extremely keen collector of books, and was fascinated by philosophical abstractions. He was 'all on fire with subjects that interest him'. Captain Ahab was similar to Melville in terms of narrow autistic obsession.

He developed wanderlust and had 'a naturally roving disposition', indicating autistic novelty-seeking. He kept an obsessional nightly inventory of what he ate and drank while he was in London.

Motor clumsiness

Melville was described as 'incorrigibly clumsy': he was 'unhandy with tools and unable to care for a large property'. He struggled with his penmanship.

Hyperactivity and impulsivity

He wrote with a nearly illegible scrawl, and at times with 'breakneck speed'. He was regarded as reckless, and showed autistic hyperactivity. Some might describe this as hypomania. All his life he enjoyed brisk hikes and climbing.

At one point he remarked that he needed '50 fast-writing youths' to help him finish current and future projects. While writing, the thoughts 'were teeming and tumbling through his brain'.

Melville could also be quite impulsive. His art was 'Dionysian, passionate, impulsive, and organic'. He had a volatile personality, and often wanted to do two incompatible things simultaneously.

He was hyperactively productive between 1846 and 1851, writing six novels at a frenetic pace. He could become totally absorbed in writing; it was noted that on occasion he did not leave his room 'till quite dark in the evening – when he for a first time during the whole day partakes of solid food – he must therefore write under a state of morbid excitement which must injure his health'.

Routines and control

He was a voracious reader and would stock up on books 'like a squirrel hoarding nuts for winter'. He was extremely controlling – he had an extraordinarily rigid daily routine that allowed him to work uninterruptedly on his books. Everybody in the house had to fit into his routine. His wife had to adapt to his moods. He was a misogynist – a feature not uncommon in persons with Asperger's syndrome (e.g. Wittgenstein, Spinoza).

He badgered the cooks at home 'about the strength of his coffee and the consistency of his oatmeal'. He could also be extremely controlling of himself – when he went to work as a customs inspector after failing to earn a living as a writer, he conformed to the rigid schedule that this required.

He was an excellent observer. He had a very sharp eye and was very visual, as can be seen from his descriptions of London. He 'guarded the secrets of his heart' closely.

Lack of empathy

Melville was quite masochistic in the sense of producing novels that the public didn't particularly want. The novel *Pierre* destroyed his credibility almost completely, and ruined his reputation. He 'violated the unwritten rule that novelists must uphold middle-class Christian values'. His family regarded him as a 'dangerous lunatic'.

He certainly had difficulties in empathizing with his son, Malcolm, who committed suicide in the house.

Depression

He suffered serious depression, as is common in persons with Asperger's syndrome. 'If genius is close to madness, Melville was close to madness from time to time. Madness was never far from his mind or the minds of those closest to him'. Melville also 'felt perilously close to the worst fate of unrecognised genius: rejection, self-doubt, and madness'.

HERMAN MELVILLE WAS a truly great American writer. His Asperger's syndrome helped him to be a great observer and to focus obsessively on his work. He had a highly fertile imagination; contrary to received wisdom, persons with Asperger's syndrome are capable of this.

FOUR

Lewis Carroll
(1832–98)

T HE PHENOMENAL SUCCESS of the children's classics *Alice's Adventures in Wonderland* and *Through the Looking Glass* ensured that the author Lewis Carroll became a household name. According to his biographer, Morton Cohen, these classics – along with the Bible and Shakespeare's works – are among the most widely quoted books in the world today (Cohen 1995).

Lewis Carroll was the pen-name of the Reverend Charles Lutwidge Dodgson, a deeply religious Victorian mathematics don whose life was mainly spent at Christ Church, Oxford. Yet Lewis Carroll remains an enigma. Cohen considers him to be

> a puzzle, on the surface a tall, straight figure dressed in black, formal, precise, exacting and proper in every detail of behaviour but his severe exterior concealed a soaring imagination, a fountain of wit, a wide-ranging and far-reaching appreciation of the human condition, and the knowledge of how to touch others, how to move them, and how to make them laugh.

Like Newton, Carroll had no difficulty in combining the scientific with the supernatural. His library contained many books on occult subjects and, indeed, he wrote widely about fairies. Undeniably, his genius rested in the primacy of his imagination and, as the journalist Will Self (2001) notes, 'a conviction that the fantastic is anterior to the naturalistic'. Cohen attributes Carroll's creative genius to a combination of his 'stern self-discipline, his determination to control thought and action, his deep commitment to the child, his friendship with the Liddell sisters, his suppressed emotional life, and his font of endless energy'.

This chapter presents the evidence that Carroll displayed Asperger's syndrome. Unless otherwise indicated, all of the biographical details and quoted extracts in this chapter come from Cohen (1995).

Family background

Born on 27 January 1832 in Daresbury, Cheshire, Lewis Carroll was the third child and first son in a family of 11. His father was a formidable High Church curate who was described as 'a pillar of righteousness and accomplishment'. Despite the restrictive and punitive environment, Carroll respected and revered his father and became a 'faithful and dutiful' son. Nevertheless, he was torn between 'filial devotion and filial rebellion'. Certainly 'the grumbling-father theme' noted by Cohen was a feature of Carroll's work as he grew older.

From the information available, it would appear that Mrs Dodgson was devoted to her eldest son; he was her 'special pet'. Indeed, in her role as wife and mother she has been described as saintly. Certainly her son 'worshipped her above all others', while she was sensitive to his 'uncommon nature'. Indeed, his first 11 years were lived in 'complete seclusion from the world'. It was a veritable 'Wonderland'. As a child Carroll had the strangest pastimes and 'numbered certain snails and toads among his intimate friends'. He also tried to encourage 'civilised warfare among earthworms'. In childhood he was often seen 'sitting or lying full length on the lawn under the noble acacia tree in the rectory garden, writing'. As she had provided such a sheltered upbringing, his mother's death brought considerable grief to Carroll at the age of 19.

Indicators of Asperger's syndrome

Social behaviour

Carroll showed impairment in reciprocal social interaction. However, despite his shy and sensitive nature, he did form friendships and during the 1860s led an active social life, with a particular fondness for the theatre and art exhibitions. Though his interests filled every minute of the day and kept him busy, Carroll's life was lonely and isolated. Even after his ordination as deacon he was the odd man out. Cohen notes that H.A.L. Fisher, Warden of New College, observed that Carroll's 'intense shyness and morbid dislike of publicity made him a figure apart'. Indeed, Carroll confessed:

> My constant aim is to remain, *personally*, unknown to the world; consequently I have always refused applications for photographs or auto-

graphs, as my features and handwriting belong to me as a private individual... I so much hate the idea of strangers being able to know me by sight that I refuse to give my photo.

There are similarities here with Jack B. Yeats (see Chapter 19).

At school he sought solitude and privacy. When sent to public school at Rugby he showed little interest in sports and was not athletic, and consequently was bullied. He was described as 'by many accounts unassertive, by some accounts, a recluse'. The dramatist A.W. Dubourg described him as a 'quiet, retiring, scholar-like person, full of interesting and pleasant conversation, oftentimes with an undercurrent of humour, and certainly with a sense of great sensitiveness with regard to the serious side of life'.

Cohen claims that he could be insensitive in some social situations – 'rude, rigid, and off-putting'. His niece Violet Dodgson reported that in his dealings with his peers, many found him 'difficult, exacting, and uncompromising in business matters and in college life'. He also showed a lack of appreciation of social cues and socially inappropriate behaviour. Indeed, he was rather like Bruce Chatwin (Chapter 8) in his manner of abruptly leaving a gathering.

Carroll had no personal interest in small talk of any description, and was often silent in adult company. Not surprisingly, he was a poor lecturer and an unsatisfactory tutor. His lectures were described as 'dull as ditchwater'. In common with many geniuses with autism, he was unable to communicate in a manner appropriate for students. Cohen notes the 'singularly dry and perfunctory manner in which he imparted instruction...never betraying the slightest personal interest in matters that were of deep concern to students'.

Cohen describes Carroll as a bachelor living a cloistered life within college walls. Undoubtedly it was a suppressed emotional life, with no desire for close personal interaction. Many of the 'dull and doleful verses' that he wrote, though not autobiographical, reflect some of his 'inner fears', according to Cohen. The themes of 'unsatisfactory love affairs and frustrated emotional states' figure highly. This can be seen in one of his poems, 'Only a Woman's Hair', which was inspired by the single lock of a woman's hair found among Jonathan Swift's effects. (Cohen notes that 'Jonathan Swift's love affair with Stella echoes [Carroll's] own frustrations, and he responds feelingly... Other similarities appear when we look at the Swift–Dodgson histories. Swift often wrote letters to Stella in baby language.')

Narrow interests and obsessiveness

Carroll was quite obsessional and focused intensely on his interests, particularly writing, mathematics and photography. His colleague T.B. Strong observed:

> [He] was a laborious worker, always disliking to break off from the pursuit of any subject which interested him; apt to forget his meals and toil on for the best part of the night, rather than stop short of the object which he had in view.

This lifestyle, of course, is similar to that of many geniuses, such as Isaac Newton.

Carroll was a perfectionist in terms of the publication of his work. He frequently made 'insistent and uncompromising demands' on publishers. Cohen notes that even in his late fifties Carroll worked 'obdurately, frantically'. He drove himself relentlessly in order to write 'purposeful, serious works which he hoped would have lasting value'.

The level of focus and concentration that Carroll brought to his letter-writing was remarkable:

> The inventive powers that drove Charles in so many directions and enabled him to reach such exceptional heights were evident in his letter writing as well. Writing letters was a ritual for him; he thought carefully about them and executed them with the greatest care and enthusiasm. He often composed letters lying awake during the night, and for those sleepless hours he invented a device, the Nyctograph, the enabled him to take notes under the covers in the dark.

Carroll also demonstrated preservation of sameness. At Oxford he always wore black clergyman's clothes except when boating on the river, when he would swap them for white flannel trousers and a white straw hat.

Cohen notes how Carroll was an inveterate collector of gadgets, toys, games, puzzles, etc. Moreover, he produced a vast amount of puzzles, stories and nonsense verse. In this respect his work can be viewed as a challenge to meaning. Cohen claims that Carroll's poem 'The Hunting of the Snark', in common with the Alice books, is 'anti-meaning': 'It is more about *being* than *meaning*, listening than seeing, feeling than thinking.' This bears similarity to Wittgenstein's anti-theoretical, anti-meaning stance (Fitzgerald 2004). Persons with Asperger's syndrome are often atheoretical.

Visuo-spatial ability

Carroll demonstrated the good visuo-spatial ability common in those with Asperger's syndrome. He could draw reasonably well from an early age, and many of his manuscripts were littered with illustrations and drawings. From his prolific output of photographs, he was clearly a first-rate photographer. Indeed, Cohen claims that he was the finest photographer of children of the nineteenth century.

In common with Wittgenstein and Newton, Carroll showed an early interest in devices and machines, particularly trains. As a child he constructed a miniature replica of a passenger railway line in the rectory garden. He also devised a timetable and rules governing its operation. 'With a carpenter's help, he built a marionette theatre, composed plays and learned to manipulate the marionettes for the presentation'. Clearly Carroll showed no evidence of motor clumsiness in these activities.

His railway interests continued throughout his life, and he became obsessed with 'the complexity of the problem of fixing time relatively'. This has echoes of Einstein. He was also fascinated by novelty gadgets, particularly those showing mechanical and technological advances, and invented a chess-board for use when travelling. Undoubtedly he was an inventor, which reflected his logical mindset. Carroll had a first-rate mathematical mind and produced first-class creative mathematics. His contribution to mathematics was recognised by Bartley (1973), who regarded him as a good logician.

Speech, language and humour

Carroll was an extraordinarily gifted man who 'in spite of a deaf right ear and an incurable stammer, lived a busy and productive life'. Indeed, there was a strong family history of stammering, affecting both Carroll and his siblings. His stammer persisted throughout his life despite long-term therapy from James Hunt, 'a foremost speech correctionist'. There is no evidence that he had language difficulties or delayed development – in fact, quite the reverse. He took great pleasure in playing with words:

> [His] early compositions in prose and poetry and his artwork showed that his handwriting was already remarkably adult, strong, confident; his vocabulary and allusions prove him well ahead of his years; and if his drawings are crude, they do not lack force or humour. So mature does he appear so early that one wonders whether he moved from childhood directly into adulthood, somehow skipping boyhood.

Opinions differ on Carroll's style of conversation, according to the Oxford don Lionel A. Tollemache. Some claimed that there could be no doubt about its brilliancy, yet it was very difficult to 'define or focus'. Others claimed the opposite:

> Dodgson was not a brilliant talker; he was too peculiar and paradoxical, and the topics on which he loved to dwell were such as would bore many persons; while, on the other hand, when he himself was not interested, he occasionally stopped the flow of serious discussion with the intrusion of a discerning epigram.

Carroll had a strong impact on his peers. Tollemache emphasizes his brilliancy, whereby words could sway his peers: 'all he said, all his oddities and clever things, arose out of conversation [and had] an odd logical sequence, almost impelling your assent to most unexpected conclusions'.

Carroll was serious in person and laughed infrequently, despite the celebrated humour of his writings. An Oxford colleague, Frederick York Powell, recalled 'the quiet humour of his voice, the occasional laugh... He was not a man that laughed, though there was often a smile playing about his sensitive mouth.'

Routines and control

Carroll had 'a compulsive orderliness' and was systematic in his approach to organizing his work and activities. Undoubtedly a severe disciplinarian, he was 'a master of regulating his life, and superhuman in today's terms, in controlling his impulses during waking hours'. Moreover, his imposition of routines and order affected those around him. According to Cohen, his 'devotion to the rigid laws of logic led to a rigid, uncompromising set of rules that governed his life and spilled over into the lives of others'.

Carroll was an indefatigable record keeper. Apart from his diary, letter register, photograph register, and the register of correspondence when he was Curator of Common Room at Christ Church, there were lists recording meals he served guests, birthdays and offers of hospitality. Most remarkable was the letter register he began halfway through his life, which showed that in his last 35 years he sent and received 98,721 letters. He was fastidious in both mind and body. One observer recalled that 'he always appeared to have emerged from a hot bath and a band box'.

Clearly, Carroll was an extremely controlled man for whom 'ritual was all'. This extended to his reading habits. Cohen notes that he was a prodigious reader and read systematically, believing that 'thoroughness must be the rule of all this reading'.

Carroll had eccentricities that formed the basis of many routines, chief among which was the belief that 'Tuesdays were his lucky days'. He had an affinity for the number 42, which he repeated in his works and letters over and over again. Other eccentricities included his method of making tea. One of Carroll's child friends, Isa Bowman, recalled him 'walking up and down his sitting room swaying the teapot to and fro for precisely 10 minutes in order to achieve the desired brew'. He also had sensory hypersensitivity: a horror of draughts led him to place thermometers near oil stoves in his room to check that the temperature was equalized.

Carroll's literary works suggest that if the world is incomprehensible for those without Asperger's syndrome, then it is even more so for those with it. At a certain level, works such as *Alice* illustrate or highlight for us this incomprehensibility.

Appearance and demeanour

According to Cohen, Carroll's face 'presented a peculiarity of having two very different profiles; the shape of the eyes, and the corners of the mouth did not tally'. This is typical of someone with Asperger's syndrome, whereby it is possible to have two different emotions simultaneously on the face. He was also described as highly strung. As an adult, his child friend Isa Bowman thought him 'almost old-maidenishly prim'. Others described him as a pensive, attractive young man.

There is evidence of clumsy body language, as observed by Alice Liddell. His gait was particularly marked. Her biographer records how, years after their rift, Alice would often catch a glimpse of Carroll walking about Oxford 'with that stiff and curiously jerky gait'. Others noted that he walked upright and 'held himself stiffly, one shoulder slightly higher than the other; in his almost over-emphasized erectness there was an old-fashioned seriousness, an air of punctiliousness'.

His friend the artist Gertrude Thompson described the extraordinarily attractive quality so commonly associated with persons of genius:

> I always had a mysterious feeling, when looking at him and hearing him speak, that he was not exactly an ordinary human being of flesh and blood. Rather did he seem as some delicate, ethereal spirit, enveloped for the moment in a semblance of common humanity… His head was small, and beautifully formed; the brow rather low, broad, white,

and finely modelled. Dreamy grey eyes, a sensitive mouth, slightly compressed when in repose, but softening into the most beautiful smile when he spoke. He had a slight hesitancy sometimes, when speaking, but though [he] deplored it himself, it added a certain piquancy, especially if he was uttering any whimsicality.

Mark Twain, on meeting Carroll for the first time, found him 'only interesting to look at, for he was the stillest and shyest full-grown man I have ever met except "Uncle Ramos"'.

Autistic superego

Like Wittgenstein (Fitzgerald 2004), Carroll had an 'autistic superego'. Cohen describes it as 'a brooding guilt'. (The typical 'autistic superego' is very harsh; it engenders perfectionism and guilt.) From his twenties onwards, Carroll chastised himself for 'unfulfilled resolves, bad habits, inconsistency'. Nearing his 31st birthday, his diary reflects his harsh conscience: 'Here at the close of another year how much of neglect, carelessness and sin have I to remember! Oh God…take me vile and worthless as I am.' Similarly, he wrote: 'I do trust most sincerely to amend myself in those respects in which the past year has exhibited the most grievous shortcomings and I trust and pray that the most merciful God may aid me in this and all other good undertakings.' Indeed, temptation became a constant concern during his mature years, which he hoped would be overcome through self-discipline: 'self-discipline must be my chief work for a long while to come'.

According to Cohen, his diary contains endless self-chastisements with fresh determination to live a holier life:

[His diary was] a steady flow of self-criticism, importunities, fresh resolves, pleas and prayers, largely adhering to the traditional pattern of Christian self-examination and resolution of other diarists. As the flow increases, however, a gnawing, deep-seated guilt emerges, accompanied by spiritual weariness and gloom: they are the cries of a man keenly dissatisfied with himself.

His mind was preoccupied with guilt, and the idea that every aspect of his life had the potential to damn him. He believed that 'a stray thought, a light-hearted indulgence, a careless pleasure could instantly damn an unrepentant soul'. Nevertheless, Carroll's diary suggests that his sins went beyond 'ordinary failings like idleness or indolence'. It is possible that he used the pen-name of Lewis Carroll to hide his scopophilia. Certainly in 1883 he wrote: 'I use the name of Lewis Carroll in order to avoid all *personal* publicity'.

Religious disposition

In common with many geniuses, Carroll showed a distinct religious disposition. Bishop Wilberforce ordained him a deacon in the Church of England in 1861. According to Cohen, he had 'a fiercely religious cast of mind, a faith worked out by his own stern rules of logic'.

Any levity on the subject of religion displeased him. His child friend Ethel Arnold recalled that 'the patriarchs, the prophets, major and minor, were as sacrosanct in his eyes as any of the great figures of the New Testament; and a disrespectful allusion to Noah...or Nebuchadnezzar...would have shocked and displeased him'. Similarly, he showed gravity in matters of social injustice and conflict, springing from his sincere humility and generosity. Indeed, his great concern was with 'rules, natural, social, religious'.

Not surprisingly, these traits made others uncomfortable. Cohen notes that his 'uncompromising moral stance, his harsh judgement of others, his occasional priggishness would be even more objectionable were they not leavened by sincere and abject humility and extraordinary generosity'. His social conscience was acute, perhaps influenced by his father's sense of Christian charity and the social reform of the time. All conflict depressed him. Furthermore, Cohen points out that 'he opposed sham and greed', though politically conservative. When he uncovered 'ugliness or injustice' he had no hesitation in putting pen to paper; he wrote 'scathing attacks and proposed reasonable remedies'.

Carroll, in common with many other geniuses, had no concern for wealth or pomp. His humility extended to his own funeral arrangements. He left instructions for his funeral to be 'simple and inexpensive, avoiding all things which are merely done for show, and retaining, only what is, in the judgement of those who arrange my funeral, requisite for its decent and reverent performance'.

Naïvety and childishness

In common with many geniuses with Asperger's syndrome, such as Wittgenstein, Carroll related better to children than to adults. Indeed, he was very much at ease in the company of younger people. According to Cohen, people testified over and over again that 'when they were children, he was as completely at ease with them as they were with him, that they found him fluent, kind, open-minded, and open-hearted'. Furthermore, Cohen claims that he was obsessed with 'child nature', in which he saw 'the primitive and pure, the noble and divine...he yearned for their favour and friendship'.

As mentioned above, his interest in children has sparked huge controversy. Undeniably, Carroll was aware that his relationships with children were out of the ordinary. For this reason he took precautions so that he 'compromised neither the child nor his own stern conscience'. Of course, his conscience was continuously compromised and he suffered a great deal of guilt. Of particular concern here is the fact that he 'put enormous energy and time into finding appropriate child sitters, then to cultivating their friendship while photographing them and amassing his pictorial oeuvres'. Cohen claims that Carroll had an 'arrested development', whereby he remained a child all his life. Undoubtedly this was the case. Commonly those with Asperger's syndrome retain a child-like outlook, which makes the company of children more satisfying. However, his cultivation of children suggests scopophilia, which is a perverse trait.

LEWIS CARROLL SHOWS that a person with Asperger's syndrome has a capacity for enormous imagination, even if of an immature kind. His Asperger's syndrome and his immature personality – part of the condition – attuned him to children and helped him to be one of the greatest writers of children's stories of all time. He had a mechanical-mathematical mind, which is highly characteristic of persons with Asperger's syndrome. Other features of the condition that helped him be successful included his workaholism and extreme self-control.

FIVE

William Butler Yeats
(1865–1939)

T HE GENIUS OF the poet and playwright William Butler Yeats, who was awarded the Nobel Prize for Literature in 1923, is well recognized. His work is renowned for its sheer beauty and symbolism and its deep love of Irish myth and landscape.

Born in Dublin in 1865, Yeats had an unconventional upbringing. Many biographers, notably Richard Ellmann (1979), have drawn attention to his tendency to construct myths, which earned him a reputation as the 'Poet of Shadows'. Keith Alldritt (1997) claims that Yeats was a master craftsman, and that one of his most skilful constructs was his own image. He distinguished himself in many fields: in the arts as poet, playwright, painter, theatre director and occultist, and as a political figure serving the newly established Irish state as senator in the 1920s.

The aim of this chapter is to show that Yeats – like his brother, the painter Jack B. Yeats (see Chapter 19) – demonstrated evidence of Asperger's syndrome.

I believe that Yeats's poetry partially conquered the autistic world in which he lived.

Family background and childhood

Yeats inherited many family characteristics that shaped his genius as a poet. Moreover, there appear to be strong indications that relatives displayed autistic-like behaviour too.

Yeats's paternal grandfather, William Butler Yeats, was a deeply orthodox rector of the Church of Ireland, and his father a complete sceptic. As a result Yeats developed, according to Ellmann, 'an eccentric faith somewhere between his grandfather's orthodox belief and his father's unorthodox disbelief'. His grandfather was described as 'a remarkable man', but his vanity was extreme: Ellmann notes that he was 'so dandiacal that he ripped three pairs of riding breeches in a day because he insisted upon wearing them so tight'. Moreover, Ellmann claims that he was an 'unusual clergyman'. It is possible that he showed signs of Asperger's syndrome. On one occasion he boxed his son's (Yeats's father's) ears and afterwards 'shook hands with him and hoped he was not offended'. Evidently he believed in harsh discipline; he sent Yeats's father to a school run by a Scotsman whose 'floggings were famous' (Ellmann 1979).

Yeats's maternal grandfather, William Pollexfen, showed signs of severe social impairment; his maternal grandmother was deeply religious and superstitious. According to Yeats in his *Autobiographies*, childhood memories of Sligo were filled with the 'silent grandfather, inspiring fear and deference, of the quiet religious grandmother interested in nature cures, of visits of the strange melancholic uncles, and of nearly wild dogs roaming the spacious lands about Merville [home of the Pollexfens]'.

There is much evidence to suggest that Yeats's father, John Butler Yeats, had autistic traits. Despite his family's expectation of a legal career, he switched to painting. He gained a considerable reputation as a painter, but led a somewhat Bohemian life. His constant search for an individual style of painting left him unsatisfied, as Ellmann notes: 'he could never be satisfied, was constantly searching for the individual style as if for the Philosopher's Stone, yet it eluded him always'. Furthermore, Ellmann claims that he was 'too exacting'. This is consistent with the perfectionist traits of those with Asperger's syndrome. It was possibly also an autistic search for perfection in creativity.

Certainly Yeats's father was a strange and eccentric man. He had little sense of financial responsibility, which impacted on his family. Alldritt (1997) states that John B. Yeats often did portraits of people 'whose faces interested him, knowing full well his sitter could not afford to buy the finished painting'. According to Ellmann, he 'always felt financial salvation was just around the corner', also possibly indicating a naïvety associated with Asperger's syndrome. The controlling element of his personality was also evident. Ellmann points to his stubborn nature, while the writer John McGahern (1999) notes how individual and independent he was – 'he disliked being forced to do what other people planned'. John Butler Yeats also demonstrated an all-absorbing interest in his work, accompanied by self-imposed social isolation.

Many biographers have remarked on the withdrawn nature of Yeats's mother. She is described as 'taciturn, withdrawn and gloomy like all the Pollexfens' (McGahern 1999) and 'sensitive...but undemonstrative' (Ellmann 1979). By all accounts the lack of desire to interact with peers was acute in her case. Brown (1999) describes her as an 'uncommunicative, apparently emotionless companion' to Yeats's father, and quotes Yeats's own words about his mother: 'she was not sympathetic. The feelings of people around her did not concern her. She was not aware of them. She was always in an island of her own.' As Yeats grew up his mother remained a shadowy figure.

Thus it would appear that genetic input was significant in Yeats. Brown (1999) states that Yeats was 'most a Pollexfen in his refusal or inability to confront in his writings in any direct way the pain of his childhood'. However, this is largely untrue, as the difficulties in understanding and writing about his childhood resulted from autism. Equally, the assertion that lack of maternal love gave rise to his inadequacies is erroneous. Harry McGee (1999) quotes Maddox: 'the secret of Yeats is that his mother did not love him'. I disagree with this view. I believe that the secret of Yeats was the impact of autism on his life and work.

Ellmann notes that Yeats remembered little from his childhood but its 'pain'. His schooling was erratic due to his family's frequent changes of abode. He was a poor student, as is often the case with Asperger's syndrome. Indeed, very few geniuses have anything good to say about their experience of school, and Yeats was no exception: according to Ellmann, he found school 'pedestrian and demoralizing'. A schoolmate described him as follows:

> [He was a] dreamy fellow, lackadaisical too, didn't go in for games...a good talker. He would argue and discuss matters with the master...he

used to spout reams of poetry to us, which none of us could comprehend as his delivery was so fast...rather fond of attitudinising.

Alldritt (1997) remarks that Yeats remembered his time at school as 'one of failure, misery and humiliation'. He failed to distinguish himself and was poor in classics, although good at science. The family wish for him to be educated at Trinity College Dublin was unrealized when he failed to meet the entrance requirements in classics and mathematics. Ellmann notes how one headmaster was sure 'he would never amount to anything'.

Like many others with Asperger's syndrome, Yeats was bullied at school. Clearly from an early age his eccentricities – collecting butterflies and moths and incessant daydreaming – made him a figure of fun. At school in England, where he was with boys of his own age, he was called the 'Mad Irishman'. Ellmann notes that 'they laughed at his awkwardness and bullied him because he was weak'.

Like many with Asperger's syndrome, such as Wittgenstein, Ramanujan and Lewis Carroll (Fitzgerald 2004), Yeats was autodidactic. As his life progressed he educated himself in many subjects, particularly philosophy and the occult.

Indicators of Asperger's syndrome

Social behaviour

There is evidence to suggest that Yeats showed severe impairment in social interaction. Certainly during his formative years and early adulthood there was a desire for isolation and lack of interaction with peers. However, he did overcome this problem to a certain extent, becoming somewhat gregarious in later life.

Many people, including his wife, tell of Yeats being shy and timid (Ellmann 1979). Unquestionably at school he was a loner; he 'felt himself set apart' (Alldritt 1997). Ellmann attests to Yeats's isolation due to a feeling of loneliness and powerlessness during his adolescence. Moreover, according to Alldritt, he took 'intense pleasure in being alone' and engaged in 'solitary wanderings'.

References to aloofness and remoteness dominate many accounts of Yeats. McGahern (1999) describes him as 'aloof and imperious'. Yeats's old friend George Russell (Æ) remarks on the lack of a personal tone in his autobiographies: 'His memories of his childhood are the most vacant things man ever wrote, pure externalities, well written in a dead kind of way, but quite dull except for the odd flashes. The boy in the book might have become a grocer as well as a poet' (Ellmann 1979). Brown (1999) also notes the autobiographies' 'curious remoteness of tone'. Certainly this autobiographical style is typical of a person with Asperger's syndrome.

Yeats's aloofness and remoteness were often interpreted as inhumanity – a common assumption about persons with autism. This preoccupied Yeats himself. Responding to his friend's, the poet Katharine Tynan's, rebuke about his bookishness, he explained that the reason he buried his head in books was that he was anxious about other aspects of life:

> I am a much more human person than you think. I cannot help being 'inhuman' as you call it... On the rare occasions when I go to see anyone I am not quite easy in my mind, for I keep thinking I ought to be at home trying to solve my problems – I feel as if I had run away from school. So you see my life is not altogether ink and paper. (Ellmann 1979)

Furthermore, Yeats provides an explanation for his lack of desire to interact with peers: 'sometimes the barrier between myself and other people filled me with terror'. In 1909, writing an unsent letter to Robert, the son of his friend Lady Gregory, he drew attention to his lack of social instincts: 'I have no instincts in personal life. I have reasoned them all away & reason acts very slowly & with difficulty & has to exhaust every side of the subject.' Ellmann notes that he attempted to build bridges to 'connect himself with humanity', which naturally were not always successful. Indeed, this is a typical Asperger aspiration. Tellingly, Yeats's wife always maintained that he 'had no interest in people as such, only in what they said or did' (Yeats 1999). This is common to many geniuses with autism. Yeats was interested in 'literary anthropology' (Alldritt 1997), and visited peasant homes around the communities of Gort, Co. Galway to collect folklore – he was not necessarily interested in the peasants themselves. This reminds one of the activities of Bartók, who travelled about the Hungarian countryside collecting folk music and who also evidenced Asperger's syndrome (see Chapter 16).

Yeats showed an ability to form and maintain a number of friendships throughout his life, but the nature of many of those friendships was autistic. In general he formed friendships only with those that shared his interests closely, such as poets and writers – Æ, Katharine Tynan and Lady Gregory.

As he grew older, Yeats overcame his shyness somewhat. This shyness had often made him hide behind masks, whereby he became the creator of multiple identities. Frank O'Connor described Yeats's relations with other men as 'a circuitous and brilliant strategy performing complicated manoeuvres about non-existent armies' (Ellmann 1979). In fact this is typical of persons with Asperger's syndrome.

One of Yeats's most defining relationships was with the revolutionary Maud Gonne. His courtship of Gonne was naïve, and its failure depressed him. This naïvety and propensity for unrequited love is typical of persons with Asperger's syndrome. For example, Wittgenstein showed extraordinary naïvety in his marriage proposal to Marguerite Respinger, which occurred a few hours before her marriage to someone else, she having had no knowledge of the depth of his feelings towards her (Fitzgerald 2004). Yeats's obsession with Gonne meant that liaisons with other women were often idealized, resulting in a lack of appreciation of social cues, and inevitably doomed to failure.

Having reached middle age, Yeats felt an urgent need to marry; in October 1917, at the age of 52, he finally did so. Lisa Jardine, in a review of Maddox (1999), points out that his decision was influenced more by astrology than by emotion, which certainly would not be unusual in a person with Asperger's syndrome:

> For almost 30 years he had pursued the impossible dream of a lasting liaison with Maud Gonne... Time was running out for Yeats if he wanted to start a family to carry on his name. Besides, the occult sources he assiduously consulted had informed him that the autumn of that year was a propitious time for him to produce a son and heir. Casting around on the rebound for a suitable bride, he settled on an unprepossessing young woman just turned 25, Bertha Georgie Hyde-Lees, who was a member of the circle of psychics he frequented in London. (Jardine 1999)

In the conduct of his affairs, Yeats often displayed socially inappropriate behaviour. On the occasion of his marriage to Georgie he thought it unnecessary to inform his two sisters of his nuptials, despite being on good terms with them both (Alldritt 1997). As we have seen, Georgie had not been his first choice of bride. He had tried to woo Maud Gonne for many years, and then her daughter Iseult, all to no avail. This is another example of autistic inappropriateness.

Yeats was lucky to have married Georgie, as it turned out. She was the perfect mother figure for him, aside from being his muse. Moreover, she organized him and devoted herself to helping him express his creativity. He settled for 'a companionate emotion-free relationship' that clearly had a stabilizing effect on him.

Interestingly, Jardine (1999) points out that a poem from this period, 'On Woman', confirms his 'thoughtlessly patronising attitude to such a partner. The merit of a good woman is her capacity to obliterate herself in the interests of the well-being of the man.' This is often seen in the spouses or partners of geniuses with Asperger's syndrome, and is not necessarily restricted to women. Examples include the submissive partners of Wittgenstein and the wives of Alfred C. Kinsey, Bartók, etc. Following his marriage, Yeats, interestingly, chose to call his wife 'George', evidently more comfortable with the masculine form of her name. This bears some similarity to Wittgenstein's close friendship with Elizabeth Anscombe, whom he addressed affectionately as 'old man' (Monk 1990).

Yeats's social impairment was most acute in his dealings with his children. When Yeats died in 1939, his son Michael did not feel any deep sense of personal loss, as Yeats had always been to him a 'formidable, towering figure' and living with him was like 'living with a national monument' (Yeats 1999).

Narrow interests and obsessiveness

Throughout Yeats's life his interests were varied, but always pursued narrowly and obsessively – he had an extraordinary ability to immerse himself in a subject. As he approached his seventieth birthday his 'literary energy and creativity lost none of their power' (Alldritt 1997). This is in keeping with many other geniuses with Asperger's syndrome who have been highly creative right to the end of their lives, such as Wittgenstein. Geniuses have an acute sense of death, and they need to produce before they die.

An affinity with animals is a common feature of the autistic person. Certainly it was evident in Yeats's case. Ellmann notes that as a child he became preoccupied with two dogs and followed them everywhere. This affinity extended to many creatures: cats, dogs, horses and, most interestingly, insects.

Yeats had the collecting instinct so characteristic of the autistic person. Like Kinsey and Bartók, he collected insects. As a young man he went on frequent entomological field trips and, according to Alldritt, collected moths and other insects, 'in which he took a serious scientific interest'.

According to his son, Yeats was afflicted 'by extreme absent-mindedness' (Yeats 1999). On one occasion at the Arts Club in Dublin he was so distracted that 'when told he had not yet eaten he believed this, and went in and had a second dinner'. Michael B. Yeats claims that at dinner parties his father became so readily absorbed in conversation that he wouldn't know what he was eating. On one occasion after eating parsnips – a vegetable he much disliked – he turned to his wife and said 'that wasn't a very nice pudding'. His family were attuned to all signs of their father lapsing into creative mode:

> One afternoon my sister Anne got on a bus on her way home to find the poet already sitting in a front seat, obviously deep in the throes of composition. So she left him alone and took a seat near the back. In due course they both got off the bus at the family gate and, as they went in, he looked at her vaguely and asked, Who is it you are looking for? (Yeats 1999)

Yeats's repetitive interest in certain topics formed the basis of his poetry. It is also consistent with the repetitive adherence to ideas and practices found in those with Asperger's syndrome. According to Ellmann (1979), Yeats 'keeps asking the same questions over and over again until they become profound: what is truth? what is reality? what is man?' Clearly he was highly motivated, driven and obsessional in his writing. Ellmann says that 'few poets have found mastery of themselves and of their craft so difficult or have sought such mastery, through conflict and struggle, so unflinchingly' as Yeats.

Clearly Yeats was predominantly visual. As a poet he had an extraordinary visual imagination. Moreover, the use of concrete images in his work is consistent with Asperger's syndrome, and is somewhat akin to Wittgenstein's picture theory of reality. This is borne out in references to Yeats's autobiographies. Ellmann quotes from Æ, who claimed that they were far from autobiography but a 'chronological arrangement of pictures'. In fact, this is typical of 'autistic biographies', those of A.J. Ayer being a good example (see Chapter 12).

The obsession with a higher order of reality meant that Yeats's poetry tended to discount material life. John Carey (1999) points out that nearly all his great poetical statements 'disparage earthly life'. Of course, dealing with 'earthly life' is highly difficult for a person with Asperger's syndrome.

However, Yeats is atypical in some respects. His attitude to money was quite unlike other geniuses with Asperger's syndrome, such as Wittgenstein, Bartók and Ramanujan (Fitzgerald 2004). According to Alldritt (1997), when Yeats won the Nobel Prize for Literature he asked the journalist Bertie Smyllie, 'How much, Smyllie, how much is it? The answer was £7,000.' That Yeats presented an atypical picture of Asperger's syndrome on this point can perhaps best be explained by the lasting legacy of his father. The poverty and hardship that the Yeats family endured through John B.'s Bohemian years had affected them greatly. Alldritt points out that Yeats was a 'dedicated careerist, a man of determined self-interest, a man preoccupied with money, a seeker after social standing'. Moreover, he was quite good at advancing his work and getting good reviews, particularly in the 1890s with the poets of the Rhymers Club in London. It can be argued that Yeats was quite narcissistic and 'always eager to promote himself' (Alldritt 1997). He was not unlike Isaac Newton in this respect.

Routines and control

Imposition of control over his interests and over others was marked in Yeats. The issue of control was hugely central to his genius, as Alldritt remarks: 'for an important part of Yeats's genius was his keen and often manipulative relationship with the turbulent life around him as well as with the turbulent life within'.

Alldritt points out that Yeats had extraordinary 'determination and perseverance', and notes his 'pushy single-mindedness'. This was evident from an early age, when his autodidactic nature became apparent – a feature common of Asperger's syndrome. In later life, Yeats's striving for perfection led him to rewrite his previously published works in prose and verse 'indefatigably' (Ellmann 1979). Undoubtedly his force of absolute conviction led to fiercely held beliefs. In fact, this is typical of geniuses with Asperger's syndrome who force others to revise their opinions in line with their own, for example Wittgenstein and Eamon de Valera (Fitzgerald 2004).

Ellmann points to Yeats's controlling nature: he became 'a terrible man in combat, who could compel by sheer force of personality, or, as he would put it, by power of his mask, a jeering crowd into silence'. He was controlling in relation not only to his own work but also to that of friends and family. According to Alldritt (1997), he tried to control Katharine Tynan's life by planning her career: 'ever the shrewd, tireless planner of his own literary career, he also sought to organize hers'.

The frequent exertion of control made him extremely powerful. Mary Colum recalls one notorious event. At a riotous debate during the performance of J.M. Synge's play The Playboy of the Western World at the Abbey Theatre, Yeats dominated the audience, 'who remembering that passionately patriotic play [Yeats's Cathleen Ni Houlihan] forgot its antagonism for a few moments and Yeats got his cheers... I never witnessed a human being fight as Yeats fought that night, nor knew another with so many weapons in his armoury' (Colum 1939).

Speech, language and humour

Yeats showed evidence of delayed speech and language development. His language difficulties and peculiarities are well documented. In fact his mother's family believed him to be mentally as well as physically defective, having failed to teach him how to read. This phenomenon is not uncommon in persons with Asperger's syndrome. Alldritt (1997) notes that Yeats showed a 'conspicuous inability to spell and punctuate' – this inability persisted throughout his life.

As with many with Asperger's syndrome, Yeats's sense of humour was simple and juvenile. According to Ellmann (1979), it took the form of 'prankishness'.

Yeats also displayed unusual voice characteristics typical of Asperger's syndrome. There are many accounts of his beautiful speaking voice, which earned him the reputation of speaking in an 'affected voice' according to his son, who preferred to call it a 'Sligo accent' with a 'strong voice' (Yeats 1999). Ellmann claims that Yeats had a 'curiously rhythmical manner of speaking' that others found hard to reproduce. Anthony Cronin, in a review of Maddox (1999), described Yeats as 'studied in manner and speech, unremittingly poetic' (Cronin 1999). A slow, mannered way of speaking is consistent with Asperger's syndrome.

Eccentricity and non-verbal communication

Yeats displayed several non-verbal communication problems consistent with Asperger's syndrome. His eyes were distinctive and the focus of much attention: Tynan described them as 'eager, dark eyes' (Ellmann 1979). A.L. Rowse observed the older Yeats as having 'a puckered look of a small child; weak eyes, visionary and estranged from the world' (Ollard 1999). St John Ervine remembered him as follows:

> A tall man, with dark hanging hair that is now turning grey, and he has a queer way of focusing when he looks at you. I do not know what is the defective sight from which he suffers, but it makes his way of regarding you somewhat disturbing. He has a poetic appearance, entirely physical, and owing nothing to any eccentricity of dress; for, apart from his necktie, there is nothing odd about his clothes. (Mikhail 1977)

Reference has also been made to Yeats's limited facial expression. According to Brown (1999), Yeats as public man seemed to many 'cold, aloof, curiously without evident affect'.

There is evidence that Yeats had stereotypies commonly found in autism. First, he displayed repetitive motor mannerisms. These stereotyped or ritualized movements were accompanied by a dissociated or trance-like state that usually occurred when he was composing poetry. Indeed, it is a classic autistic state. Alldritt (1997) describes how he roamed 'the streets of Dublin…sometimes flapping his arms about as he recited or composed poems aloud'. Tynan described their long walks around Dublin, where Yeats would 'flail his arms around in a violent way that…intrigued policemen'.

A second stereotypy involved a speech element. Alldritt quotes from John Butler Yeats's recollection of the times when Yeats would compose poetry at home:

> …oblivious to everyone else, [he] would start to murmur, developing lines of poetry. Then he would speak them louder and louder. And louder. Then, still utterly preoccupied, he would chant and declaim. Finally, as John Yeats remembered, 'his sisters would call out to him, "Now, Willie, stop composing!"'.

The chanting and ritualized movements generally occurred at the beginning of a period of composition, which was likely to happen at any time, as Michael Butler Yeats (1999) pointed out:

> All the family knew the signs, we were careful to do nothing that might interrupt the flow of thought. Without warning he would begin to make a low, tuneless humming sound, and his right hand would wave vaguely as if beating time. This could happen at the dinner table, while playing croquet, or sitting in a bus, and he would become totally oblivious to what was going on around him.

Clearly, Yeats had an extraordinary effect on people in much the same way that geniuses with great originality generally have on their followers. When working on *Blake's Prophetic Books* with Edwin Ellis, Yeats unnerved Ellis's German wife to a bizarre degree:

> …she became alarmed by the shabbily dressed mystical poet who would throw his arms about rhythmically in her drawing-room, as though conducting an orchestra… On one occasion she threw him out of the house for, said Yeats, she was entirely convinced that he had thrown a spell on her. (Alldritt 1997)

Autistic aggression

There are many accounts of Yeats's violent temper and aggressive behaviour, especially towards family members. This leads one to suggest that he possibly had 'autistic aggression' (the typical propensity for uncontrollable bouts of temper found in persons with autism). Alldritt (1997) describes him as 'a combative man with a violent temper that sustained him in many nasty quarrels... a brawler and scrapper'.

Identity diffusion

Yeats manifested the problem of identity diffusion to an extraordinary extent. Identity diffusion is common to many with Asperger's syndrome. Certainly to the general public he presented several distinct personae – the poet, the dramatist, the nationalist, the politician – whereas Yeats the painter and the occultist were less well known. It was not surprising that Ellmann titled his biography of the poet *Yeats – The Man and the Masks*. Similarly, Desmond McCarthy highlighted the issue of identity in 1934 (in *The Sunday Times*) with his reference to Yeats's 'Mask or Anti-self'. I believe that the mask or anti-self is a manifestation of his autistic persona, and indicates the cognitive intellectual approach typical in ASD/Asperger's syndrome.

It is clear that from early adolescence Yeats showed significant dissatisfaction with his 'self'. According to Alldritt (1997), as a young man Yeats spoke 'only of the terrible inner turmoil, the churning sense of inadequacy within. As he approached his twentieth birthday his sense of self was unformed, still volatile and a mass of contradictions.' The multiple personae were arguably the outcome of a restless mind, rooted in insecurity over personal identity.

This insecurity led to an interest in the occult and astrology, and hence to his belief that the transmutation of the soul could facilitate the remaking of the self again and again. In this regard, Ellmann (1979) notes how Yeats believed that 'the human mind had power to control the universe, to make and unmake reality'.

In later life Yeats showed a certain dissatisfaction with masks and the multiple personae he presented. Ellmann compares him to 'Melville's Ahab', whereby he sometimes wanted 'to break through all masks'. This could be interpreted as an attempt by someone with Asperger's syndrome to make real contact with other people. Yeats did change, grow and develop, as persons with Asperger's syndrome certainly can do.

Many commentators claim that by immersing himself in masks and creeds – often of an esoteric nature – Yeats distanced himself from reality (or, more specifically, common sense). Certainly Carey (1999) holds this view. He points out that 'as time went on, [Yeats] accumulated a bizarre panoply of creeds that could liberate him from the prison of common sense – Rosicrucianism, reincarnation, cyclical patterns of history based on the phases of the moon'. I disagree that Yeats wanted to be liberated from common sense: indeed, he lacked common sense and therefore could not be liberated from it. Moreover, with marked social impairment, lacking empathy and understanding, he was incapable of common sense.

Ellmann remarks that Yeats went into long sieges of self-criticism from 1908 to 1910. In 1908, he began to keep a diary recording dissatisfaction with his life and his attempts at reformation. This has echoes of Wittgenstein and Lewis Carroll, both of whom displayed an 'autistic superego'.

Sometimes he was content to think that his real self was in his verse. 'My character is so little myself,' he wrote, 'that all my life it has thwarted me. It has affected my poems, my true self, no more than the character of a dancer affects the movements of a dance' (Ellmann 1979).

Politics

Following the foundation of the Irish State, Yeats became a distinguished senator and held progressive ideas on education and equality. He was involved in drafting a new Copyright Act and helped develop a new Irish coinage (not unlike Newton's work in the Royal Mint), although he had little knowledge of economic questions and practical politics.

In common with many persons with features of Asperger's syndrome, who are attracted to fundamentalist forms of governance, Yeats's political leanings were controversial. During the 1930s he was attracted to Mussolini's elitist government and got involved with an Irish political group, the Blueshirts, known for its fascist persuasions. Ellmann (1979) notes that Yeats also advocated eugenics and individualism during this time, and refers to the period as his 'flirtation with authoritarianism'. However, it can be argued that Yeats's 'hostility to democracy' was due to his political naïvety. This is not a surprising trait in persons with Asperger's syndrome, as they lack empathy and show little reciprocal social interaction, as with de Valera and Keith Joseph (Fitzgerald 2004). Nonetheless, Yeats later became aware of the dangers of political fanaticism.

Religion and esotericism

Persons with Asperger's syndrome are frequently attracted to the supernatural and esoteric subjects. Newton had a considerable interest in occultism.

Yeats's interest specifically in 'psychical research and mystical philosophy' grew out of dissatisfaction with himself and an awareness of his own imperfections, according to Ellmann (1979). More significantly, it increasingly became the key inspiration for his poetry. As he grew to maturity, Ellmann notes that 'he wanted not merely to protect the inviolability of his own mind, but to ferret out more and deeper secrets which were withheld from logicians and literalists'. Certainly his obsessive need for the esoteric, and the ambiguity that it entailed, was central to his autism and his genius.

Arguably, the practices and beliefs associated with occultism facilitated Yeats's social naïvety. Consequently, many critics and commentators have raised the issue of his gullibility, given that occultism has a reputation for drawing people not always of rational mind. Alldritt (1997) believes that Yeats's venture into occultism was bizarre in so far as it was 'theologically and socially perverse'. Undoubtedly, the ritual, magic and mystery associated with the hermetic Order of the Golden Dawn held particular appeal for the poet.

Co-morbidity

Ellmann notes that Yeats talked about his 'dreadful despondent moods', leading one to believe that he may have suffered from a recurring depression. Certainly depression is associated with Asperger's syndrome.

Motor clumsiness

There is evidence that Yeats showed signs of motor clumsiness. His awkwardness and physical weakness as a child kept him from being a favourite of his mother's family, who were excellent athletes. Ellmann notes that it upset Yeats's father that he 'did not learn to ride well', nor had he the physical courage to make up for his lack of horsemanship.

WILLIAM BUTLER YEATS meets the criteria for Asperger's syndrome, and resembles the other people described in this book in terms of problems in social relations, problems with empathy and eccentric interests.

SIX

Arthur Conan Doyle
(1859–1930)

ARTHUR CONAN DOYLE was born in Edinburgh on 22 May 1859 ('Conan' was originally his middle name; he later adopted it as part of his surname). Having trained in medicine, he achieved immortality as creator of the hugely popular fictional detective Sherlock Holmes – his first Holmes novel, *A Study in Scarlet*, was published in 1887, and many other novels and stories followed. These were so successful that Conan Doyle was able to give up his medical practice. When he tried to kill off Sherlock Holmes, the outcry was so great that he was forced to bring him back to life.

Louise Hawkins, whom Conan Doyle married in 1885, died in 1900. He married Jeanne Leckie in 1907, and had five children in all.

Conan Doyle served as a doctor in the Boer War, and was knighted for defending Britain's record in that conflict. He was very interested in spiritualism, especially after his son was killed in the First World War.

Conan Doyle died on 7 July 1930, aged 71. This chapter considers the evidence that he had Asperger's syndrome, and proposes that Sherlock Holmes was the autistic creation of an autistic mind. All of the biographical details and quoted extracts in this chapter come from Stashower (1999).

Background

Arthur Conan Doyle's paternal grandfather was the Irish political cartoonist John Doyle, who revolutionized political caricature in the early Victorian era. One of John Doyle's sons, Richard (uncle of Arthur) was a prominent caricaturist and illustrator.

Like many geniuses, Conan Doyle resented 'the soul-deadening' quality of the education he received. He was a good athlete and a keen boxer, but a 'lonely student'. He 'read with an indiscriminate passion' – many persons with high-functioning autism tend to read tremendously. He went on a whaling voyage, and once said that 'several times in my life I have done utterly reckless things with so little motive that I have found it difficult to explain them to myself afterwards'.

Conan Doyle suddenly gave up his medical practice and went to Vienna to train as an eye surgeon, but found it difficult to follow the lectures in German. He returned without qualifications and set up a practice in London, which was unsuccessful. Then he began to write about a character called Sherlock Holmes and his friend, Dr John Watson – he wrote an average of 3000 words a day.

Indicators of Asperger's syndrome

Social behaviour

Conan Doyle had 'a rigid sense of honour, the code of chivalry that guided his life and shaped his fiction'. Nevertheless, his 'temper flared often. He took offence easily, and could be curt with associates.'

Narrow interests and obsessiveness

A fellow writer stated that Conan Doyle 'would sit at a small desk in a corner of his own drawing room, writing a story while a dozen people around him were talking and laughing'. He had enormous resilience and energy, and researched his topics in great detail.

It appears that the satisfaction that Conan Doyle got from setting and solving puzzles was purely intellectual – he wasn't interested in financial recompense. He suffered very severe depression, and 'his black moods became more frequent and longer in duration' as he grew older. He was also an insomniac. Writing served as an antidepressant for him.

Conan Doyle applied his powers of detection with some success in real life, defending with a 'religious fervour' those that he felt had been falsely accused of crimes. He was instrumental in securing the release after 19 years of Oscar Slater, a German Jew who had been wrongly convicted of murder. It is interesting that 'like Holmes he possessed a powerful memory and an encyclopaedic knowledge of crime'. When he came across a miscarriage of justice, he wrote, 'I was called upon to do what I could to set it right'.

He had a 'passion for cricket' which embraced statistics. It is not uncommon for persons with Asperger's syndrome to be very interested in cricket statistics.

He showed autistic novelty-seeking: he was a risk-taker who went up in a hot-air balloon and a biplane, and was enthusiastic about motoring. While novelty-seeking is usually associated with attention deficit hyperactivity disorder (ADHD), it can also be associated with Asperger's syndrome, as for example in the case of Bruce Chatwin (Chapter 8).

Routines and control

Conan Doyle was a workaholic who imposed a punishing schedule on himself and thus produced a large body of writing.

Speech, language and humour

According to Stashower, Conan Doyle 'had no natural facility for public speaking – his manner of speech is said to have been clipped and hesitant'. He had 'a nervous halting voice whose burrs recalled the banks and braes of Scotland'.

Appearance and demeanour

A friend described Conan Doyle as a 'great, burly, clumsy man with an unwieldy-looking body that was meant for a farm bailiff, with hands like Westphalian hams'. Stashower points out that 'behind the placid, sleepy eyed demeanour was a man of strong convictions, some of them absurd'.

Naïvety and childishness

According to Stashower, Conan Doyle had 'too much scruple and not enough guile…for deception'. He wrote a history of the First World War, employing, as usual, 'exhaustive research and painstaking accuracy', but was rather naïve in accepting what British commanders told him.

He showed enormous gullibility in relation to paranormal phenomena.

Lack of empathy

Conan Doyle's first wife, Louise, developed tuberculosis and died after a long illness. It appears that he failed to notice her deteriorating health until it was at a very advanced stage.

Spiritualism

Conan Doyle was always interested in the spirit world, like W.B. Yeats. He developed an interest in automatic writing, and appeared to see no contradiction in being an advocate of logical reason on one hand and a committed spiritualist on the other. Stashower points out:

> 'Fairies, ghosts and that' have been the millstone of Conan Doyle's reputation for the better part of a century. Toward the end of his life, Conan Doyle came to believe that communication with dead souls was possible. His efforts to spread this message, which he considered the most important work of his life, proved to be his undoing. The British public watched with growing incredulity as he made one foray after another into the spirit realm. On any given day he might pronounce upon a ghostly photograph of fallen World War I soldiers, or speculate on a possible literary collaboration with the late Charles Dickens. In America, where such reports were less frequent, it was possible to remain sympathetic, if bemused. In Britain, the general public's tolerance began to fray. 'Poor Sherlock Holmes,' ran one headline, 'Hopelessly Crazy?'

Stashower entitles two of his chapters 'Is Conan Doyle mad?' and 'Away with the fairies'. It appeared at this point that Conan Doyle 'believed in fairies'.

Autistic superego

According to Stashower, 'Conan Doyle's private sense of honour mattered more to him than public opinion. His daughter Jean once wrote: "he seemed to us to be the very personification of the chivalry of stories of King Arthur's Round Table".' Persons with high-functioning autism very often have high moral and ethical standards.

Personality

Stashower describes Conan Doyle as 'a perfectly impossible person'. For one of his plays he took on the role of impresario and rented a theatre himself for six months: clearly he had a 'take-charge personality'. The financial cost was great; he ended up with 'heavy debts and an expensive lease on an empty theatre'. He then wrote a new play – The Speckled Band – from 'blank page to full production in little more than three weeks'. This allowed him to recover his financial losses.

Val McDermid, in a review of Stashower (1999) (Sunday Tribune, 5 March 2000), points out 'a yawning gap at the heart of this book…[in] the place where insight should be. Reading this, it is hard to form any sense of Conan Doyle's interior life or his personality.' McDermid continues: 'Conan Doyle was reticent about most of the private areas of his life. On several occasions, his version of key events underwent several transformations, each reflecting better on him than the previous one' (indeed, the same could be said of Hans Christian Andersen). McDermid notes that 'at a time when biography is expected to provide more penetrating insights into its subjects, *Teller of Tales* is, ultimately, a disappointment, skimming surfaces rather than probing beneath them'. However, I believe that Daniel Stashower has done an extremely good job in writing about Conan Doyle, and has told what there is to tell. It is very difficult to find the central self of a person with Asperger's syndrome, because this is a central deficiency in Asperger's syndrome. It is impossible to build up a sense of oneself without a good theory of other people's minds; in Asperger's syndrome, this is lacking.

Sherlock Holmes

Interestingly, Sherlock Holmes – a fictional character – shows the characteristics of a person with Asperger's syndrome. One interpretation of the stories is that Holmes represents Conan Doyle and Dr Watson represents a non-autistic person.

Holmes's phraseology is very precise, pedantic and scientific – he is 'the perfect reasoning and observing machine', i.e. a kind of 'autistic machine'. Apparently there is little non-verbal communication. Personal relationships are very functional. Holmes:

- is a loner
- has weak central coherence and is highly observant of small details
- is very intellectual and well read
- is highly knowledgeable, with a vast store of information
- wants everything to be in due order
- has a great sense of omnipotence and total control
- is so brilliant that he is almost megalomaniacal – a feature of persons with Asperger's syndrome and genius.

There is very little emotion in what Holmes says; he is like a computer analysing a forensic problem.

Holmes states in 'The Stockbroker Case' that he rarely goes anywhere except on professional business – this has an autistic flavour. In 'The Adventure of the Copper Beeches', Holmes keeps saying, 'I need data, I can't make progress without facts.' He spends entire nights on chemical researches. In 'The Red-Headed League' he is very interested in music and indeed is a composer – some of the greatest composers, such as Beethoven (Chapter 14) and Bartók (Chapter 16), had Asperger's syndrome.

In 'The Adventure of Gloria Scott', Holmes describes his childhood. It is full of 'cerebral' fact. Everything is spoken of in a computer-like manner. At the very end of the story, Holmes says 'those are the facts'. Persons with Asperger's syndrome are interested in facts. They have acute powers of observation – they are 'lookers' and can see small details that other people would miss; this is evidence of low central coherence and would clearly be very useful in detective work. (Happé (1999) defines central coherence as 'the everyday tendency to process incoming information in its context – that is, pulling information together for higher-level meaning – often at the expense of memory for detail'; she notes that 'weak central coherence may underlie many of the "modular talents" found in autism'. Sigman and Capps (1997) point out that in autism, 'a deficient drive for central coherence…accounts for…the obsessive desire for sameness, repetitive and stereotypical movements, restricted range of interest, and fragmented sensations'.) Persons with Asperger's syndrome are often 'anti-theory', as Hermelin (2001) has pointed out – theory must not be allowed to precede the facts.

The language in the Holmes stories is very precise – almost formulaic. There are tremendous twists to stories, which keep the excitement high. These twists appear to be brought about by new observations that a person with little central coherence has the capacity to make.

Sherlock Holmes shows total control – cerebral control, cognitive control, certainty. He dominates the relationship with Watson, displaying an 'autistic narcissism'.

What interests Holmes most is not status but the problems that he is asked to solve. It is puzzles that fascinate Holmes – the intellectual aspects of cases. These satisfy his curiosity. He is clearly bored by social gatherings of affluent people, parties, etc. His interests are narrow: he reads only the criminal news and the agony column. This is a perfect example of autistic narrowness of interests.

Other characters in Holmes stories also appear to be autistic. Professor Moriarty, the arch-criminal, is an extraordinary mathematician, but Conan

Doyle gives him hereditary criminality (this sounds very modern in the 21st century). It appears that Moriarty is an autistic psychopath. He is a classic high-functioning person with autism – a genius, mathematician, philosopher, abstract thinker; he has a deep criminal mind and shows diminished non-verbal communication. The discussion between Moriarty and Sherlock Holmes at the beginning of *The Adventure of the Final Problem* is a classic dialogue of a rather stilted kind between two persons with Asperger's syndrome, with few words spoken.

CONAN DOYLE IS a classic example of a novelist of genius who had Asperger's syndrome. His fictional legacy is as interesting to us today as it ever was. Like another genius, W.B. Yeats, he also had highly eccentric interests, partly because of a certain naïvety and difficulty in recognizing deception.

SEVEN

George Orwell
(1903–50)

'GEORGE ORWELL' WAS the pseudonym, adopted in 1933, of Eric Arthur Blair. Orwell was a prolific novelist, non-fiction writer, political thinker and intellectual. His best-known novels, *Animal Farm* and *1984*, have been translated into more than 60 languages and have sold more than 40 million copies. He was born in Bengal, where his father was a colonial official, and moved to England as a baby. He served in the Indian Imperial Police in Burma in the 1920s, and fought on the Republican side in the Spanish Civil War, in which he was wounded. He died of lung disease in 1950.

V.S. Pritchett called Orwell 'the wintry conscience of a generation'. He showed integrity, idealism, commitment, and an 'obstinate search for moral values', but suffered from a 'chaos of self-doubt'; He had 'a noble character', but was also 'violent, capable of cruelty, tormented by guilt, masochistically self-punishing, sometimes suicidal' (Meyers 2000). His books are still fresh and relevant.

This chapter considers the evidence that Orwell had Asperger's syndrome. All of the biographical details and quoted extracts in this chapter come from Meyers (2000).

Family background

Orwell's great-great-grandfather, Charles Blair of Winterbourne, Dorset, was the absentee owner of tropical plantations and 'wretched slaves in Jamaica'. His mother, Ida, was described as having 'an acute mind'; she 'dressed rather picturesquely and was fond of oversized jewellery: jet beads, amber necklaces and dangling earrings'.

His father, Richard Walmesley Blair, may have had an autism spectrum disorder. He has variously been described as weak, passive, tyrannical, autocratic and distant; an 'unsmiling and rather forbidding figure who rarely spoke'. He was 'completely self-absorbed' and took no interest in children; he was 'henpecked and narrowly focused on the cinema, bridge and golf'. He and Orwell's mother had separate rooms and separate interests. Orwell's relations with his father were strained.

Richard Blair joined the British forces for the First World War at the age of 60 – apparently his wife was glad to be rid of him. Ida Blair 'could not be bothered to see her small children' even during their holidays – a rather eccentric type of mothering. She led a 'self-absorbed life'.

Childhood and education

At 18 months, Orwell contracted the lung disease that would eventually lead to his death at the age of 46. He was described as a weak, miserable child.

His education comprised five years at St Cyprian's Prep School followed by four years at Eton. He suffered a great deal at school, and had highly unpleasant experiences with teachers – this is not uncommon for persons with Asperger's syndrome. A teacher beat him savagely for bed-wetting. According to Meyers, 'his cynicism about the school's ethos and arrogance about his own ability made him unpopular with the other boys'. He was described as 'not an affectionate little boy…there was no warmth in him… Reclusive and often weeping, he was bullied by the louts who were jealous of his intelligence and despised his awkwardness – he read books and was no good at games – and were angry at his difference from the herd.' This is typical of Asperger's syndrome. As Orwell himself put it, 'I had no money, I was weak, I was ugly, I was unpopular, I had a chronic cough, I was cowardly, I smelt'.

Orwell was interested in natural history, vampires and the supernatural. He was a highly intelligent student, and 'genuinely different from the other boys'. At Eton he appeared to be 'unusually grown up, literate and satirical', and his 'subversive intelligence undermined the traditional values of the school'. Cyril Connolly stated that 'his mind worked in rather different ways, his reactions were different from the ordinary boys… He loved airing his knowledge, particularly to the masters who were slightly shocked to find someone so well read.' A classmate stated that 'he never seemed to love anybody'; he also 'didn't really like other people. He liked their intellectual

side, someone to talk to, but friends didn't really mean anything to him.'
Again, these are classic signs of Asperger's syndrome. He hated the school,
and in 1939 was delighted to hear that it had burnt down. Many persons with
Asperger's syndrome hate their school experience.

Indicators of Asperger's syndrome

Social behaviour

In a review of *1984*, Julian Symons noted that Orwell was 'a novelist interested in ideas, rather than in personal relationships'. He was repeatedly
described as having no close friends (or, as is typical with Asperger's
syndrome, only one friend), and as being very much the odd man out. Arthur
Koestler stated that 'the closer one came to him, the more there seemed to be a
barrier against warmth and personal contact' (Meyers 2000). Orwell spoke of
'the star-like isolation in which human beings live'.

He had quite a few physical relationships with women, but these had 'absolutely no warmth of contact' on his part. He always found it difficult to
'reveal his inner self, express his deepest feelings and get close to people –
even during sexual intimacy'. A woman with whom he had a relationship said
that there was no great romantic passion: Orwell wasn't that sort of man. He
didn't open up with her, even when they made love.

One of his pupils described him as an introvert whose mind was elsewhere. He was aloof, austere, detached and remote, yet guilty about his inability to belong. In Burma he kept very much to himself. An Englishwoman who
knew him there characterized him as 'a delicate and shy man, brusque and
unsociable, with no small talk'.

Apparently he 'believed he was ugly and felt that women, whose needs he
did not fully understand, did not welcome his attentions'. He was 'shy, inhibited and self-conscious', and 'thought English women were distant and unattainable'. According to Meyers, 'in his [Orwell's] experience women were
quite insatiable, and never seemed to be fatigued by no matter how much
love-making', adding that Orwell 'suspected that in every marriage the
struggle was always the same – the man trying to escape from sexual intercourse'.

Orwell married Eileen O'Shaughnessy in 1936. She was 'the only person
who ever got very close to him'. Eileen was herself an unusual personality and
'rather gawky' – perhaps this is why she was able to have a close relationship
with him.

The couple lived in rough accommodation, grew vegetables and ran a village shop. He was grossly insensitive to his wife and neglected her health; 'she lost the satisfaction of her own professional career, and had to endure harsh conditions, boring work with animals, tedium in the shop and isolation in the village, while he was constantly absorbed in his writing'. She suffered a great deal in the marriage, and died during an operation in 1945, at the age of 39. Afterwards he 'impulsively proposed marriage to several attractive younger women whom he scarcely knew'. He had a bizarre deathbed marriage to a woman named Sonia Brownell, which was highly inappropriate for all concerned.

Orwell wrote of wanting to find some way of getting out of the respectable world altogether; he was 'drawn to the marginal, the destitute and the dispossessed'. Persons with Asperger's syndrome are very much outsiders. He was said to be 'really at home only with animals and children', and was 'a mine of information on birds and animals', to the point of being a bore. Again, this is very typical of persons with Asperger's syndrome. Like Ludwig Wittgenstein, who also had Asperger's syndrome, 'with bright or normal children, he was an excellent teacher'.

Narrow interests and obsessiveness

'Orwell's main interests in life were narrowly focused on his ruling passions – literature and politics'. He 'always worked tremendously hard, rarely took any time off and – except when he was ill or during the war – began his next book soon as he'd finished his last one'.

The characters in Orwell's books have been described as 'one-dimensional'. Norman Collins, a reader for the publisher Gollancz, regarded him as 'bizarre' and an 'in-house madman'. Collins said

> it is perfectly clear that he had been through hell, and that he is probably still there. He would certainly be a plum for a practising psycho-analyst. There is in his work, either latent or fully revealed, almost every one of the major aberrations. Indeed, the chaotic structure…would suggest some kind of mental instability.

Orwell 'wrote most effectively about things he had actually observed, deliberately sought out experiences he could use in his work'. Persons with Asperger's syndrome are better with concrete things, and tend to like classic realistic novelists – Orwell liked Somerset Maugham because he had the 'power of telling a story straightforwardly and without frills'. Also, Orwell focused on 'aspects of things that no one else would have noticed'. Seeing things from a different angle is an Asperger's trait.

A friend described Orwell as 'gloomy and complaining...he didn't really understand people...women in particular, he couldn't give himself...writing was the one great thing in his life. Nothing – not even people – got in the way of that.' The socialist historian John Morris described him as possessing 'benevolence and fanaticism' (Meyers 2000).

Orwell admired the poet W.B. Yeats, who also had Asperger's syndrome (see Chapter 5).

Routines and control

Orwell tended to be very domineering and dogmatic. He was highly independent, and would never 'desert his own individualistic standards to conform to a different, more socially acceptable mode of behaviour'. He had a 'mania about personal cleanliness', and was very squeamish and sensitive to smell.

Orwell was an extremely controlling man; he was 'absorbed in his own work, needed an unusual amount of privacy and independence, and also wanted the freedom to have other women'. This shows a gross lack of empathy for his wife, who noted that 'for him his work comes before anybody'.

He was 'a strict disciplinarian: while teaching he kept a thick cane near his desk, used it frequently and 'would cane you unmercifully at the slightest provocation'. This reminds one of Wittgenstein, who used brutal corporal punishment on the children he taught.

In Burma, Orwell was 'strongly attracted to the uniform, the money, the adventure, the danger, the authority and power of the quasi-military police force, which would put him in charge of a small bit of Empire'. In the Burma police you had 'a certain amount of independence and responsibility. You were on your own quite a lot'.

Speech, language and humour

Orwell was described as having a 'flat dead voice'. His housekeeper stated that he would 'make a highly satisfied sort of squeaky whine, rather like a puppy, if he was eating pudding that he really enjoyed'.

In Burma he showed tremendous linguistic skill: he picked up new languages relatively easily, and could speak eight languages.

He disliked frivolity.

Naïvety and childishness

Juan Negrín, prime minister of the Spanish Republic from 1937 to 1939, described Orwell as

> a decent and righteous gentleman...[with] a too rigid, puritanical frame, gifted with a candour bordering on naiveté, highly critical but blindly credulous, morbidly individualistic but submitting lazily and without discernment to the atmosphere of the gregarious community in which he voluntarily and instinctively anchors himself, and so supremely honest and self-denying that he would not hesitate to change his mind once he perceived himself to be wrong.

According to Victor Gollancz, his publisher, Orwell had 'great difficulty grasping what constituted libel in this country, even when the legal position has been clearly explained to him, or the very real dangers involved'. He was also 'naïve about household affairs'.

Lack of empathy

Because of his lack of empathy or understanding of the rules of social relations, Orwell could be extremely tactless in his personal relationships with women. One woman described him as 'too prickly to be nice, too cynical, too perverse, too contradictory, too paradoxical, a strange mix of shyness and assertiveness, endowed with a fundamental honesty and commonsense that she never questioned along with small-minded...prejudices'.

Appearance and demeanour

As a small child Orwell showed evidence of 'a stiff posture'. He was 'always shy and awkward'; at school he was 'a bit like a hamster' and 'a stork-like figure, prematurely adult, fluttering about the school yard in his black gown'. Later he had 'a commanding presence (intensified by his ascetic gauntness)'. Like many people with Asperger's syndrome, he was physically courageous.

In Spain he had an eccentric appearance, and wore a very odd mixture of clothes. At other times he didn't wear proper clothes during bad weather, and got very sick.

His friend John Morris said that 'Orwell always reminded me of one of those figures on the front of Chartres Cathedral; there was a sort of pinched Gothic quality about his tall thin frame...in repose his lined face suggested the grey asceticism of a medieval saint carved in stone and very weathered'.

Autistic aggression

> For most of his life Orwell had a tendency to violence, settling scores
> with his fists at school, kicking servants in Burma, holding his own in
> the rough Paris kitchens and using the cane freely on unruly school-
> boys. Quarrelling with an elderly but contentious taxi-driver in Paris,
> en route to Spain in 1936, he exclaimed: 'you think you are too old for
> me to smash your face in. Don't be too sure.

Rayner Heppenstall, who once shared a flat with Orwell, stated that the latter
knocked him unconscious in a fight. Heppenstall said that when he became
conscious Orwell pushed him back,

> armed with his shooting-stick...poking the aluminium point into my
> stomach. I pushed it aside, and sprang at him. He fetched me a dreadful
> crack across the legs and then raised the shooting-stick over his head. I
> looked at his face. Through my private mist I saw in it a curious blend of
> fear and sadistic exaltation.

Orwell was capable of extremely aggressive thoughts, and once stated that
'the greatest joy in the world would be drive a bayonet into a Buddhist priest's
guts'. He was 'fiercely combative in his polemical writings'.

Autistic superego

Orwell had 'a deep sense of guilt that pervaded his personality and his
writing'. V.S. Pritchett described him as 'a kind of saint'; his biographer Noel
Annan observed 'a biting, bleak, self-critical, self-denying man of the idealist
left...[he] spoke with the voice of ethical socialism...he was the first saint of
Our Age, quirky, fierce, independent and beholden to none' (quoted in
Meyers 2000).

A woman who had known him in Burma remarked on the 'minute care
with which he sifted each case, his passion for justice, his dislike of prejudiced
remarks about anyone, however lowly, and his sense of utter fairness in his
minutest dealings'. Cyril Connolly stated that Orwell 'could not blow his nose
without moralising on conditions in the handkerchief industry'. He showed a
'scruffy asceticism...idealism, self-sacrifice, honesty and independence eventually became identified with his literary work'. The poet Edouard Roditi
described him as having a 'gnawing social conscience'.

Orwell relished 'his monkish poverty' (as an aside, it is interesting that
Keith Joseph, who also had Asperger's syndrome (Fitzgerald 2004), was nicknamed 'the Mad Monk'). 'Tormented by a social conscience, he felt uneasy

(even when relatively poor) about having more money than anyone else.' This is reminiscent of Ludwig Wittgenstein and Simone Weil (Chapter 11).

The author Mark Benny wondered 'whether Orwell revered tradition or was slightly mad'. Orwell's friend Richard Rees noted his capacity 'to be painfully scrupulous while painfully uncomfortable'. The deprivations of the Blitz suited him very well, and he was very much at home in it. He had a 'pared-down personality'.

Orwell took 'personal responsibility for creating a morality based on humanistic socialism. His constant disregard for his own health, especially on the remote and sodden island of Jura [in the Scottish Hebrides], cut his life short at the age of 46'.

Depression

Orwell suffered from depression, and compared himself to an Old Testament prophet: 'you complain about the gloominess of my letters...this age makes me so sick that sometimes I am almost impelled to stop at a corner and start calling down curses from Heaven like Jeremiah or Ezra'.

Oppositionality and autistic hyperactivity

'In a famous autobiographical passage in *The Road to Wigan Pier*, he explained that after his experiencing Burma he became violently opposed to a settled, normal, prosperous, comfortable middle-class way of life, and saw tramping as a kind of expiation.' Gaud, one of his teachers at school, also found him quite oppositional. The writer Cyril Connolly described him as a 'rebel...[with a] supercilious voice, he was one of those boys who seemed born old' (Meyers 2000).

To join the Burma Police after Eton seemed an extremely odd and eccentric decision. The tradition was for people to go to Oxford or Cambridge from Eton. However, persons with Asperger's syndrome don't follow the beaten path; his decision not to go to Oxford or Cambridge was part of his oppositional behaviour, which is a characteristic of Asperger's syndrome.

His fascination with tramping revealed two important aspects of his character: the wanderer and the outsider. 'He could never remain in one place for long and he only felt right with the world when he stood at a slight angle to society'.

As a child he showed evidence of autistic hyperactivity.

Perverse behaviour

Orwell had a 'self-consciously perverse attitude'. There were certainly strong sado-masochistic elements in his personality. He beat his servants, and was quite masochistic. The poet Ruth Pitter stated that he was 'a wrong-headed young man'; she was well aware of the cruel elements in his personality.

After Burma he began his expeditions as a tramp, and

> continued, on and off for the next four years, the self-punishing experiments that mystified his family and friends. To go from policeman to tramp was a radical venture: part expiation, part social exploration, part self-scrutiny. Tramping won him time to examine his life, to find his purpose, to focus his aspirations. It gave him original material to write about, made him more worldly and less self-absorbed. But like so many other aspects of his life, guilt provided the initial impetus – an irrational yet deep-rooted guilt that fed on past guilt and formed a kind of disfiguring hump that he always carried around with him.

In fact a great deal of this was autistic behaviour. Orwell was somewhat like Wittgenstein in being attracted to very simple, manual jobs, and to 'isolation and hardship'.

Of his tramping days, Pitter remarked that he was 'exposing himself in such weather in totally inadequate clothing. It wasn't just poverty. It was suicidal perversity.' His health had been poor even before he started all this.

Jura was an isolated place where the climate was damp, and it was uncomfortable to live in. Orwell's moving there reminds one of Ludwig Wittgenstein going to Bergen. Once again Orwell was showing his 'self-destructive impulse'.

The writer Herbert Gorman 'noticed Orwell's masochism and shrewdly observed that he "rather enjoys being down and out"'.

Brenda Salkeld, a close friend of Orwell, described an incident that he recounted to her:

> I nearly died of the cold the other day when bathing, because I had walked out to Easton Broad not intending to bathe, & then the water looked so nice that I took off my clothes & went in, & then about 50 people came up & rooted themselves to the spot. I wouldn't have minded that, but among them was a coastguard who could have had me up for bathing naked, so I had to swim up & down for the best part of half an hour, pretending to like it. (quoted in Meyers 2000)

Orwell had 'a sadistic streak, a talent for writing about animals and an ability to add new phrases to the English language'. He gambled recklessly with his health, his reputation and his future.

GEORGE ORWELL MEETS the criteria for Asperger's syndrome.

EIGHT

Bruce Chatwin

(1940–89)

THE NOVELIST AND travel writer Bruce Chatwin was born in Birmingham in 1940. After working at Sotheby's of London as an art expert, he embarked on a series of eccentric and restless journeys that provided material for unusual and thought-provoking books, several of which won major prizes. His writings included *In Patagonia, The Viceroy of Ouidah, On the Black Hill, The Songlines* and *Utz*.

At the age of 25 Chatwin married an American woman, Elizabeth Chanler. Their 23-year marriage (punctuated by a judicial separation) was a highly unconventional one, as the couple spent long spells apart and he had many affairs with men and women. He died of an AIDS-related illness at the age of 48.

Chatwin is generally seen as a highly enigmatic character. This chapter sets out to explore his personality, and to present the evidence that he may have had Asperger's syndrome. Unless otherwise indicated, all of the biographical details and quoted extracts in this chapter come from Shakespeare (2000).

Family background

On his father's side there were Milward ancestors who had a reputation of being 'adventurers, corner-cutters and embezzlers'. Robert Milward was dismissed by the Duke of Marlborough for 'gross incompetence'; his 'extravagance matched his recklessness'. He was imprisoned for fraud. These traits may have surfaced in Chatwin, for whom, according to Shakespeare, 'theft, plagiarism, pick-pocketing…were writer's skills'. The art critic Ted

Lucie-Smith stated: 'Bruce was a great intellectual thief. He had no respect for intellectual property.' Stella Wilkinson, a friend, described him as a 'street urchin'.

Bruce's father was a 'big, socially awkward, decent man and bossy as some shy people are'. His mother, Margharita Turnell, was 'highly strung'. Hugh Chatwin, Bruce's brother, stated that his mother was 'a bit of Scarlett O'Hara trying to burst out'. Shakespeare says that 'she was a giggler, but her vivacity camouflaged a nervous side'. Bruce was very good at giving tips on what clothes she should buy; she dressed him up in her clothes for fun when he was six years old. His father was away at the war at this time. Psychoanalysts have observed this kind of background in persons who are later homosexual, yet to attribute Chatwin's later difficulties with identity to such incidents would be simplistic in the extreme.

Bruce's grandfather used to 'draw meticulous plans of houses that were never built'. His grandmother, Mary Mathieson, had 'plenty of Romany temperament': according to Bruce, she was 'an addict of the Ouija board and horoscopes' and 'given to any kind of gambling'.

When he was seven, Bruce told his brother Hugh that 'Erasmus says it is possible to be a great genius and a complete fool'. Hugh replied, 'Then you, Bruce, must be a great genius'. There is a lot of truth in what Erasmus said.

Education

Chatwin was bored at school. His headmistress said that 'this child is different from the others'. He was extremely sensitive to teasing: 'occasional lapses into gullibility...made him a natural target for teasers'. He was not popular with the other boys.

An early school report stated: 'He is rather a careless worker and his attention soon wanders. He is still very young and hardly out of the egocentric stage; his behaviour is childish and very noisy at times!' According to a later report, he had difficulty in remembering facts and 'only the bizarre or trifling really appeals to him'. He was also described as 'somewhat dreamy and vague'. Chatwin himself said: 'I was hopeless at school, a real idiot, bottom of every class. I was also innumerate.' Like many persons with Asperger's syndrome (e.g. Isaac Newton, Ludwig Wittgenstein), he was essentially an autodidact.

At Marlborough, 'There were complaints of his disorderly mental processes, his vagueness and bewilderment, his resignation, his insouciance to everything.' He was clearly uninterested in the regular curriculum; he was egocentric and wanted to do his own thing. Educational and behavioural problems are common in the childhood of artists.

Work

Chatwin worked in Sotheby's, the upmarket London auction house, for eight years, describing himself as 'a rather unpleasant little capitalist in a big business in which I was extremely successful and smarmy'. He was seen as a potential chairman of Sotheby's.

According to a colleague, Chatwin had 'a genius for self-promotion'. Like T.E. Lawrence, he 'had this ability to make you believe he was a born aesthete and passionately pursuing the aesthetic life since he was 16'. (Ludwig Wittgenstein, another person with Asperger's syndrome, had a similar genius for self-promotion.) Another colleague said that 'he was not a team player...he'd come in late, leave early, was never around when the crunch was on'.

According to Shakespeare, 'Bruce's talent was to dig up extraordinary facts and link them'. A friend described him as 'an intellectual gibbon who swung from connection to connection with incredible ease'. He possibly tended to elaborate things rather than always producing original creativity.

Indicators of Asperger's syndrome

Social behaviour

Chatwin had major difficulties with social and emotional reciprocity. He was described as 'wantonly dismissive' and as 'someone who eats off another's plate'. From a financial point of view 'his host could pay dearly for his visits'. He tended to use his hosts, and could be extremely tactless. It was said that 'he demanded attention. He was heroically selfish, but not purely self-indulgent or egocentric.' He had a tremendous capacity for superficial relating, but found a deep and prolonged relationship more or less impossible to achieve. He was also described as cunning – there is a myth that persons with Asperger's syndrome never show this trait.

A female friend said: 'I chose Bruce as a friend. But I never had a deep personal affection for him. I think it was not possible.' She also said: 'Bruce had no passion. It was all cerebral.' He was described as 'not loving at all...couldn't care less'. Nevertheless, his future wife Elizabeth stated that 'he was more fun to be with than almost anyone I knew'.

According to Shakespeare, 'many of those who had loved Bruce speak of his frigidity, his emotional unwillingness, his lack of connection'. The writer and critic Susan Sontag stated that he was 'profoundly solitary and therefore conducted his sexual activity as a way of connecting with people. At such an industrial rate it meant not an inclusive or intensifying connection: it meant he had a connection.' A young art dealer with whom he had a relationship said that he was 'a cold fish' with a 'limited emotional attention span' – 'You had only a part of him.'

A colleague at Sotheby's stated that Chatwin 'viewed himself as apart from himself'. This detachment was a recurring trait. According to Shakespeare 'few came close. At the point where his lovers might want to talk personally, Bruce would be incapable.'

The reason for his getting married, he told Hugh, was 'to stop myself from going mad'. Hugh understood Bruce to be saying that he needed Elizabeth as an anchor against nervous collapse. Elizabeth was a very suitable wife for a person like Bruce – one wonders whether they had an 'Asperger marriage'. She had 'the ability not to be emotionally clinging', just like W.B. Yeats's wife.

Elizabeth said that Bruce was 'a marvellous guest but a terrible host'. Even his own guests quickly bored him. During a dinner party he would 'simply leave the table and disappear because he had thought of something he wanted to write. He had awful manners in lots of ways. He'd push his plate away when he'd finished and he had a complete aversion to washing up.'

Shakespeare quotes the journalist Neal Ascherson: '…to be unfindable and untraceable – that is an English dream! It is an idea of liberty which allows the individual to be present only when he or she chooses, but to retain the right and capacity to melt away.' This describes Chatwin perfectly.

Like many with Asperger's syndrome, Bruce was good with children and able to see the world through their eyes, but not good with peers. Despite his major difficulties with social relationships he was an interesting person, as persons with Asperger's syndrome often are. Of course it's their intellectual pursuits and the power of their minds that people find interesting.

Narrow interests and obsessiveness

Chatwin was a collector from childhood – a feature common in persons with Asperger's syndrome. He had a rather strange collection of items. According to Shakespeare, he later 'collected people just as he collected objects'. The jazz musician George Melly said 'what amused me was his tunnel vision… He knew everything there was to know about Persian miniatures, but he'd never heard of the Muppets.'

Like many people with Asperger's syndrome, Chatwin had a fascination with intellectual matters: he was attracted to 'intellectual passion' and liked 'adventures of the mind'. He was like the French writer André Malraux, who was 'archaeologist, aesthete, art smuggler, adventurer, compulsive traveller and talker'.

Chatwin's wife Elizabeth said that 'he reads piles and piles of books and writes away like mad… During the week he spends all day in the Bodleian or one of the other libraries in Oxford and says he's accomplishing a lot.'

He had a phenomenal memory. In his work 'he learned to look with close attention to detail and to remember what he had seen'.

Routines and control

The journalist Francis Wyndham said that 'reading Chatwin one is acutely conscious of the authorial control – and therefore, simultaneously and intoxicatingly, of the alluring danger of loss of control, of things getting out of hand'. Shakespeare notes that 'Bruce hated to lose possession of himself'. Control is an important issue for persons with Asperger's syndrome.

Speech, language and humour

Chatwin's voice was 'pitched low for his age, and with a most unusual timbre – a bit like one of those brassy middle-aged women with an impossibly deep suntan and too many bangles'. Persons with Asperger's syndrome sometimes have problems with the tone of their voice. One of his teachers referred to his 'rather monotonous tone'.

Naïvety and childishness

Immaturity of personality is a central feature of persons with Asperger's syndrome. Chatwin was always socially immature, and his personality was not fully developed. Even shortly before he died he had 'the animation of a schoolboy'.

Shakespeare notes that 'he did not know what he wanted and his frustrations came out, like a child, in mean outbursts'. It was said that he was 'very childish and needed looking after', and that 'like a child, he took everything'.

The fact that he 'couldn't live within his income' is further evidence of a poorly functioning personality with immaturity and lack of reality testing.

Lack of empathy

Bruce 'had no scruples about rattling family skeletons'. He could be extremely tactless in writing about people (for example in *In Patagonia*), hence showing his lack of empathy. He did his own thing, and people were there to be used as he saw fit.

While at college in Edinburgh, Bruce would go for a meal with his teacher and overstay his welcome, showing a lack of empathy.

Appearance and demeanour

When people observed Chatwin they noticed his shyness, his unusual non-verbal behaviour and his large head. He was described as 'painfully shy, despite his bluster'. As a child he was 'an isolated little boy with a large head in comparison to the rest of his body, self-contained in the world'; his head was 'almost a perfect square in all directions, like an Oxo cube', with 'huge blue eyes that never seemed to blink'. His brother Hugh described him as having 'the mad eyes of a nineteenth-century explorer'.

Bruce was a mimic 'after the manner of Gustave Flaubert and Konrad Lorenz…at various moments he would lose himself so completely in the role that he lost the scent and became the person he was mimicking'. This is an autistic form of mimicry. He was 'very theatrical'. Ludwig Wittgenstein was also a great mimic.

Motor clumsiness

Chatwin had the classic motor problems of a person with Asperger's syndrome. He was described as clumsy. A schoolmate said that when he was running 'his legs went sideways instead of straight and one never imagined he would get anywhere'.

According to Elizabeth, 'he would cut himself and go septic over and over again'.

Autistic imagination

When asked, 'Where in your work is the division between fiction and non-fiction?', Bruce replied, 'I don't think there is one.' Contrary to received wisdom, persons with Asperger's syndrome can show evidence of tremendous imagination, as Chatwin did.

Sandra Wheeler in *The Independent* pointed out that Shakespeare's book shows us a 'psychic landscape peopled by the fearful monsters that Chatwin kept mostly at bay by continuously moving and reinventing himself'. His brother Hugh reckoned that 60 per cent of the content of Bruce's stories was true, the rest embellishment.

As a child, he had an imaginary friend, Tommy, who talked to him a lot and to whom he would tell stories. A teacher said: 'I think he lived in a fantasy world and was quite genuinely incapable of distinguishing fact from fiction. It wasn't a pretence.' According to Shakespeare, 'In the tearoom at Sotheby's, there was a phrase, "doing a Bruce". It meant wrapping up something in a bit of myth and making a story out of it.' Martha Gellhorn said that Chatwin and Hemingway 'are not conscious liars. They invent to increase everything about themselves and their lives and believe it. They believe everything they say.'

Jeremy Swift, an economic anthropologist, noted that Chatwin didn't seem to have read things central to his task. Swift also stated that

> he wasn't cautious. That was one of the wonderful things about him. He would dramatically be plotting out several moves ahead, and you can't do that if you are a researcher. His method was not scientific. Bruce fixes on a beautiful idea, a poetic idea, and marshals evidence to support his hunch. Sadly, that doesn't work. His canvas is too vast.

His autistic imagination was the driving force.

His wife said that he had 'a funny sixth sense about lots of things'; Bruce himself stated that his 'temperament is definitely towards the fantastic'.

Shakespeare points out that towards the end of his life he 'actively denied his illness, even to himself'. Reality was what his imagination told him it was.

Identity diffusion

Chatwin was 'a solitary antisocial person, working very hard at creating an identity for himself'. His life and work were a search for identity. Identity diffusion is a central issue for persons with Asperger's syndrome, and Bruce was 'a chameleon'. At one point in his life he considered becoming an actor – an occupation that might have suited him.

He has been described as

> a German admiral, a curate, a fallen angel, an unfledged baby sparrow, a farmer, a St Bernard, but the image fixed in most minds is that of a pink-cheeked schoolboy, slightly bumptious, with Robert Louis Stevenson's ability to render those he met 'slaves to a rare, authentic and irresistible charm'.

It was said that 'the trouble is, Bruce wanted to be Genghis Khan, but he would have preferred living in Byzantium'; similarly, 'half of Bruce despised being European and longed to be a Mauritanian nomad, renouncing everything; the other half was a worldly, acquisitive collector with an eagle's eye for the unusual who longed to go riding with Jackie Onassis'.

The actor and theatre director Peter Eyre remarked that Chatwin showed 'the malleability of all-knowing Proteus, eluding questions by changing into a lion, a serpent, or fire. His whole life was spent transforming.' Sheila Chanler, his wife's sister-in-law, said: 'I think I hardly knew him, there were so many of him.'

In terms of sexuality, his head of house, Robin Garran, said 'he wasn't particularly anything really'. Colin Thubron said that 'Bruce's sexuality went a long way to explaining his fascination with crazed people out of their context, for the ambiguous, the odd, the peculiar'. I believe that his Asperger's syndrome was of much greater significance.

Perverse behaviour

Autistic perverse behaviour is far more common in Asperger's syndrome than is generally realized, and perversion is often very closely linked to creativity. Chatwin appears to have had masochistic and scopophiliac tendencies.

Patricia Morrisroe, in her biography of the photographer Robert Mapplethorpe, stated that his studio was a 'port of call for men with every perversion' (Morrisroe 1997). Bruce went there often. An acquaintance said: 'I think Bruce had a lot to hide. I think he liked danger. I always assumed he liked being violated in some way and preferably by brigands, gypsies, and South American cowboys. It was part of his nomad pattern.' Bruce said that he 'experimented with everything' in New York. 'He wasn't interested enough in people to have a proper sexual relationship.' Novelty-seeking is often seen in persons with Asperger's syndrome (e.g. Arthur Conan Doyle, see Chapter 6).

Shakespeare notes: 'Bruce's tendency to view himself as a separate self gave him enormous freedom to misbehave. Promiscuity provided release for a streak of masochism. Bruce's notebooks make frequent mentions of "the pleasures of pain".' David Sulzberger, a dealer in Islamic art and a friend of Chatwin, once drove with him and Elizabeth to T.E. Lawrence's cottage in Dorset: 'Bruce was aware that comparisons were being made. He was very silent. He loved it. I found it very sinister: tiny, faux-monastic, sadomasochistic.'

Chatwin was a kind of sexual psychopath or predator: a user rather than an abuser. He compartmentalized his life in different 'autistic boxes' and kept multiple affairs going at the same time. Miranda Rothschild described him as 'a polymorphous pervert... He is out to seduce everybody, it doesn't matter if you are male, female, an ocelot or a tea cosy.' She said that he engaged in love-making with 'great speed and savagery, as if he wanted it to be over quickly'. After her experience with him she felt 'lacerated as if by a Bengal tiger'.

Autistic hyperactivity and novelty-seeking

Chatwin embodied what Diane Kennedy calls the ADHD–autism connection (Kennedy 2002). One of the greatest mistakes of psychiatry researchers in the 20th century was the excessive (and almost exclusive) focus on categorical diagnosis. This error put a lot of psychiatric research off course. In my clinical practice I observe that many persons with ADHD (attention deficit hyperactivity disorder) have features of Asperger's syndrome that are often missed. Failure to intervene with the Asperger-type features as well as the ADHD can lead to failure in treatment.

Chatwin showed some overlap of Asperger's syndrome and ADHD traits. While novelty-seeking is usually associated with ADHD, it can also be associated with Asperger's syndrome.

Chatwin had enormous energy and colossal interest in and curiosity about life. Salman Rushdie observed that 'everything he did, he did very noisily'. He spoke extremely rapidly in a hyperkinetic fashion, and 'never stopped talking'. He was described as 'the mother of all grasshoppers'. The novelist David Plante said that 'he has the ability to act rapidly and to talk rapidly at the same time, as if he were two people, one all motion, the other all talk, and sometimes one distracts the other, but mostly, amazingly, they converge'.

It is hardly surprising that nomads fascinated Chatwin. It appears that he was absolutely fascinated with his wanderlust, and wanted to understand it better. Clearly he didn't know that he had autistic hyperactivity, and was trying to understand what was driving him.

Piggott, his teacher in Edinburgh, stated that Bruce was 'running away from himself by travelling'. His hyperactive travelling was part of his sensation-seeking. According to his wife, 'he was constantly gyrating on his own axis, to cause a sensation, to find a sensation. That's what made him so exciting, but you couldn't get close to him.'

At the age of 26, Chatwin left his job at Sotheby's to study archaeology in Edinburgh, but he had 'an Indiana Jones notion of archaeology'. His attention wandered when confronted by detailed work; he 'had no patience at all' and 'wanted to find everything immediately'. Academic discipline and 'piles of old pots' were incredibly boring for him.

The art critic Robert Hughes said that Bruce 'liked the offbeat. He liked the monstrous. He liked things that suggested an inadvertent crack in the seamless world of cause and effect.' This can be interpreted as autistic novelty-seeking.

Autistic narcissism

This is also a central feature of persons with Asperger's syndrome. There was 'probably ... nobody Bruce loved more than himself' and 'nothing meant more to him than his own written word'. While in Patagonia, he was described as 'very arrogant, very sure of himself, very narcissistic'.

Psychological stress, depression and hypochondriasis

Persons with Asperger's syndrome very often experience depression. Bruce wrote of being in a mood of insufferable depression, and said that he was 'given over to much private melancholy'. An eye specialist, Patrick Trevor-Roper, stated that 'he had feelings of fatigue, discomfort and vague subjective unease'. Trevor-Roper felt his problem was due to being 'a bright, sensitive, rather neurotic young man trying to cut a dash'. He then had a breakdown and took time off in the Sudan. Around the time he left Sotheby's, he thought he was going blind: he said it was because he hated Sotheby's.

Asperger-type depression is associated with difficulties in social relationships, mental confusion, and difficulties with work. Problems with identity increase mental confusion.

Bruce was also 'a terrible hypochondriac'; 'he was always worried about his stomach', and his suitcase 'was stuffed with pills'.

His secretary, Sue Goodhew, stated that 'he was a volatile person to work for. One moment he was in good form. The next he was not.' Emotional volatility is a feature of Asperger's syndrome.

Bruce said that 'travel was an immense relief – it got rid of the pressure from above and from below. If you're out on the road, people have to take you at face value.' It was his antidepressant and his outlet from autistic claustrophobia caused by human relationships. It allowed him to lose himself in the wider world.

SHAKESPEARE NOTES THAT when Bruce Chatwin died, 'many people felt a sense of loss out of all proportion to their expectation'. The travel writer Colin Thubron described him as 'a complex, flamboyantly gifted and rather tragic figure', and said: 'He was expansive; he opened horizons; you always felt with Bruce he was capable of coming back with the key to everything.'

The evidence presented in this chapter suggests strongly that Chatwin had Asperger's syndrome combined with hyperactivity and sensation/novelty-seeking traits.

PART II

Asperger's Syndrome and Philosophers

A S STORR (1988) has pointed out, most of the greatest philosophers of the Western world since the Greeks have not lived normal family lives or formed close personal ties. This is true of Spinoza, Kant and Ludwig Wittgenstein. Storr notes that the capacity to be alone becomes linked with self-discovery and self-realization; with becoming aware of one's deepest needs, feelings and impulses. According to Storr, 'The artist or philosopher is able to mature primarily on his own. His passage through life is defined by the changing nature and increasing maturity of his work, rather than by his relations with others.' This certainly describes persons with Asperger's syndrome.

The high points of many creative persons' lives occur when they make a creative breakthrough. They also tend to show hypersensitivity, and can appear to be paranoid. These phenomena are all associated with Asperger's syndrome.

Murray (1989) points out that 'many philosophers insist upon autonomy at all costs, are reluctant to acknowledge debts to others, and sometimes assert that they are almost incapable of reading the work of other philosophers'. This is a typical autistic position as demonstrated by Wittgenstein and Kant, who had Asperger's syndrome.

According to Murray, Kant and others

> insisted that their contributions to philosophy depended upon having freed themselves from the influence of their predecessors and pursued their own autonomous paths irrespective of the past. So did Wittgenstein, who is another example of a philosopher who was intro-

verted, who particularly prized solitude, who claimed that he was largely impervious to influence, who had certainly found his main source of self-esteem in his work. He is generally counted to be the most original and influential philosopher of the twentieth century.

Extreme intellectual interests are a feature of philosophers. They often think of themselves as being extremely logical and rational beings; some philosophers think of themselves as 'pure reasoning machines'. Not surprisingly, Kant wrote that 'about ourselves we are silent' (Kuehn 2001).

It has been stated in this book that literary writers with Asperger's syndrome often write about matters that they have difficulty with. The same can be said about philosophers: for example, the greatest philosopher of the 20th century, Ludwig Wittgenstein (who had Asperger's syndrome), focused his philosophical work in the area of language. He always experienced great difficulty in communicating with people through language, and felt he was never understood. The Asperger philosopher could be described using Anthony Kenny's words as 'not a citizen of any community of ideas' (Fitzgerald 2004).

Persons with Asperger's syndrome often have problems with narrative, as Sigman and Capps (1997) point out: 'individuals with autism do not use the present tense as a rhetorical device; rather, they seem unaware of narrative convention'. This narrative problem means that they have difficulty telling stories that have happened in the past as if they were happening in the present.

Sigman and Capps also point out that

> highly intelligent autistic people struggle to understand social affective matters as if they were solving a maths problem. While they are often able to come up with adequate, albeit strange, accounts of social and personal situations, the process is laborious, operating outside of intuitive notions about how they and others ordinarily feel and think in various situations. Thus despite diligent, genuine, and often courageous effort, even the most intelligent autistic person cannot compensate for their limited access to a commonality that is effortlessly entered by most of us as we give conventional narrative form to life experiences.

This would certainly apply to Wittgenstein (see Fitzgerald 2004).

Sigman and Capps note the Asperger/high-functioning autism (HFA) person's problems with developing a theory of other people's minds, but also in 'identifying meaningful aspects of human activity'. This is apparent in philosophers with Asperger's syndrome. Persons with Asperger's syndrome/HFA have problems with narration, i.e. the forging of 'connections between settings, characters' behavioural and emotional responses, and consequences' (Sigman and Capps 1997), and thereby in allowing people to share their experiences. The writing of persons with Asperger's syndrome often embodies idiosyncratic themes and has problems in giving the gist of events.

Normal human development necessitates an understanding of other minds, other persons and the social context that one finds oneself in. The greatest human capacity is the capacity to understand other human beings – something that is deficient in Asperger's syndrome.

Jill de Villiers (2000) notes the language deficits in autism, and that some individuals with autism may be pushed intellectually to represent an understanding of other persons that does not come naturally. This can probably lead to a certain 'oddness' in their work – excessive pedantry, for example.

Problems with the development of 'an experiencing self' (Jordan and Powell 1995) and language difficulties will also lead to thinking problems – autistic thinking. This will be reflected in the literary and philosophical writing of persons with Asperger's syndrome.

Nevertheless, according to Amy Wetherby, Adriana Schuler and Barry Prizant (1997), 'because the processing of written language is not dependent on sequential analysis, superior written word-skills in individuals with autism are readily explained'. This partly explains why persons with Asperger's syndrome can write interesting material.

The problem the 'Asperger philosopher' has could be summed up by Wittgenstein's statement that there is no such thing as private language. Future research on 'Asperger philosophers' should focus on the possibility that they have a metarepresentational deficit, i.e. difficulties in working out theories about other minds and autistic problems with inner speech. Philosophizing can be a kind of 'philosophic therapy' for Asperger philosophers, somewhat similar to music therapy for persons with Asperger's syndrome.

Philosophers with Asperger's syndrome have some problems with language, particularly in the semantic pragmatic area. This can lead them to experience 'knotted thinking'. Their philosophic efforts are then aimed at resolving this knotted thinking. Of course the 'neurotypical' philosophic community often finds these unravellings helpful. One of the limitations of the 'Asperger philosopher' is that his or her philosophizing is often too narrow, like that of Wittgenstein. Indeed, Wittgenstein was called the 'engineering philosopher' – the 'philosopher of machinery' (Fitzgerald 2004).

The weak central coherence of Asperger's syndrome and the 'Asperger philosopher' leads to a focus on detail, a narrow philosophical position.

NINE

Spinoza
(1632-77)

S PINOZA WAS ONE of the greatest philosophers of the 17th century. Many aspects of his personality and work suggest that he had Asperger's syndrome, which occurs mainly in males who are socially odd, naïve, and inappropriate as well as being egocentric and hypersensitive. They tend to have good grammar and extensive vocabularies but are long-winded, literal and pedantic, and have circumscribed interests, while their intelligence is often normal or in the superior range. They are capable of producing remarkably original ideas but tend to lack common sense. This chapter will attempt to show that Spinoza demonstrated these traits. All of the biographical details and quoted extracts in this chapter come from Gullan-Whur (1998).

© Lebrecht Music & Arts Photo Library

Life history

Baruch (or Bento, or Benedictus) Spinoza was born in Amsterdam on 24 November 1632, into a Jewish family that had fled persecution in Portugal. His father, Michael (or Miguel) de Espinosa, was a merchant and member of the Stock Exchange who married three times; Spinoza's mother, Hana Debora, died when he was a young boy.

Spinoza had a lifelong interest in optics and astronomy and, after turning away from his father's profession of merchant, earned a living by grinding and polishing lenses. Having been expelled from the Jewish community for heresy in 1656, he left Amsterdam in 1660 and lived in various parts of Holland for the rest of his life. Inhalation of glass dust, as well as heavy tobacco-smoking, contributed to his death from tuberculosis on 21 February 1677, at the age of 44.

Work

Spinoza wrote philosophical and theological tracts that for a long time were seen as subversive and atheistical. Some of these were banned; most were published anonymously. *Theologico-Political Treatise*, dealing with the Bible and Christian theology, was published in 1670 and banned in 1674. *Ethics*, his major work, was published posthumously in 1677.

Spinoza's work propounded the idea of philosophical freedom as opposed to faith, and of a God identical with nature as opposed to a personal God. He believed that truth was derived from reason rather than revelation, and that a beneficent metaphysical system could be deduced with mathematical certainty – 'I shall consider human actions and appetites just as if it were a question of lines, planes and bodies'. Mathematics was the paradigm of adequate knowledge, and mathematical rationality could provide sufficient practice in deductive inference to control imagination, opinion, passion and prejudice. Logical inference was his yardstick for drawing conclusions in all aspects of human concern, including emotion. The root of human problems was an inability to reason properly. Spinoza offers an autistic solution to problems in that he expects each person to reason things out for himself.

It is possible that Spinoza became less autistic around 1676, when for the first time, 'universal knowledge' displaced reason as the primary element in his philosophy – 'those who believe that a crowd, or people divided over public affairs, can be induced to live by reason's dictate alone, are dreaming of the poets' golden age or of a fairy-tale'. This mirrors Wittgenstein's shift from a picture theory to a tool theory of philosophy when he became less autistic, at around the same age (Fitzgerald 2004).

Indicators of Asperger's syndrome

Social behaviour

Spinoza had severe social difficulties: he has been described as intellectually supercilious, arrogant, testy, brusque, sarcastic, odd, and short with people. He shunned company, was rigid in his views, would not allow disagreement, and showed little sympathy for anyone who expressed distress at an illness. At his excommunication from the Jewish faith he showed insolence and contempt rather than remorse or repentance.

Spinoza had very low levels of social intuition; he believed that intuition was a kind of knowledge rarely enjoyed by humans. 'Mathematical intuition' was largely what was available to him. Problems with empathy meant that he had to work things out intellectually. This is one of many similarities between Spinoza and Ludwig Wittgenstein.

Spinoza scorned the social structure of his community, which left him 'vulnerably naked', and he was clearly 'handicapped emotionally'. He was an intellectual gypsy who moved from one location to another throughout his life in Holland, often to get away from people. In about 1660 he 'took precautions to avoid all intercourse with his friends'. He had contempt for intellectual people, and 'when he spoke to them he felt himself as thwarted by prejudice, triviality, and superstition as he had among his father's people'. His isolation can be seen in his correspondence, where contact is limited to 'temporary and fragile associations of convenience' and loneliness, archness, naïvety, egotism, sycophancy and parsimony are evident. He had no steadfast patron, no ready readership, no supportive students of high social standing to guarantee a benign reception for his ideas.

Spinoza never admitted that he was wrong, or apologized; he very rarely asked for advice, and (like Wittgenstein) did not consider that he was intellectually indebted to earlier philosophers. He rarely deferred to anyone, and was a 'supremely uncompromising rationalist'. He ruthlessly lectured correspondents on their misguided opinions and gave instant alternative doctrines which were outlined laconically, as if their thrust were evident to anyone but a fool. Gullan-Whur writes that 'disagreement and mental alienation were... habitual and not discomforting states of mind for Spinoza'.

Spinoza's attempt to show how reason could remove the destructive power of affects is not surprising, since affects are bewildering for a person with Asperger's syndrome. For Spinoza (like Wittgenstein), the power of the mind was defined by knowledge alone. There are further parallels with Wittgenstein in that Spinoza turned away from a commercial career, lived in rented rooms, had major problems in social relationships, moved lodgings often, tended to live in isolation from people, refused to be controlled by others, lived in a self-enclosed world, turned his back on institutional religion, had few possessions at the time of his death, and felt that his work would be misunderstood. Also like Wittgenstein, he was preoccupied with confused thinking and felt that the evidence of the senses was often false.

Narrow interests and obsessiveness

Spinoza's focus on philosophy was narrow and intense in an autistic way, i.e. he attempted to 'act solely through reason'. Wittgenstein's focus on language was equally narrow, and he denied the existence of private language because of his autism. They both tried to deal with bewildering social worlds by this retreat into all-encompassing philosophy.

Wittgenstein and Spinoza were citizens of an 'autistic' community of ideas. It is not true that they were 'citizens of no community', to use Wittgenstein's phrase, since they were both philosophers in the 'autistic mode'.

Spinoza had a geometrical mind, and he wanted to find the reason for everything. This is the classic cognitive style of persons with Asperger's syndrome. He felt that the correct method of seeking the truth requires us to reason from first principles, and to do this we must hone our reasoning faculties.

Routines and control

Spinoza was a man of absolute routine, and worked at philosophy and grinding lenses throughout his life with an extraordinary intensity. When he became angry, he would retire from company for fear of losing control. It has been suggested that he used the geometrical method as a form of self-discipline. Also, he was offered a professorship at Heidelberg but turned it down: he did not want to be controlled by any institution.

Naïvety and childishness

Spinoza was naïve to expect that the *Theologico-Political Treatise* would not offend people when, as Gullan-Whur puts it, 'at each cutting of his quill, he guaranteed offence'. Yet he was so surprised at the adverse reaction to this work that he published no others in his lifetime.

Idiosyncrasies

Spinoza took enormous narcissistic pride in his intellect: he did not see how any intelligent person could disagree with his philosophy, and became very annoyed with any confusion or dissension. His standard was the mathematical standard. He was so certain of his correctness that he put 'QED' at the end of his philosophical writings.

Wittgenstein showed similarities to Spinoza in regard to narcissism. Both considered their philosophical researches to be of the greatest importance, and their lack of empathy had a narcissistic side. Asperger's syndrome is sometimes mistaken for a narcissistic personality disorder.

Like Wittgenstein, Spinoza showed a high level of animosity towards women, making 'negative pronouncements on their whimpering, partiality, foolish pity, superstition, inconstancy, deceptiveness, weakness and mental inferiority'. Gullan-Whur feels that this misogyny indicates 'a chasm between his principles and his opinions' in that he argued for the common human nature of ethnic groups, and one might logically infer from his principles a common male–female mentality.

Spinoza never married, and saw sexual relations with women as degrading: he dismissed a link between happiness and sexual desire, emphasizing post-coital misery instead. According to Gullan-Whur, 'No evidence has been found…for an attraction to men.' He appears to have been celibate.

Gullan-Whur writes that 'humour was, for Spinoza…an aspiration, not a disposition'.

Conclusion

The 'autistic mode' of conducting philosophy placed considerable limitations on the philosophical contributions of both Spinoza and Wittgenstein. However, the latter at least recognized the limitation of the 'picture theory' of philosophy represented by the *Tractatus Logico-Philosophicus* when he moved to his 'tool theory' of philosophy in the *Philosophical Investigations*, where he discovered the importance of social relationships. More broadly based theories of philosophy require the philosopher to have a significant capacity for empathy, which is largely diminished in persons with Asperger's syndrome.

THE EVIDENCE OUTLINED above suggests that Spinoza meets the criteria for Asperger's syndrome set by Asperger (1944) and Gillberg (1991, 1996).

TEN

Immanuel Kant
(1724–1804)

THE GERMAN PHILOSOPHER Immanuel Kant, one of the most influential figures in Western philosophy, was born in the city of Königsberg, Prussia (now Kaliningrad, Russia) on 22 April 1724. He taught at the local university, and spent his entire life in Königsberg. He published scientific works on astronomy and physical geography in the early part of his career; his major contributions to philosophy (*Critique of Pure Reason, Critique of Practical Reason, Critique of Judgement*) appeared from 1781 onwards and earned him his fame, although his emphasis on rationalism rather than religious revelation brought him into conflict with the authorities. His *Perpetual Peace* (1795) advocates a world federation of free republican states. Kant's system of philosophy formed the basis of the systems developed by

Hegel and Marx. He died on 12 February 1804.

On the subject of biographies, Manfred Kuehn (2001) makes some observations that are relevant to this book. He states:

> Biographies of philosophers have been relatively scarce in the recent past. One of the most important reasons for this has to do with the way philosophy is being done in America, Australia, and England. To an analytically minded philosopher, the biography of a thinker is simply irrelevant, since it says nothing about the truth of his position and adds nothing to the soundness of his arguments. While this is, strictly speaking, true, the lack of context – or perhaps better, the substitution of an anachronistic context – often stands in the way of appreciating what a philosopher wanted to say.

He goes on to state:

> Ideally, a biography of any philosopher would be both philosophically and historically interesting, and would integrate the story of the philosopher's life with a philosophically interesting perspective on his work.

> While both life and thought need to be addressed, this cannot mean that these two different concerns should simply be given equal time. Matters are more complicated. A biography must integrate the two in some way. It must make clear how the life and thought of a philosopher are connected. Though it is a difficult and perhaps impossible task to establish why a certain philosopher held the views he held and wrote the works he wrote, any biography that does not address this question will probably be of limited interest.

Kuehn then raises the question of the source of biographies' appeal:

> I do not really know what makes biographies so fascinating to so many readers. Is it simply curiosity about how the 'famous' have lived? Is it voyeurism, an unsavoury desire to glimpse the dirty little secrets of the 'great'? Is it escapism, an attempt at vicarious living, a kind of romance for the more intellectually inclined?

Kuehn quotes Virginia Wolff as observing that biographies are difficult, if not impossible, to write, because 'people are all over the place'. Nevertheless, Kant was not 'all over the place' – he was focused and very much routine-bound. You could set your clock by him.

Family and childhood

Kant was the eldest son of Johann Georg Kant, a harness-maker, and Anna Regina Kant (née Reuter), the daughter of another harness-maker. Only three of his eight siblings survived childhood; his mother died when he was 13 years old.

His school days at the Collegium Fredericianum were not happy. According to one of his friends, Theodor Hippel, Kant 'used to say that terror and fear would overcome him as soon as he thought back to the slavery of his youth' (Malter 1990). One of Kant's early biographers, Johann Mortzfeld, spoke of the 'leaden atmosphere of punishment' in this school. Indeed, Kant stated that school years 'are the hardest years because one is very much subject to discipline, seldom has a friend, and even less often has freedom' (Kant 1990).

According to Kuehn (2001), Kant felt that 'the kind of discipline he experienced amounted to a particularly harsh form of slavery that was not only *not* very useful, but also positively harmful'. 'In school there is coercion, mechanism, and the shuttle of rules. This often robs people of all the courage to think for themselves, and it spoils the genius' (Kant 1990). It is interesting that, like Ludwig Wittgenstein, he regarded it as highly important that people learn to think for themselves.

According to Kuehn, 'Kant later complained that it would be better if schools taught "the spirit" and not merely "the phrases" of authors'. Again this is similar to Wittgenstein. Not surprisingly, in later life Kant rejected the 'servile attitude' inculcated by the pietistic religion of his community. Autonomy was hugely important to him.

Indicators of Asperger's syndrome

Social behaviour

Christoph Heilsberg, a friend of Kant, stated that 'Kant did not like any frivolities and even less "going out on the town", and he converted his listeners little by little to the same tune' (Kuehn 2001).

Johann Metzger, a professor of medicine at the University of Königsberg, said that he was not particularly hard-hearted, but he did not have a particularly kind heart either. Kuehn notes that 'Metzger intimated that he probably had never given any money to anyone except his immediate family. He concluded from the evidence that Kant had once refused to contribute to a collection for a colleague whose house had burnt down that he "was an egoist to a quite considerable degree".' Yet on the day after his death, a local newspaper ascribed to him the virtues of 'loyalty, benevolence, righteousness, and politeness' (Vorländer 1911).

Kuehn refers to Kant's 'autonomous, self-reliant, and self-made character'. He did not have a close relationship with his siblings, and 'remained aloof'.

According to Kuehn, 'Organized religion filled him with ire. It was clear to anyone who knew Kant personally that he had no faith in a personal god. Having postulated God and immortality, he himself did not believe in either.' He was averse to marriage, like Spinoza.

Narrow interests and obsessiveness

Like Ludwig Wittgenstein, Kant once wanted to become a medical doctor. He spoke of 'a thirst of knowledge'. According to Kuehn (2001), 'his studies were more important to him than anything else'. After he had written his first work, while still a student, he stated: 'I have already prescribed the route I want to take. I will begin my course and nothing shall prevent me from continuing it' (Kant 1990). Kuehn points out that in a sense, he was 'going over the heads of his professors, bypassing the discussion within the university, as it were, and asserting his right to be an equal participant in the philosophical discussion of the period'. (This also has echoes of Ludwig Wittgenstein.) 'He was concerned with philosophical truth, and he wanted to be known for having advanced philosophical truths.'

It took Kant over 11 years to write the *Critique of Pure Reason*. For many years he lived mostly for his work.

Kuehn points out that Kant's 'philosophical work is so dense, abstruse, and technical that it is difficult to make it accessible to the general reader' (the same could be said of Ludwig Wittgenstein's philosophy). He constantly strived to live in accordance with reasoned principles.

Kant's biographer Reinhold Jachmann reported that 'the writings of his enemies he could understand only with the greatest effort because he could leave his own original conceptual system only for short periods' (Kuehn 2001).

Routines and control

Kant favoured self-control as one of the highest virtues. Kuehn remarks that 'Kant, it would seem, actually succeeded in turning himself into a machine'. The poet Heinrich Heine wrote:

The history of Kant's life is difficult to describe. For he neither had a life nor a history. He lived a mechanically ordered, almost abstract, bachelor life in a quiet out-of-the-way lane in Königsberg, an old city at the northeast border of Germany. I do not believe that the large clock of the Cathedral there completed its task with less passion and less regularity [*sic*] than its fellow citizen Immanuel Kant. Getting up, drinking coffee, writing, giving lectures, eating, taking a walk, everything had its set time, and the neighbours knew precisely that the time was 3.30 p.m. when Kant stepped outside his door with his grey coat and the Spanish stick in his hand…eight times he would walk up and down the little alley lined by Linden trees – every season, no matter whether the weather was cloudy or whether the clouds promised rain. One could see his servant, the old Lampe, anxious and worried, walk behind him, with an umbrella under his arm, like an image of destiny. (Heine 1962)

Certainly Heine's description is that of a classically autistic person.

Kant stated that 'All change makes me anxious, even if it seems to contribute greatly to the improvement of my situation. I believe I must pay attention to this instinct of my nature, if I still want to lengthen somewhat the thread, which fate spins very thinly and delicately for me' (Kant 1990).

Like Ludwig Wittgenstein, he was extremely upset by the noise of neighbours. He even moved his place of residence because of this. He led a very regular, ritualized life. Again like Wittgenstein, 'Kant's furnishings were by all accounts simple and inexpensive. He was opposed to opulence in principle' (Kuehn 2001). Kuehn described Kant's domestic arrangements: 'His servant Lampe took care of all practical matters. He saw to it that Kant had clean clothes, that he woke up on time, that he had the needed supplies.'

It is interesting that, according to Kuehn, 'Kant was not the most effective administrator. Hippel observed that, while the philosopher could recite long passages from mathematical and philosophical books "almost verbatim or verbatim" and memorize name registers with lightning speed, he could not even keep track of three different things in administration.' Kuehn describes him as having an extremely good memory, but he was incapable of living a businesslike life (Rink 1805). Associates described him as a theoretician.

Kant was very controlling, and allowed no disagreement. Kuehn points out that 'he mistreated his servants. Even his own uneducated sister, who took care of him during his dying days, was not allowed to eat at his table.' Like Wittgenstein, he could be 'quite insulting when someone dared to disagree with him'. Kuehn notes that 'he was interested not only in teaching philosophical theories to his students, but also in teaching them how to live, by recommending a certain way of life'. The philosopher Moses Mendelssohn, Kant's contemporary, described Kant as 'all-crushing'; Johann Hamann stated that 'he likes talking better than listening' (Hamann 1776).

Kant felt that keeping emotions in check was important. Like Wittgenstein, he disliked ostentation.

Speech, language and humour

Kuehn (2001) notes that Kant had 'a deadpan character. Spontaneous laughter or uncontrolled joy did not seem to be in his nature.' Nevertheless, according to Kuehn, Kant did have a sense of humour, albeit an unusual one. He 'could be funny in a direct and obvious way when he was in the company of his equals', and 'could also be subtle and witty in noble society'.

Lack of empathy

Kant was celibate. Although he was theoretically in favour of marriage and considered it in his early life, he never took the final step because 'he calculated income and expenses and delayed the decision from one day to the next' (Malter 1990). Later he formulated the maxim 'One mustn't get married.' According to Kuehn, 'whether Kant ever really understood women is an open question'. Kant wrote: 'A woman narrows a man's heart. The marriage of a friend usually means a loss of a friend' (Kant 1990).

Kuehn (2001) points out that 'Kant thought little of common soldiers. Someone who could endure the life of a soldier, with its lack of autonomy, had to have a mean…character, from his point of view.' While a student, Kant showed a lack of empathy by writing material that 'could make him seem presumptuous and make enemies for him in Königsberg'.

The 19th-century philosopher Georg Simmel, according to Kuehn, 'spoke of the "incomparable personal trait of Kant's philosophy", which he saw in "its uniquely impersonal nature". Kant was "a conceptual cripple", his thinking was the "history of a mind" and not that of a real person.' Other commentators referred to a deformed, 'mechanized' life.

Like Wittgenstein, Kant thought he was a bad teacher: 'probably the worst private teacher…who ever lived'. As a lecturer he 'cultivated a certain kind of obscurity that made it very difficult for students to understand him. He gained the reputation of being a difficult philosopher' (Kuehn 2001). Kant himself said that 'I have almost no private acquaintance with my listeners, and it is difficult for me even to find out which ones might have accomplished something useful' (Kant 1967). Kuehn goes on to say that by 1778

Kant had 'isolated himself almost completely from his students. For the most part, he did not know them, and they seem not to have known him.'

Naïvety and childishness

Kant could be tactless: Kuehn points out that he 'knowingly provoked the censors in Berlin' regarding his book *Religion within the Boundaries of Mere Reason.*

Kant wrote that 'it is the fortieth year' in which we reach maturity (Kant 1990). This would ordinarily be considered very late to attain maturity, but for a person with autism and delayed emotional growth there might be some truth in it.

Appearance and demeanour

According to Kuehn (2001), Kant 'embodied the ideal of an intellectual and man of letters'. He was short and slender, with a sunken chest, and 'had a serious appearance'.

There was some discussion of his eyes, and how arresting they were. This reminds one of Ramanujan, who also had Asperger's syndrome (Fitzgerald 2004).

Co-morbidity

Kant described himself as having 'a natural inclination to hypochondria, which in my earlier years bordered on despair of living' (Kant 1990). It would appear that he suffered from anxiety and depression. He hated noise.

In later life he was anxious about the state of his bowels. According to Hamann (1776), he would undertake

> the most careful observation of his *evacuations,* and he ruminates often at the most inappropriate places, turning over this material so indelicately that one is often tempted to laugh in his face. The same thing almost happened today, but I assured him that the smallest oral or written evacuation gave me just as much trouble as his evacuations *a posteriori* created for him.

Kuehn points out that 'delicate and sensitive, he was also subject to allergic reactions. Freshly printed newspapers would make him sneeze.'

IT WOULD APPEAR that Kant displayed the criteria for Asperger's syndrome.

ELEVEN

Simone Weil
(1909–43)

SIMONE WEIL WAS a French writer, teacher, social philosopher and political activist. She came from a Jewish family, and was a precocious child and a brilliant student. Her early death was associated with a form of self-starvation.

This chapter examines the evidence that Simone Weil had Asperger's syndrome. All of the biographical details and quoted extracts in this chapter come from Gray (2001).

Life history

Simone Weil was born in Paris on 3 February 1909. Her father, a medical doctor, was 'kind, loving, and thoroughly enlightened, but taciturn and easily overwhelmed by his forceful spouse'. Her elder brother, André, went on to be a brilliant mathematician. Gray describes their mother, Selma, as 'a genius factory of sorts, masterminding every move in her children's intellectual training, tapping every available educational resource to assure the fulfillment of their talents'. Both siblings attended more than a half dozen schools, and were instructed by scores of private tutors.

Selma Weil was very fearful of germs: she imposed her own compulsive hand-washing on her children. By the time Simone was four, she 'disliked being kissed, even by her parents, and for the rest of her life she displayed repulsion for most forms of physical contact'.

According to Gray, when her mother tried to wean her at eleven months,

Simone, in an early struggle of conflicting wills, refused to eat from a spoon. She became so thin that several doctors gave her up for lost; until the age of two she did not grow in height or weight, and had to be fed mush from bottles into which increasingly large holes were pierced.

This difficulty with food is common in persons with Asperger's syndrome. At the age of five, her mother described her as 'indomitable, impossible to control, with an undescribable stubbornness that neither her father nor I can make a dent in'. Clearly she was an extremely intelligent and eccentric child: Gray points out that at the age of three she had already turned down a wealthy relative's gift of a jewelled ring on the grounds that she 'disliked luxury'. At ten years of age she read several newspapers a day. Fascinated by world events, she was becoming politically conscious. During summer holidays, Simone, 'increasingly uncomfortable with the sense that she belonged to a very privileged elite, assembled the bellhops, chambermaids, desk clerks and porters at the hotel where her family were staying, chided them that they worked too hard, and urged them to form a trade union'. (It is interesting that others with Asperger's syndrome, such as the mathematician Paul Erdös and Ludwig Wittgenstein, have been concerned about having too much wealth (Hoffman 1998; Fitzgerald 2004).)

Simone's brother, André Weil, was born in 1906 and 'was solving the most advanced mathematical problems by the time he was nine; by the age of twelve he had taught himself classical Greek and Sanskrit and become an accomplished violinist'. There is no doubt that he was a mathematical genius. 'At the age of fourteen, three years below the minimum age required by the government, he obtained a special dispensation to take his *bachot* – the state-sponsored baccalaureate exam – and passed it with the highest score in the nation.'

André taught his sister to read when she was aged five, giving her intense tuition up to six hours a day. Not surprisingly, he succeeded in teaching her only too well. Gray states that once, on a tram, the two children were talking on such a level of intellectual virtuosity that another passenger angrily exclaimed, 'How can anyone train children to be such parroting savants!' Simone became acutely depressed at 14, partly due to her brother's perceived superiority.

Weil taught philosophy in schools and also did manual work. An accident curtailed her involvement with the Republicans in the Spanish Civil War. She worked for the French Resistance in London, and formed a mystical feeling for the Catholic faith without actually joining it. She died on 24 August

1943, and is buried in Ashford, Kent. Her writings have been published post-humously in several books.

Indicators of Asperger's syndrome

Social behaviour

Simone remained as averse to physical contact as she had been in childhood, shunning even the most casual hugs or comradely linking of elbows (her dread of sexuality seems to have been deepened in early adolescence by the sight of an exhibitionist in the Luxemburg Gardens). She was oblivious to 'normal' boy–girl relationships. (Paul Erdös was also terrified of sexual contact.) Her mother called her a 'poor troll' and unmarriageable.

Weil was impetuous. If she saw an unfavourable trait in one of her friends, she was capable of brusquely ending the friendship. She tolerated no discrepancy between people's beliefs and their way of life: 'What I cannot stand is compromise', she used to say about people (this is precisely like Ludwig Wittgenstein and his relationship with Bertrand Russell). She was like Wittgenstein in the 'ruthless manner in which she could cut off friends who in some small way displeased her'. She had an aggressively contentious streak: according to Gray, 'she retained the argumentative, eccentric style she had evolved in her mid-teens, and which had become even more intransigent'.

She could be quite insensitive and insulting; for example, she never once consulted the mentor she had chosen – the philosopher Léon Brunschvicg – while she was working on the thesis he was supposed to direct. A classmate, Camille Marcoux, was a friend of Weil's for years, but Weil castigated him ferociously and cut off all contact because she disagreed with something in a presentation he had made. Later she told her comrades that for her Marcoux was 'dead'; it took over a year for her to reconcile with him.

The philosopher and author Émile Chartier (pen-name 'Alain') lectured to Weil at the Lycée Henri IV, and was an important mentor to her. He may also have had Asperger's syndrome. He 'refused all earmarks of literary celebrity and shunned almost every kind of traditional comfort. He even declined marriage, stating that domesticity might diminish the energy of his writing, and only in his 80s agreed to marry the woman who had shared his life for forty years'. This has echoes of Paul Erdös. He was certainly an eccentric lecturer, and would commence lectures without any acknowledgement or social ritual. Persons with Asperger's syndrome are often drawn to each other.

It is interesting that one of Weil's professors called her 'my little Martian'. There are many references to other planets, particularly Mars, in relation to persons with Asperger's syndrome. Temple Grandin, who has Asperger's syndrome, reversed the usual perspective by saying that she felt like an anthropologist on Mars. The 'alien' metaphor undoubtedly corresponds to autistic 'alienation'.

Narrow interests and obsessiveness

Like Isaac Newton and Ludwig Wittgenstein, Weil had extraordinary powers of concentration and could study for days on end without food or sleep. Because she loved geometry, she was fascinated by the large blocks of stone that were unloaded near Austerlitz Bridge in Paris, which she associated with geometric shapes. When Marcoux came to meet her she would be 'kneeling on the pavement of the quay, the world shut out, immersed in the book before her, occasionally tugging at a lock of her hair'.

In terms of trade union agitation, Weil was hyperactive, 'writing scores of articles a year, teaching full time at the lycée, making the six-hour round trip to St Etienne on weekends to hold her fastidiously prepared classes at the workmen's education center'. Like Paul Erdös, she would give any excess money to the unemployed. At the École Normale, fellow students would try to avoid Weil because of 'the blunt, thoughtless way she had of confronting you with your responsibilities by asking for your signature on a petition…or a contribution for some trade union strike fund'.

Like Ludwig Wittgenstein, she put great emphasis on manual labour, believing that work is the truest road to self-knowledge; she put this into practice on farms and elsewhere. A fisherman with whom she worked, Marcel Lecarpentier, described her as 'a real ragamuffin'. Lecarpentier noted her total neglect of physical comfort, and said that she loved solitude and the sea. He and Weil became friends, and she helped him to continue his own education.

She kept very extensive journals, which remind one of the notebooks of Paul Erdös, Ludwig Wittgenstein and others.

Routines and control

Weil was quite obsessional. The writer and critic Susan Sontag said that she was one of those who are 'repetitive, obsessive, and impolite, who impress by force – not simply by their tone of personal authority and by their intellectual ardor, but by the sense of acute personal and intellectual extremity'. Gray writes that she was regarded as the 'Categorical Imperative in skirts' because 'of her need to draw all ideas to their ultimate logical conclusion'.

She was extremely controlling. A friend, Clémence Ramnoux, stated that 'she always had to be involving you in demonstrations, urging you to get signatures, sending you out with leaflets. I withdrew.'

Her 'self-mastery' could be seen in her efforts to do a better writing script and to become a sportsperson. At one point, she decided not to heat her apartment 'out of sympathy with the unemployed who could not afford heating fuel'. There is a question of whether she fused with the unemployed and almost could not see herself as separate from them.

Speech, language and humour

Weil was reading the evening paper aloud to her family when she was five, and mastered Greek and several modern languages in her early teens. She and André often communicated with each other in spontaneously rhymed couplets, or in ancient Greek. Gray notes that 'the young Weils' conversations…were so laced with literary and philosophical allusions that they were barely accessible to outsiders'. Alain described her as a 'very fine student, greatly gifted, who should, however, be on guard against over-abstruse reflections expressed in almost impenetrable language'. Here he was referring to 'autistic-type language' without knowing it.

Her voice was 'high-pitched'. As a teacher she was

> constantly rumpling her hair as she spoke in an unchanging monotone…after sitting in on one of her classes, an inspector from the Ministry of Education reported that hers was 'a distinguished mind…impressive in its sincerity and conviction'; but he found her lectures to be 'diffuse and even quite confused', although 'abundant and rich in details'.

The writer and philosopher Gustave Thibon said that she had a 'keen sense of humor', and that 'she went on ad infinitum in an inexorably monotonous voice… I emerged from these endless discussions literally worn out.' She gave the impression of an 'eccentric, stridently left-wing intellectual and labor organizer'. She had a black 'ironic sense of humor'.

A priest that Weil went to see, Fr Raymond-Leopold Bruckberger, described her 'battling aggression' – 'her conversation was all dialectic, irony, attacking the front or the flank, disdaining all explanations, all rejoinders, all apologetics… Were we or were we not, she demanded, the Order whose specific vocation was to reconcile the intellect with revelation?' Yet, as Gray observes, she 'accepted the doctrines of the Trinity, the Incarnation, the Crucifixion, and the Resurrection of Christ', and was devoted to the Eucharist.

A priest who visited her in London, Fr René de Naurois, said that she spoke 'rapidly and in a low voice, in sentences interspersed with silences'. He described her mental processes as like 'the acrobatics of a squirrel in a revolving cage'. He also said her thought was 'highly abstract and abstruse, of a rapid dialectic, and very "feminine"…a thought that was elusive and at the same time prodigiously rich…which would not accept any fixed starting points from which to advance or retreat'. Like Ludwig Wittgenstein, even when approaching death she still spoke about the future.

According to Gray, 'the language of paradox and contradiction familiar to all mystics abounds in Weil, and is made even more cryptic by her very terse aphoristic style'. Gray refers to her

> penchant for speculative reconstructions of history and her hazardously subjective manner of interpretation (when her brother, André, contested a particularly far-fetched judgment of hers, commenting that it was 'not based on anything', she replied: 'it's based on what is beautiful, and if it's beautiful, it must be true').

Her aphorisms remind one of the style of writing of Ludwig Wittgenstein. Gray notes that the early period of Weil's writing 'already reveals the terse, paradoxical style of her later work. Her epigrams recall, in turn, the enigmatic abruptness of Zen aphorisms ("Void is the only plenitude").'

Naïvety and childishness

Weil was naïve in various ways throughout her life. As a child, she once demanded 'that the entire class be assigned to learn Racine's *Athalie* by heart!' She was also capable of bursting out with such sentiments as 'I wish my parents had been born poor!'

In later years Weil was not unlike Ludwig Wittgenstein in her 'naïve idealization – if not canonization – of the proletariat, which she saw as a form of contemporary sainthood'.

Appearance and demeanour

She was 'a strikingly beautiful girl with dark limpid eyes'. Gray quotes a former schoolmate as stating that 'physically, she was a little child, unable to use her hands, but of extraordinary intelligence…she looked as if she belonged to another order of being, and her mind didn't seem to belong to our age or our milieu. She felt like a very old soul.'

Gray describes that in adolescence

> a mass of uncombed black hair and huge tortoiseshell-framed glasses nearly obscured her small, delicate face. Those who met her for the first time were bound to notice the large, bold, inquisitive dark eyes that scrutinized others with an almost indiscreet curiosity. Her gestures were lively but brusque and awkward, and she was pitifully thin.

Clearly here she was showing social interactional deficits as well as clumsiness and awkwardness.

She dressed in 'clumsy clothing with which she covered her angular body. They were the clothes of a ragtag soldier or a poor monk. Her garments were always of the same monastic, masculine cut – a cape, boyish flat-heeled shoes, a long, full shirt, and a long body-obscuring jacket in dark colors'. Loosely fitting clothes and shoes are a common feature of persons with Asperger's syndrome, and suggest problems with touch.

Other common features of Asperger's syndrome worth mentioning here are a preference for heavy things over things that touch lightly, and a high pain threshold, both of which Weil showed.

During the Second World War, the poet Jan Tortel described her as

> a kind of bodiless bird, withdrawn inside itself, in a large black cloak down to her ankles that she never took off, still, silent...alien yet attentive, both observant and distant... Extremely ugly at first sight, thin, ravaged face under her large black beret, thick ragged hair, only heavy black shoes to be seen under her ankle-length cloak – she would stare at you...her eyes very much to the fore as also her head and her bust, centering on whomever she watched with her invasive shortsightedness, with an intensity and also a kind of questioning avidity that I've never encountered elsewhere... The eagerness in Weil's eyes was almost unbearable. In her presence, all 'lies' were out of the question...her denuding, tearing and torn gaze...would grasp and render helpless the person she was looking at.

She had a similar impact on people to that of Ludwig Wittgenstein.

Gustave Thibon said that she was

> prematurely bent and old looking due to asceticism and illness...her magnificent eyes alone triumphing in this shipwreck of beauty... I had the impression of being face to face with an individual who was radically foreign to all my ways of thinking and feeling and...to all that

represented the meaning and savor of existence...one who refused to make any concession whatever to the requirements and conventions of social life.

At a miners' function, a miner who asked her to dance was 'amazed by the fact that she could not keep time with him, and did not know the basic steps of the simplest dances'. This highlights Weil's dyspraxic tendencies. One student remembered 'the clumsiness of her gestures, above all her hands...her piercing look through the thick glasses, her smile – everything about her emanated a feeling of total frankness and forgetfulness of self, revealing a nobility of soul that was certainly at the root of the emotions she inspired in us'.

Whenever she was breaking off contact with someone who did not fulfil her very demanding standards of conduct, she accompanied this judgement with a horizontal, violent cutting gesture of her hand, which she repeated.

Motor clumsiness

Weil seems to have been very uncoordinated and physically awkward. She also appears to have been rather hyperactive.

At 19, she had an 'awkward gait'. 'Her hands, disproportionally small for her fairly large-boned body, were unusually weak and maladroit. So she wrote sloppily and slowly, never finishing in time with her classmates.' Taking notes was an excruciating effort:

> Because of the slowness with which she wrote, Simone often had to borrow her friends' notes...to complete hers. Her clothes were frequently ink-splotched from the improperly closed bottle of Waterman's she always kept in her pocket... Out on the street she put herself and anyone accompanying her at constant risk, talking and gesticulating as she walked through traffic with long, jerky steps, totally heedless of cars and escaping them by sheer chance.

She was an outstanding student except in cartography and drawing.

As a teacher, 'at first the students were amused by her awkwardness, her clumsy way of holding chalk, the total anarchy of her clothes'. She would often put on her sweater inside out.

She signed up for service in the Spanish Civil War: 'noting her awkwardness, her fellow volunteers immediately decided to avoid walking anywhere near her rifle's line of fire'. She saw no military action, because she injured her leg severely by stepping into a huge pot of boiling oil (which was at ground level to avoid giving away the volunteers' position). It took her many months to recover – meanwhile, Franco's army annihilated the unit she had served with.

Religion and masochism

At the age of 21, the possibility of contact with a personal God seemed very remote to Weil. In her view, the existence of God could neither be affirmed nor denied. Later she wrote that 'the conviction suddenly came to me that Christianity is pre-eminently the religion of slaves, that slaves cannot help belonging to it, I among others'.

She asked a peasant family, the Bellevilles, if she could work for them, and later asked to live with them full-time and pay rent. They refused the latter request, because as well as peppering them with embarrassing questions,

> not only did she never change her clothes…but she failed to wash her hands before milking the cows, and when they offered her a fine cream cheese she pushed it away, saying that the Indochinese were hungry. 'The poor young girl,' they commented. 'Too much study has driven her out of her wits.'

She began to accuse herself of laziness: indeed, a lot of her self-criticisms were similar to those of Ludwig Wittgenstein. It is interesting that she was attracted to Spinoza, who had Asperger's syndrome – she referred to Spinoza and Charlie Chaplin as two great Jews.

Gray points out that a 'notable feature of Simone's personal summing up – some might call it masochistic – was her growing interest in the redemptive value of suffering'. This is not unlike Ludwig Wittgenstein when he was at the front in the First World War. One wonders whether psychological mechanisms of a masochistic kind were at work. Simone, according to Gray, had an 'almost pathological receptiveness to the sufferings of others, and [a] strong tendency to cultivate her own'.

She had a 'life-changing experience' at the Chapel of Santa Maria degli Angeli in Assisi. She said that 'something stronger than myself compelled me, for the first time in my life, to go down on my knees'. She was increasingly attracted to Christianity. Her teacher, Alain, detected a mystical streak in her. Indeed, Bertrand Russell noticed the same kind of mystical streak in Ludwig Wittgenstein after the First World War: it seems that Wittgenstein had a conversion at this time, and it appears that something similar happened to Weil later. Her brother became a conscientious objector in relation to the Second

World War, and was put in prison. Gray points out that 'Weil's religious vision was deeply affected by Pascal, whose sense of cosmic alienation, of the far-awayness or absence of God, resonates throughout her work'. One wonders whether this was a sense of autistic alienation. One also wonders whether Weil's mysticism, in counterpoising the scepticism and 'scientific' standpoint of male philosophers with Asperger's syndrome such as Ayer, points to innate gender differences within Asperger's syndrome.

She said 'when I think of the Crucifixion, I commit the sin of envy'. This sounds extraordinarily masochistic. According to Gray, 'only this experience of detachment, of acute voidness – the *via negativa* of medieval mysticism – might create interstices through which God can enter and touch us'. This sounds a bit like autistic thinking. According to the writer Graham Greene, Weil stood 'at the edge of the abyss, digging her feet in, refusing to leap like the common herd…demanding that she alone be singled out by a divine hand on her shoulder forcing her to yield'. The critic Leslie Fiedler wrote that she symbolized 'the Outsider as Saint in an age of alienation'.

She wrote in 1941: 'I did not mind having no visible successes. What did grieve me was the idea of being excluded from that transcendent realm to which only the truly great minds have access, and wherein truth abides. I preferred to die rather than live without that truth.' Persons with Asperger's syndrome are very much 'truth seekers'. A friend once described her as having a strong taste for 'gratuitous risk and futile sacrifice'.

Food

Weil 'ate very slowly and sparingly, as if masticating food were a painful chore'. Gray attributes her fraught relationship with food, which finally killed her, to anorexia. She advocated research to find a means by which humans could live on sunlight and certain minerals. At various times in her life she refused to eat because people in other places did not have enough food.

Weil adhered rigidly to a standard diet each day (at one point, one brown roll). This is reminiscent of Wittgenstein, who, on his travels, often asked for exactly the same food each day, and even at every meal. Weil also became obsessive about eating fresh and, eventually, uncooked food. A very restricted diet is not uncommon in persons with Asperger's syndrome. (Gillberg (2002) points out that girls and women may be diagnosed with an eating disorder when Asperger's syndrome would have been a more appropriate and helpful diagnosis.)

Identity diffusion

Weil probably also suffered from identity diffusion. Her parents referred to her as 'our son number two'. Her brother referred to her as *la trollesse*, in reference to 'troll', the androgynous imp of Norse mythology. She joined the first women's rugby team in France. This kind of complex gender identity seems to be a feature of persons with high-functioning autism/Asperger's syndrome.

Gray refers to

> the despair caused by her general sense of unworthiness, her sense that she was plain and somehow incomplete and could not be loved as a woman, her deep unease about issues of gender. There was only one source of strength about her identification with men: although terrified of any sexual contact, she got along with them marvellously as 'comrades,' far better than with women.

One wonders whether her sense of unworthiness was related to her difficulty in deep emotional relating.

SIMONE WEIL MEETS the criteria for Asperger's syndrome.

TWELVE

A.J. Ayer

(1910–89)

T HE ENGLISH PHILOSOPHER A.J. Ayer was born in London on 29 October 1910. He had a difficult birth, and was an only child. His autobiography, *Part of My Life* (1977), reveals a highly intelligent child, somewhat 'highly strung' and suffering considerably from childhood terrors. A clumsy boy, he was very much given to reading. He was self-righteous, and had a very clear definition of right and wrong.

Ayer was a keen collector of books, stamps and cigarette cards, and remained fascinated with games, such as soccer, throughout his life. Board, card, and spelling games also interested him. He had a phenomenal memory for facts, and could be classified as a savant because of this. He was something of a loner as a child; according to Rogers (1999) he was 'quarrelsome and hard to control' and developed 'a rich, consoling and rather narcissistic fantasy life'. He always adored praise.

Ayer (who was generally known as 'Freddie') regarded himself as an outsider, and put considerable emphasis on the extent to which he created himself. He showed the characteristics of a self-made man and an autodidact.

Ben Rogers (Ayer's biographer) and Dee Wells (Lady Ayer, Ayer's widow) got to the heart of the matter after they both read Oliver Sacks's book *An Anthropologist on Mars* (Sacks 1995) and discussed Ayer in terms of autism. They felt that it would fit his 'constant fiddling and tendency to gabble – but also deeper psychological traits, like his devotion to games, love of facts and figures, and remarkable memory. Most obviously, it might have accounted for the remoteness that he sometimes displayed' (Rogers 1999). Unfortunately, Rogers later decided that this approach was 'unfruitful'. Unless otherwise indicated, the biographical details and quoted extracts in this chapter come from Rogers (1999).

Family background

Ayer's father was fascinated by statistics, and was very interested in games and puzzles. In 1984, Freddie described his father as a very clever man. However, he was narrow, rule-bound and pedantic, and probably also had some features of an autism spectrum disorder or the broader phenotype. He went bankrupt speculating on foreign exchange. Later in life his greatest interest was in cross-word puzzles. According to Rogers, Freddie's maternal grandmother was an eccentric: on her death she left money to London Zoo so that the monkeys could have bananas on bank holidays. She clearly had some genetic input into Freddie's personality as well in terms of eccentricity.

Freddie's maternal grandfather was also a collector, and showed savant ability in mental arithmetic. It was said that 'he could run his eyes down a long page of figures and in seconds tell you their sum'. A cousin of Freddie's had a similar ability. Freddie's paternal grandfather was a linguist who wrote text-books and statistical surveys. He was obsessed with facts.

Freddie seemed to identify with outsiders or orphans: Ben Rogers points out his interest in Dickens's stories that focus on enterprising orphans 'of excellent abilities with strong powers of observation, quick, eager, delicate, and soon hurt bodily or mentally'. This could almost describe Freddie himself.

Education

Ayer went to a preparatory school at the age of seven. He was rather timid and hard to control. School was a distressing time for him; he later described it as 'a little Belsen'. He came across as a rather immature and unmasculine boy, and was small in stature. Not surprisingly, he was bullied severely: he would retreat to the toilets during break times to avoid bullying. His fascination with reading helped him survive. According to Rogers, at football matches he would plump arbitrarily for a team, and had the capacity to identify himself entirely with its fate. It is as if he almost fused with the team. This could be an example of identity diffusion and lack of a clear identity, which is common in persons with autistic spectrum disorders.

Freddie progressed to Eton, where he was caned frequently. He was very much an autodidact there, and worked on his own. He was not popular;

Rogers points out that he 'was in many respects an unpractical and badly co-ordinated boy. He could barely swim or climb a rope or change a plug.' However, he was good dribbling a ball.

At Eton he was singled out for bullying, and was savagely beaten on at least five occasions. He had a lack of empathy in dealing with teachers, and would tend to answer back rather than staying silent. This only aggravated matters. One teacher said to him, 'Now, you are already an oddity. You don't want to be even more different from the other boys than you are' (Ayer 1977).

At school he was basically a loner with few friends, shy and often alienated from other boys. Other pupils didn't invite him to their parties. It is hardly surprising that he was lonely. He was described as odd and 'a one-off', and it was said that he had a kind of 'chip on his shoulder'. Ayer himself said that he never knew when he was not wanted (Ayer 1977). He had a major lack of empathy: he tended to harangue people in an insensitive way, which they naturally found tiresome. He could be intellectually over-controlling with his contemporaries.

Interests

Like Ludwig Wittgenstein, Ayer rejected mysticism. According to Rogers, he was committed to a broadly scientific view of the world, and believed in 'the importance of scepticism, rigour and clarity of thought. Philosophy was not a science, but Ayer agreed with Russell that it needed to be put on a scientific footing.'

He had a rather autistic relationship to nature, which made little sense to him. He said that 'so long as the bounds of logical possibility are respected, it is not for the philosopher to set any limit to the marvels of nature' (Ayer 1980).

The philosopher Isaiah Berlin stated that Ayer said to him, 'there is philosophy, which is about conceptual analysis – about the meaning of what we say – and there is all of this' – an excited sweep of the hands – 'all of life'. It was his autism that separated his philosophy from life. Philosophy was an intellectual pursuit for Ayer; it was separate from life, which was for living.

Berlin also stated that Ayer 'was the best writer of philosophical prose since Hume, better even than Russell, but he never had an original idea in his life. He was like a mechanic, he fiddled with things and tried to fix them.' This sounds remarkably like Wittgenstein's *modus operandi*: Wittgenstein was fascinated by mechanics and of course was trying to fix philosophy with his own style of philosophy. They were both trying to straighten out philosophy.

Ayer thought that the job of philosophy was to systematize and simplify. For him, philosophy was a 'fairly abstract activity…concerned mainly with the analysis and criticism of concepts, and of course most usefully of scientific concepts'. For Ayer, philosophy was an analytic discipline. It is interesting that when Ben Rogers originally read Ayer's books *Language, Truth and Logic*, *The Problem of Knowledge* and *The Central Questions of Philosophy*, he reassured himself that 'the world could not possibly be reduced the alien place they seemed to describe'. Here he had a major insight into Ayer: he was describing an autistic philosopher and the philosophy of an 'alien' in England.

Penny Price, who wrote an academic reference for Ayer in 1935, noted his

> narrowness of interest and the certain indifference and contempt for some quite respectable but old-fashioned ways of thinking. Perhaps we might say that Mr. Ayer has at present both the defects and the merits of the man with a system… It must be admitted too that his uncompromisingness in controversy has antagonised a certain number of people, including some of those who would admit on reflection that they have learned a good deal from him.

These are classic high-functioning autism/Asperger's traits.

Because of his Asperger's syndrome, Ayer lacked

> the deep feeling for human motivation, for the great range of forms that human values can take, that goes into the best political theory. But it was also true that Ayer himself had so narrowed the scope for moral and political thought, reducing it to the clarification of ethical concepts, that what was left could hardly satisfy the intellectual ambitions or seem adequate to the exigencies of the moment.

Persons with autism are often said to be 'lacking something'. The writer Cynthia Kee said that there was 'something deficient in Freddie's make-up – somehow he had been nipped in the bud as a child'.

Indicators of Asperger's syndrome

Social behaviour

Because of his high-functioning autism, Ayer had great difficulty in understanding other people's minds. According to Rogers, he felt it was an analytic truth that 'one cannot experience other people's experiences…any experience one has is by definition one's own'. Ayer admitted that 'none of my philosophical preoccupations have given me as much trouble as the problem of our knowledge of other minds'. This is the central problem for a person with autism.

According to Isaiah Berlin, 'Freddie always wanted to be the centre of attention in any room'. The playwright John Osborne described Ayer as the most selfish, superficial and obtuse man he had ever met.

According to Jocelyn Richards, with whom he had a relationship, Ayer had deep anxieties and would cry out 'no, no, no' during sleep. He said that 'I am always on the outside...looking in' – a common perspective for persons with autism.

Ayer had to win at games, and with women. He scoffed at 'old-fashioned ideals of fidelity, friendship, and married love'. He was a philanderer and used women, although they did tend to retain some affection for him. He once stated that he 'kept women at a distance'.

He was quite narcissistic, and liked to perform in front of an audience and bask in its admiration. He liked the attention associated with being on the radio, and made an interesting statement: 'I am famous, therefore I exist.' This shows that his sense of self depended on admiration.

In terms of philosophy he had the same anti-authoritarian attitude as Wittgenstein and Spinoza. It is not surprising that he was attracted to Wittgenstein's work, particularly the *Tractatus Logico-Philosophicus*.

His daughter, Wendy Westbrook, wanted him 'to see who I was, and instead I found him fixed on himself'. The playwright Fredrick Raphael, in a 1977 review in the *Sunday Times*, stated that 'a systematic prejudice against speculation has created, it seems, a Narcissus incapable of seeing himself, and hence others'. Clearly Ayer had a disorder of self – probably what psychoanalysts would call a narcissistic personality disorder. He was often fearful of being found to lack substance.

Celia Paget, who had a relationship with him, described him as 'perfidious in the extreme' in regard to women, and said that he was

> a man in whom intellect and the senses were unusually highly developed at the expense of the faculties of feeling and intuition. In these he was very deficient, as indeed he realised himself: only a few days after I first met him he told me he was 'a hollow man'...he was subject to sudden bursts of affection when he felt particularly happy and in good form, on the whole he was completely indifferent and would not go a step out of his way – would not even cross the floor at a party – to see them [friends].

His letters, like his relationships, were formulaic. His wife Dee stated that 'he loved pets – he identified with them in a way he couldn't always with people'. She felt that he was remote and lacked deep feelings, and noted:

> He was observant about people and a good judge of intelligence, but he was not interested in their psychology. He did not try to understand them as an analyst does and most of us do to some extent. If someone died he would not miss them – he enjoyed their company while they were there but that was all. If a cleaner or a secretary or someone left, he never mentioned them again. It was out of sight, out of mind… He knew he was different.

A colleague stated that when Ayer came into the army 'they had never met anyone like him before'. This is a typical comment about a person with high-functioning autism; it was also said about Wittgenstein. Ayer had problems with military discipline.

Ayer's lack of social connectedness was also seen in his lack of reaction to death (see 'Lack of empathy' below).

Narrow interests and obsessiveness

After Ayer's death, the philosopher Anthony Grayling in *The Guardian* described him as 'perhaps the last great figure of the Cartesian tradition, that tradition of thought in which our understanding of ourselves and the world has to be built outwards on data of consciousness'. This is very much a place from which a person with high-functioning autism would come. Around the same time, the writer and philosopher Roger Scruton in the *Sunday Telegraph* criticized him, quite rightly, for 'enormously narrowing the range of philosophical enquiry' and 'destroying the conception in which the wisdom of humanity reposes'. A person with Asperger's syndrome has no choice but to be narrow in their philosophy, just like Wittgenstein. Nevertheless, he was absolutely committed to truth, again like Wittgenstein.

Ayer's philosophical style was clearly cerebral; not surprisingly, he didn't see philosophy as having much connection with real life. He focused on conceptual analysis in the classic autistic mode. It is interesting that he admired W.B. Yeats – someone with a very similar problem to himself.

Ayer was obsessional in that he always had to be writing something.

Routines and control

Ayer could work 'in almost any circumstances'. Dee was amazed at how he could shut himself off from the hubbub around him, and noticed that he worked in 'a world of his own' – clearly an autistic world.

One of his three wives felt that his detachment was tied up with unusual traits that she noticed: the way he had to have a chain to play with when he worked (she kept spare chains around the house); how, when working, he could shut himself off from the rest of the world; his devotion to games; his love of routine; the minute handwriting; and his 'complete inability to visualise'.

In relation to his autobiography, *Part of My Life*, Rogers points out that 'Ayer's wry, measured, urbane tone denies us any insight into his inner life. Ayer's motivations…remain a mystery – as perhaps they were to Ayer himself.' Rogers then remarks that 'as befits someone who denied the existence of a substantive self, the book has no centre'. This lack of a sense of self or centre is pivotal to Ayer's autism.

The reviews of *Part of My Life* were revealing. In the *Sunday Telegraph*, Mary Warnock stated that 'there seems to be a lack of curiosity and particular lack of inquisitiveness about other people' – deep down, she wrote, Ayer seems 'bored'. John Sturock in the *New York Times* noted the engrossing detail, but remarked that there was 'strangely little self to go with it. Ayer's record of experience is all fact and no feeling.' Foster (1985) claimed that Ayer's 'logical construction of the physical world' was his great achievement. This predilection for logic is certainly consistent with Asperger's syndrome.

Mark Bonham-Carter, the editor of Ayer's final volume of autobiography, *More of My Life*, wrote tellingly to him about the book:

> …we are introduced to a large cast of characters, but they sometimes remain merely names – I find it difficult to tell the difference between Angelica Weldon, Alvys Maben and Jocelyn. Ryle and Price remain philosophers rather than colleagues whose personalities must have had some impact on you. I think what I am saying is that I could do with more light and shade, more contrast, that the equable flow of your prose sometimes appears to conceal you rather than reveal you, your mind and your feelings – which is after all one of the purposes of an autobiography.

This was an extremely perceptive description of the style of a person with Asperger's syndrome.

Speech, language and humour

Clearly Ayer had a great mastery of language, as persons with Asperger's syndrome often do. William Outram stated that he was 'a ready talker and appeared to be fond of arguments, discussions, often drawn out into wordy locutions on almost any subject – such as some people might dispose of in a few phrases'.

Isaiah Berlin remembered hearing him say: 'I don't think in the first person but the third person singular: I say not "I am going to do this or that" but "Freddie is going to do it".'

On the radio his voice was 'like a Martian who had only recently mastered talking – almost nasal and slightly grating, but it lilted in a bizarrely attractive way'. It is very interesting that persons with autism are often described as being 'from Mars'.

Ayer does not appear to have been a particularly humorous person, although there are some references to his wit.

Lack of empathy

People with Asperger's syndrome often lack empathy, and this was certainly the case with Ayer.

It was evident, for example, on the day his daughter Valerie died of Hodgkin's disease. On hearing the news, Ayer focused on the clinical details and once he had got the facts straight in his mind, he felt the conversation was over.

Dee said that:

> He did not know how, but he knew he did not know what the rest of us were talking about when we spoke of feelings. It was strange because when I met him, I knew here was a good, kind man. And he really cared passionately about justice and fairness. But certain things were missing. The first time I got an inkling of this was when, in very early days, I said rather wistfully, after a great old friend of mine had died 'I am feeling sad. You know how all my friends keep dying,' and he responded 'No, how?'

Angelica Weldon was a woman with whom Ayer had an affair, and who committed suicide. He described this episode in a very factual, autistic way: 'She rang me on the night of her death, without giving me any hint of her intention, which may not yet have been formed. I do not think that I could have done anything to save her' (Ayer 1984).

Ayer's wife Renee was concerned with his lack of empathy for people in authority at university, and tried to get him to be more empathic with them. She did her best to repair social damage that he might have done.

Naïvety and childishness

Ayer was immature in personality. He was naïve, and was often described as being without malice and as having a child-like innocence. Even his vanity came across as guileless.

Appearance and demeanour

Richard Wollheim, who succeeded Ayer as Professor at University College London, noted Ayer's

> constant movement, of head, hands, fingers, hair – the playing with the watch-chain, one bit rubbed against another, the feet going backwards, forwards, shuffling, tapping, turning on his heel and *sotto voce* a stream of 'Yes, yes, yes' – it was this incessant movement, this constant stream of excitement, that so impressed me. (Wollheim 1992)

At university, Ayer was said to have walked with a 'manner and gait quite unlike other undergraduates' and to have stared straight ahead. He was described as having a 'foreign appearance'; in the army in Algeria he was regarded as 'an odd-looking individual'.

Identity diffusion

Ayer was a complex, contradictory and chameleon-like figure. He may have lacked a 'core' self, like W.B. Yeats; another interpretation is that he 'put on' various identities in an effort to connect to people: this is common in persons with Asperger's syndrome, who often want friendships very much but have little idea of how to establish them. He had great difficulties in understanding emotion. According to Rogers, Ayer found hard to communicate emotion; this problem is central to an understanding of his personality. The style and the topics of philosophy that interested him were those that gave him some anchor in the world.

Ayer took identities 'off the shelf', so to speak – from Oscar Wilde, Noel Coward and others. At one stage he modelled himself on the classical scholar and wit Maurice Bowra, copying some of his mannerisms of speech and his style of humour. Ayer's problems with a sense of self led to 'a certain affectation of both manner and matter' and perceived 'intellectual snobbery'.

Vanessa Lawson, Ayer's third wife (he remarried his second wife, Dee, shortly before his death), stated that 'Freddie's face looks fat, but really it is thin'. Rogers interpreted this as 'sometimes he seemed one thing, sometimes another'. This again shows his identity diffusion and lack of a sense of a stable self.

Ray Monk, in his review of Rogers (1999) in the *Sunday Times*, observed that 'we can find Ayer's self-centredness touching, but unless we have some insight into the self upon which he was centred, we will still find ourselves faced with the empty "autistic space" in the plaster mould'.

Ayer argued that a person is a person because of a 'sensible continuity' of thought and feeling. According to Rogers, this meant that 'two experiences belong to the same self if they occur at the same time or immediately after one another, or are linked indirectly by a chain of directly related experiences, or alternatively, if one of them represents, directly or indirectly, a memory of the other'. Rogers points out that Ayer 'gave excessive weight to mental over bodily continuity' and that his Jamesian analysis didn't quite work, because

> it depended on a concept of memory which itself depended on the concept of a person, and was thus circular. The rather lame conclusion at which Ayer was forced to arrive was that both physical and mental criteria enter into the ascription of personhood, although these might, at least in theory, collide: in such cases 'there would not be any true or false judgement of identity'.

Rogers notes that Ayer went on in a similar vein to 'examine the concept of time, space, and the material world, all of which, like the self, he attempted to present as theories with respect to raw experience'. Time and space was a matter considered by another person with Asperger's syndrome, Albert Einstein. It is uncertain whether persons with Asperger's syndrome are particularly attracted to concepts like time and space.

It is of interest to see what Ayer had to say about the issue of identity, since this was one of his core problems. In *The Problem of Knowledge*, Ayer stated (as summarized by Rogers) that there is

> no one defining feature of a person's identity. Almost any aspect of an individual – his parents, time of birth, character, race or appearance – could be very different without making him a different person from the one he is, although of course there will be a point at which identity ceases to hold.

It appears that Ayer didn't think much of origins, and indeed felt that 'there was no reason to value an authentic El Greco more than a perfect reproduction of one'. This is clearly a bizarre statement.

In 1971 Ayer stated that:

> I wonder whether I do even have an image of myself? I suppose if you ask me questions about my character, I would have opinions about most of them, I would say: 'Yes I am X' or 'I'm not Y' [but] I don't think that I have an image of myself in the sense that I am much concerned with my own character. I don't think I'm all that much interested in myself. I'm much more interested in trying to solve philosophical problems, or in what's happening around me, or how my little boy is getting on.

Again we can see his identity diffusion, lack of a sense of self, and lack of a capacity for self-reflection.

Thinking style

Ayer was described as highly unvisual, an always admitted to being a very poor visualizer. This is consistent with Asperger's syndrome, where verbal skills tend to be more developed than visual ones.

Ayer was once asked what he saw when he thought of Paris – whether it was the Eiffel Tower or perhaps Notre-Dame. He thought for a moment before replying 'A sign saying "Paris"'. This is classically autistic.

A.J. AYER MEETS the criteria for Asperger's syndrome.

PART III

Asperger's Syndrome
and Musicians

PERSONS WITH ASPERGER'S syndrome are often interested in music and song. It is easy to pick out great composers that had Asperger's syndrome, such as Bartók and Beethoven.

Winner (1996) points out that 'the earliest clue that a child is gifted in music is a strong interest and delight in musical sounds'. There is also an exceptional musical memory. A tremendous memory capacity is common in persons with Asperger's syndrome – Mozart had it. Winner states that 'musically gifted children…sing with great accuracy, demonstrating the ability to match pitches with precision by their second year'. According to Winner, 'the core ability of the musically gifted child involves a sensitivity to the structure of music – tonality, key, harmony, and rhythm… In fact giftedness in music may appear earlier than giftedness in any other domain of skill.'

Winner also points out that Mozart could instantly play a piece that he had not seen before, and the pianist Glenn Gould (who also had Asperger's syndrome) said that he could read notes before words.

According to Rimland (1978), musical ability (not of genius proportions) is the most common form of autistic savantism. Uta Frith (1989) points out that the capacity for absolute pitch, 'which might be an example of an unusual focus on the elements of melody', occurs in musical savants and in many persons with autism.

Francesca Happé (2001) observes that persons with autism are detail-focused in their information-processing style – Uta Frith calls this 'weak central coherence'. Happé notes the finding of 'perfect pitch…even in musically naïve children with autism'; this could be seen in the detailed focusing style.

Beate Hermelin (2001) quotes Leon Miller in discussing absolute pitch ability: 'a skill in identifying and labelling specific notes without reference to an external standard...may provide the building blocks for the implicit understanding of the higher musical structures'. Hermelin states that 'musical savants can extract, remember and use musical structures – i.e. the "grammar" of music'. She also notes that they can reproduce 'what they have heard, they can also improvise, transpose and invent their own musical compositions', and that 'an extraction of structures can be transposed to other new tasks, as shown by the improvisations and transpositions by savant musicians'.

'Autistic musical savant' is the term used to describe musical talent in the context of general learning disability. Musical composition of genius can occur not in this context but in the context of musical ability of genius proportions and high-functioning autism (HFA)/Asperger's syndrome. It requires good intelligence. (Of course musical creativity of genius proportions usually occurs without HFA/Asperger's syndrome.)

Hermelin (2001) points out that the independence of intelligence and savant ability applies more to the areas of art and music than to numerical and linguistic abilities. Sula Wolff (1995) states that 'music and drawing, while not necessarily tied to general intelligence, usually depend on an overall high intellectual level of outstanding achievements but...extraordinary feats...for example musical reproduction or artistic products, are performed by some people with autism who function overall at quite low ability'. Hermelin (2001) also notes that 'although some painters or musicians may be generally much brighter than others, this need not influence their modular, domain-specific level of excellence'.

Blakemore (1988) notes that the 'right side of the brain seems to be the home of the interpretation and reading of music – skills that in some ways are very similar to language'. According to Schultz *et al.* (2000), it has been proposed that autism 'is specifically a disorder of the right hemisphere'.

Mottron and Burack (2001) point out that persons with autism show

> increased ability to detect changes to musical stimuli in the condition with the changed contour as compared to that with preserved contour and ability to detect change in musical stimuli in the transposed melody condition...persons with autism were better able to detect change in non-transposed contour preserved melodies, that are used to assess local processing. These findings support the notion of a 'local bias' in music perception among individuals with autism. In this domain the

enhanced localising that is evident in the processing of elementary physical properties of auditory stimuli...[is seen] as compensation for deficit in higher level mental operations.

As Lorna Wing (1996) points out, 'music can be the focus of repetitive routine...most autistic people are fascinated by music and may play the same tunes over and over again. They may know one conductor's interpretation of a piece and object strongly if they hear another rendering.' At another level, musical composers are searching for properties in the patterns of musical symbols that they are creating.

Tony Attwood (1991) emphasizes that 'listening to music can maintain movement fluency. It is interesting that certain types of music have proved beneficial...music with a clear and consistent structure and rhythm, as occurs in baroque and country and western music.' Attwood quotes a personal account of autism: 'When I am feeling angry and despairing of everything, music is the only way of making me feel calm inside.'

Oliver Sacks (1995) describes a boy with autism as 'losing' his autistic persona while he sang; the 'autistic persona' immediately returned once he stopped singing. Not surprisingly, music therapy is helpful to persons with autism and Asperger's syndrome.

THIRTEEN

Wolfgang Amadeus Mozart (1756–91)

I N HIS SHORT life, Mozart showed himself to be one of the greatest musical geniuses, raising the musical forms of the day to new and sublime heights. From an early age he was an extraordinarily talented musician and a prolific composer, but he suffered from depression, had difficulties in his relationships with patrons, and never managed to attain financial security.

This chapter reviews the evidence for Asperger's syndrome in relation to Mozart, and goes on to review the evidence for attention deficit hyperactivity disorder. Unless otherwise indicated, the biographical details and quoted extracts in this chapter come from Kolb (1937).

Life history

Wolfgang Amadeus Mozart was born on 27 January 1756 in Salzburg. His mother, Anna Marie Certl, had seven children but only two survived: Maria-Anna (Nannerl), born in 1751, and Wolfgang.

His father, Leopold Mozart, was a violinist and composer. At the age of four, Wolfgang was a musical prodigy; at the age of six, he was highly skilled on keyboard instruments and violin, and was composing pieces that are still played today. In 1762 he commenced a series of concert tours of Europe with his father. In 1769 he was appointed concertmaster to the archbishop of Salzburg. In 1782 he married Constanze Weber – the sister of Aloysia Weber, a singer with whom he had fallen in love but who had married another man. They had six children, of whom two survived, and Mozart supplemented his income by teaching.

He composed concertos, symphonies and operas – over 600 works in all – before dying at the age of 35, probably of typhoid fever, on 5 December 1791. There were few, if any, mourners at his funeral. His grave is unmarked, and his wife did not attend the funeral.

Indicators of Asperger's syndrome

Social behaviour

Mozart had great faith in his father. He himself was ineffectual and lacked comprehension of the usual mercenary proceedings that one has to undertake in order to advance in life. His father was overbearing, but his mother had great faith in him: he was the apple of her eye. In his early years he was described as spoiled and hypersensitive.

He said 'I have far too sensitive a heart'. In later life he was 'never able to live comfortably and free of cares', although he was always confident that he would one day be rich, and was upset at seeing 'wretched bunglers' succeed. He had enormous difficulty in negotiating jobs, and when a post fell vacant, he was always passed over in favour of someone else.

He behaved in a cavalier fashion to persons of rank. Although acutely conscious of his uniqueness and rank as an artist, he was too naïve to grasp that the world must also be convinced of it, and that powerful allies would be necessary if he was to achieve this. In relation to personal social interactions he was regarded as being simple-minded. He little valued his 'public'. As a teacher, he could not manage his pupils properly and would sometimes give lessons for free. He lived only for the day.

Narrow interests and obsessiveness

In 1777 he wrote to his father:

> I cannot write poetically, for I am no poet. I cannot arrange my phrases
> so skilfully as to give light and shade, for I am no painter. Neither can I
> express my feelings and thoughts by gesture and pantomime, for I am
> no dancer. I can, however do so in music.

He also said: 'I am completely absorbed in music, so to speak, that it occupies
my thoughts the whole day long, that I like speculating, studying, reflecting.'
He was capable of concentrating intensely on his composing at times of great
crisis in his life.

He set 'great store by clothes' and was regarded as rather arrogant.

Routines and control

Kolb observes that a submissive tone was alien to his character: he wanted
others to fall in with his plans immediately.

Speech, language and humour

Mozart 'was somewhat free in his utterances and not always discreet'. He was
described as garrulous, impetuous and caustic of tongue. His letters to his
sister were 'full of jocularities and witticisms', and he indulged in all sorts of
buffoonery. It was noticed that he tended to indulge in 'fooling, his drollery,
his love of jollity and laughter'.

Naïvety and childishness

His father told Mozart that he looked on everything 'as gold which turns out
in the end to be nothing but tinsel'. He also said to him, 'you know too little of
the world but when you are home again you will remember my letters and all
my forebodings and predictions of human ingratitude', and that 'you have too
good a heart. There is no evil in you. It is merely that you are heedless.' Mozart
had many 'schemes'; his father was indignant at his 'grandiose plans'.

He was childish in relation to life and to people, and could not judge
them. He lacked all sense of the meaning and value of money.

In 1776 his mother went with him on a tour because he was so 'reckless in
practical matters and so credulous a dreamer in dealings with people who flat-
tered him that he would have been too great a risk to allow him to set off
alone'. Whenever he had money, he found it impossible to refuse it to any

'needy wretch', and was 'shamefully fleeced'. He was incapable of perceiving the dangers of life, and couldn't read others' intentions; therefore he was easily exploited by means of flattery.

Physical appearance

He was sometimes mentioned as having an unusually large head, which is often associated with autism.

From the evidence presented above it seems possible that Mozart had Asperger's syndrome.

Attention deficit hyperactivity disorder (ADHD)

There is no doubt that Mozart had the three core clinical symptoms of attention deficit hyperactivity disorder in adults, i.e. (a) inattention and distractability, (b) impulsivity and (c) hyperactivity (Wilens *et al.* 1995).

Inattention and distractibility

Mozart daydreamed frequently, and was described as a credulous dreamer. He was easily distracted by internal thoughts (e.g. fantasies of riches) or external events. As we have seen, he paid little attention to details of social relationships, especially with important and powerful people who could have advanced his career, and indeed found it difficult to listen to them. He had poor concentration except for playing or composing music.

Impulsivity and hyperactivity

Mozart showed all the hyperactivity and impulsivity symptoms of adult ADHD. His father said that he 'roamed the world like a Gypsy'; his mother regarded him as 'impulsive and wayward'; his whole life could be seen as a succession of arrivals and departures. He was extremely impatient, and this was a major factor in his lack of success in Paris in 1778. He did not remain long enough in the city to make progress in musical circles.

He was possibly hyperactive, and even before the age of 18 he involved himself in 'an incessant round of composing and performing'. A musician noted during a rehearsal 'how the agile and restless little composer frequently jumped up from the piano, which stood on the stage, leaped over the prompter's box into the orchestra, and then after an animated discussion with the musicians clambered back just as swiftly onto the stage'. His sister-in-law, Sophi Haibl, stated that even 'when he washed his hands in the morning he would pace up and down his room, never still for a moment, knocking his heels one against the other, lost in thought the whole time'. His hands and feet were never still; he was always playing with something, for example his hat or watch chain, as though it were a clavier. His father said that he was 'too impatient, too hasty and unable to wait for anything'. At the table he would often take the corner of a napkin, screw it up, and absentmindedly draw it back and forth under his nose, apparently unaware of what he was doing and often grimacing. He was clearly a very restless person.

Hallowell and Ratey (1994) describe a number of features in people with ADHD. Mozart had every single feature they describe, including high energy, creativity, intuitiveness, resourcefulness in relation to music, tenacity in relation to music, a hard-working and never-say-die approach, as well as being warmhearted and excessively trusting, and indeed also excessively forgiving: he forgave his wife when he was being sued unjustifiably for breach of promise. He also showed extreme sensitivity, but could hurt other people. He showed flexibility in his movement from one style of composition to another, was extremely loyal and had an excellent sense of humour.

This all suggests that ADHD is a diagnosis that fits Mozart much more easily than Asperger's syndrome. There is little doubt that, clinically, patients with ADHD do have social functioning deficits.

Affective disorder

In relation to Mozart this has engendered considerable discussion over many years. The possibility that Mozart had manic-depressive illness or cyclothymia has been raised (Jamison 1993). Peter Davies (1987, 1989) has argued that Mozart had manic-depressive tendencies consistent with a diagnosis of cyclothymia. Kolb notes that from the age of 17 he had 'moods of depression which...his father shared'. Slater and Meyer (1960) state that Mozart had a melancholic side but that he did not become very depressed until he was a dying man. It is also interesting that, according to Biederman (1998), mania has sometimes been mistaken for ADHD.

IT WOULD APPEAR that Mozart had ADHD and depressive symptoms, which are very commonly associated with ADHD, as is Asperger's syndrome.

FOURTEEN

Ludwig van Beethoven
(1770–1827)

THE COMPOSER LUDWIG van Beethoven was born in Bonn on 17 December 1770, one of three surviving children in a family of seven. His father was a court musician who, on noticing young Ludwig's talent, began to teach him with a view to creating 'the next Mozart'; however, Ludwig would achieve immortality in his own right and in his own way. He gave his first public performance at the age of eight, and published his first work when he was 12 years old. In June 1784 he was appointed organist at the court of the Elector of Cologne.

He went on to have a brilliant but troubled career as a musician and composer, gaining a reputation for being impulsive an difficult but also as a supreme artist and a gargantuan creative force. Very often he was an extremely innovative composer, whose compositions represented a marked advance over their predecessors (Solomon 1998), and indeed became a turning point in the history of music itself. But he had problems with his finances and his health, including an advancing deafness, clashed with family members, and did not find happiness in his personal life.

Ludwig van Beethoven died on 26 March 1827 at the age of 56. A great crowd attended his funeral; Franz Schubert and other musicians carried the coffin.

All the biographical details and quoted extracts in this chapter come from Solomon (1998).

Family background

His paternal grandfather, also Ludwig van Beethoven, was a singer and kapellmeister who strongly opposed the marriage of his son, Johann, to Maria Leym in 1767. Ludwig senior felt that Johann 'would never amount to anything', and wasn't far wrong in this view. Johann had a 'flighty spirit' but 'lacked the energy to pursue his fantasies'. He spent a great deal of time 'in the taverns or wandering through the town with his friends, arriving home in the middle of the night or early morning'. An attempt to defraud his employers was discovered, and his position deteriorated. Gradually he became a 'comic figure'; he would 'walk conspicuously through the neighbourhood drinking wine from a flask', and became embroiled in debt and reckless ventures.

Johann was eccentric, odd, insensitive, and incapable of providing for his family. He conducted his son's musical education in a 'brutal and wilful' manner, administering beatings to the young boy. Solomon notes that 'Beethoven's first steps towards expression of his genius were manifested in free fantasies on the violin and clavier, improvisations that were quickly silenced by his father'.

Ludwig's mother, Maria, was described as very serious and as a 'quiet, suffering woman', but also as being 'hot-tempered and argumentative'. She had a very negative and unhappy view of marriage and of women's state within it. She died of consumption on 17 July 1787, when Ludwig was 16.

Education

Beethoven had 'a lonely, withdrawn childhood', and did not play games with other children. His 'external appearance was marked in a quite extraordinary way by uncleanliness, negligence'. At school, he was described as isolated and neglected. He showed an 'inability to make progress at school'; 'he learned absolutely nothing in school' and 'not a sign was to be discovered in him of that spark of genius which glowed so brilliantly in him afterwards'. This is characteristic of many geniuses with Asperger's syndrome. He showed a 'life-long inability to learn arithmetic beyond addition'.

Indicators of Asperger's syndrome

Social behaviour

As a child, Beethoven's 'happiest hours were those when he was free from the company of his parents, which was seldom the case – when all the family were away and he was alone by himself'. Solomon also notes 'the early signs of withdrawal in Beethoven, who remained indifferent to all praise, retreated, and practised best when he was alone, when his father was not at home'. This is also a characteristic of schizoid personality disorder. He occasionally engaged in physical violence with his brothers: some aggression is common in persons with Asperger's syndrome.

Beethoven had major difficulties in social and emotional reciprocal relationships. It was said that 'outside of music he understood nothing of social life; consequently he was ill-humoured with other people, did not know how to converse with them, and withdrew into himself, so that he was looked upon as a misanthrope'. Nonetheless, he was interested in 'conversation with good minds': persons with Asperger's syndrome are most interested in intellectual conversations, rather than in ordinary social discourse.

In the company of strangers, Beethoven was 'reserved, stiff, and seemingly haughty'. His 'studied rudeness' was commented upon. But his defensive exterior masked a fragile sensitivity to slights, real or imagined. He would storm away from an aristocratic dinner in fury because he had not been seated at the main table. Exaggerated or false attentiveness disturbed him equally.

He made many strange and unsuccessful attempts to form relationships with women: he had the desire but not the 'know-how'. He also appeared to fear greatly a relationship with a woman. He made a proposal of marriage without encouragement or preparation; it was rebuffed because he was 'ugly and half-crazy'. This reminds one of Ludwig Wittgenstein's proposal of marriage to Marguerite Respinger – he told her of his feelings for her on the day of her wedding to someone else (Fitzgerald 2004).

Solomon points out that 'young Beethoven was unable to establish a love relationship with any woman', and this upset him. Most women in whom he was interested were already attached to other people, and thus in a sense it was 'safe' for him to express an interest. He wrote in 1801, 'I certainly could not marry...for to me there is no greater pleasure than to practise and exercise my art'. As Solomon puts it, 'the self-deception of Herculean heroism, the pretence of romantic masculinity, was at an end; Beethoven's marriage project was abandoned, and his attitude towards marriage took on a cheerless character'.

'If he did not establish his own family, he repeatedly attempted to participate, by reflected light as it were, in the family of others': he attached himself 'to a series of families as a surrogate son or brother'. This is reminiscent of Hans Christian Andersen (see Chapter 2).

In a hotel that he visited, Beethoven would sit

> in a distant corner, at a table which, though large, was avoided by the other guests owing to the very uninviting habits into which he had fallen... Not infrequently he departed without paying his bill, or with the remark that his brother would settle it... He had grown so negligent of his person as to appear there sometimes positively dirty.

This is somewhat like Antonio Gaudí – yet another creative person with Asperger's syndrome.

As well as arguing with the musician Friedrich August Kanne over musical keys, Beethoven had 'quarrels with patrons, perpetual postponements of his cherished benefit concerts, delayed publications, and contract difficulties... Nevertheless, his personality was at that time sufficiently resilient that he could withstand these and other pressures with relative equanimity.'

Ludwig's brother, Kaspar Karl, died on 15 November 1815. He had written that he wished the guardianship of his son Karl to be exercised by both his wife and Ludwig, but the latter disliked the former and pursued, in an extremely conflictual fashion, the wresting of the guardianship from her. This legal battle showed Beethoven to be unempathic, insensitive and indeed paranoid. He was at his controlling and tyrannical worst in this battle, and was totally obsessive. He won a Pyrrhic victory in 1820, and wrote 'I have fought a battle for the purpose of wresting a poor, unhappy child from the clutches of his unworthy mother, and I have won the day – Te Deum laudamus'. His behaviour and his accusations about the mother were grossly inappropriate; indeed, he was 'beginning to have trouble distinguishing fantasy from reality'. He developed paranoid delusions (brief psychotic episodes are not uncommon in persons with Asperger's syndrome), and even wrote 'I am now the real physical father of my deceased brother's child'. (Isaac Newton, who also had

Asperger's syndrome, had a similar brief irrational episode.) Ludwig treated his nephew harshly; the boy was eventually given back to his mother.

Narrow interests and obsessiveness

Beethoven was hyper-focused on his musical work. It was a narrow focus. He wrote 'I live entirely in my music', and, in the very same letter in which he announced his deafness, stated that 'hardly have I completed one composition when I have already begun another. At my present rate of composing, I often produce three or four works at the same time.' Music occupied virtually all his waking hours. Solomon states that 'with the aid of his music, Beethoven wrapped himself in a protective cloak of his own daydreams'.

He sketched musical ideas constantly, wherever he happened to be. 'I always have a notebook...with me; when an idea comes to me, I put it down at once' he said. He also stated that 'I even get up in the middle of the night when a thought comes, because otherwise I might forget it.' He filled a large number of sketchbooks during his lifetime, and retained them until his death. 'I dare not go without my banner,' he said, 'quoting Schiller's Joan of Arc, when asked why he always carried a sketchbook with him'. Such notebooks were also a strong feature of other creative artists with Asperger's syndrome, e.g. Bruce Chatwin, van Gogh and Wittgenstein. Solomon notes that 'a theme of yearning for the unattainable' is central to much of Beethoven's work. In psychoanalytic terms he had a very demanding ego ideal.

Beethoven loved the countryside, where 'he was able to find tranquillity, seclusion, and contact with nature, which he worshipped in an almost religious fashion'. This reminds one of Wittgenstein in Norway and the west of Ireland. His creativity required 'peaceful, conflict-free external surroundings... Perhaps in pursuit of an unattainable tranquillity, Beethoven changed his lodgings almost as readily as his moods.' He showed a great deal of restlessness.

According to Solomon, Beethoven was attracted 'to stage projects dealing with the mythical and the magical, the sombre and the supernatural'. Asperger people are attracted to this kind of issue. Solomon notes that 'his late music, to an extent never previously seen in the history of music, would be created out of the composer's imagination and intellect rather than through a combination and amplification of existing musical trends'. Again, this is redolent of Asperger's syndrome. Creative people with Asperger's syndrome tend to start anew rather than builing on others' work. Hans Asperger noted that, unlike other children who struggled to pregress from mechanical learning to original throught, children with Asperger's syndrome (or autistic psychopathy, as he called it) were capable only of forming their own strategies (Mesibov, Shea and Adam 2001).

Routines and control

> Beethoven's daily life was organised so as to maximise his creative productivity. He arose at daybreak, breakfasted, and went directly to his desk, where he normally worked – with occasional time out for a short walk – until midday; he retired early, usually at 10 o'clock, but sometimes continued to write for many more hours through the night until a creative surge was exhausted.

He was a 'workaholic' as well as working with an obsessive regularity.

He was extremely controlling, and did not take other people's feelings or views into account. He was an autodidact, and 'preferred self-education through voracious reading on everything from Greek and Roman literature to esoteric writings on theology and science'; this was part of his controlling nature. 'It never occurred to him that his brothers knew how to conduct their own lives: he repeatedly interfered in their affairs, asserting his supposed prerogatives as the eldest brother and guardian.'

According to Solomon, 'Beethoven's difficulty with Haydn was that he learned too much from him – more than he could acknowledge'; he had a huge desire to 'be his own master'. He 'despised tyranny' even though he was extremely tyrannical towards himself and others. In May 1804, on hearing the news that Napoleon had proclaimed himself emperor of France, he destroyed the 'Bonaparte' inscription of the Third Symphony because he felt that Napoleon would become a tyrant.

Solomon notes that his eccentricities 'cannot be explained solely in terms of his need to demonstrate his independence and assert his equality with his patrons as a human being'. It is not surprising that Beethoven became a 'freelance' semi-feudal composer and virtuoso, 'moving towards relative independence from aristocratic sponsorship'. Nevertheless, he tended to worry a lot about money. In these respects he was similar to Glenn Gould, who also had Asperger's syndrome (see Chapter 17).

Speech, language and humour

Beethoven had some speech and language difficulties. 'He remained shy and monosyllabic because he had little thought of communication with others.'

Both his mother and his sister died when he was about 16 years of age. Solomon points out that 'the inability to verbalise his sense of loss at the deaths of those he loved – such as certain of his patrons, friends, and teachers – was characteristic of Beethoven throughout his life'.

Solomon notes that 'He hummed and howled in an off-key voice.'

Naïvety and childishness

Beethoven was always emotionally immature (emotional immaturity tends to go with creativity). The journalist Friedrich Wehner stated that he had a 'childlike naiveté' and was like an 'amiable boy'.

When the composer Friedrich Himmel 'slyly wrote to him from Berlin that a lamp for the blind had been invented, Beethoven unhesitatingly broadcast the remarkable news to all his friends'.

The other members of the orchestra played tricks on him because of his naïvety. On one occasion when they were in a restaurant in 1791, several musicians prompted the waitress 'to play off her charms upon Beethoven. He received her advances and familiarities with repellent coldness; and as she, encouraged by the others, still persisted, he lost his patience and put an end to her importunities by a smart box on the ear.'

Appearance and demeanour

Beethoven showed significant non-verbal difficulties. His head was described as 'unusually large' – this is not uncommon in Asperger's syndrome. He dressed in such a 'negligent, indeed even slovenly way' that he had the appearance of a beggar.

On the street, his eccentric appearance and behaviour made his nephew, Karl, ashamed to walk with him.

Motor clumsiness

'He was totally lacking in physical grace: his movements were awkward and clumsy, and he constantly overturned or broke things and tended to spill his inkwell into the piano.' His cheeks were covered with cuts from shaving. Although, upon his arrival in Vienna, he noted in his diary the name and address of a dance master, he never learned to dance in time to music. Awkwardness and clumsiness are characteristic of Asperger's syndrome.

Personality

Beethoven's personality was of a hypersensitive type. Goethe described it as 'utterly untamed'. His closest friends suffered his moods and sudden rages – most often followed by expressions of boundless penitence. Occasionally his temper crossed the boundary into physical violence: he was seen to throw an unwanted entrée at a waiter's head, and to pelt a housekeeper with eggs that he found insufficiently fresh.

He showed evidence of 'iconoclasm and rebelliousness'. Persons with Asperger's syndrome tend to be very oppositional and rebellious.

Solomon claims that he 'acquired an unshakeable faith in his ability and [became] imperiously aware of the quality of his genius', which he described as 'my divine art'. On one occasion he 'exhibited withering scorn towards a man who would not automatically grant him a place beside Handel and Goethe in the pantheon of genius' – which is where he undoubtedly belonged. According to Solomon, 'one need not take such utterances literally, but in them one may see the strengthening of a boundless self-esteem, which was surely a necessary precondition for the formation of Beethoven's sense of mission and, consequently, it may be, of his "heroic" style'. For a time he had a 'nobility pretence', but he had to abandon this in a court of law. This suggests 'autistic narcissism'.

Solomon points out that Beethoven

> introduced elements into instrumental music that had previously been neglected or unwelcome. A unique characteristic of the *Eroica* Symphony, and its heroic successors, is the incorporation into musical form of death, destructiveness, anxiety, and aggression as terrors to be transcended within the work of art itself.

Some of this probably arose from his Asperger's syndrome, where aggression is not uncommon.

Autistic superego

According to Solomon, 'few people could live up to Beethoven's high standards of morality, and many of his relationships were undermined by a suspiciousness that in later years took on a somewhat ominous cast'. Beethoven said 'never, never will you find me dishonourable'. The organist Wilhelm Karl Rust stated that he was 'always satirical and bitter' but also 'very childlike and certainly very sincere. He is a great lover of truth and in this goes too far very often.' He had an autistic superego, which is very common in persons with Asperger's syndrome.

Solomon notes that Beethoven's diary began to express his sense of guilt and even revulsion concerning sexual activity: 'Sensual gratification without a spiritual union is and remains bestial…afterwards one has no trace of noble feeling but rather remorse.'

Beethoven wrote that 'all evil is mysterious and appears greater when viewed alone'. He was much more aware of evil in others than in himself. He tended to project this aspect of himself onto others and view them as evil.

Psychological and physical disorders

There is no doubt that Beethoven suffered from depression; indeed, he wrote in September 1787: 'I have been suffering from melancholia, which in my case is almost as great a torture as my illness'. Solomon discusses his 'inevitable melancholic moods'. His creativity was 'generally richer during the warmer months'. He may have suffered from seasonal affective disorder (SAD). He became an alcoholic, and developed cirrhosis of the liver.

At various times Beethoven wrote that he would like to die, or that he had considered suicide. Solomon points out that 'on occasion, he used the threat of suicide as a means of compelling obedience from members of his family or concern from his friends. It was quite another matter, however, to write of suicide in his private ruminations.' Music was his antidepressant and saved his life. Depression and suicidal behaviour are not uncommon in persons with Asperger's syndrome.

As noted above with reference to his dealings with his nephew, Beethoven's thinking was often somewhat paranoid. He felt that people were deceiving him, that Haydn was envious of him, or that students would steal his ideas. This reminds one of Wittgenstein and his philosophy. Late in life he showed 'sudden rages, uncontrolled emotional states, and increasing obsession with money, feelings of persecution, ungrounded suspicions…reinforcing Vienna's belief that its greatest composer was a sublime madman'. He was described as crazy, a lunatic, a misanthrope, a recluse and mentally unbalanced.

He had a great fear of catastrophe – in 1801 he had a sense of 'impending personal shipwreck'. He wrote:

> My wretched health has put a nasty spoke in my wheel; and it amounts
> to this, that for the last three years my hearing has become weaker and
> weaker. I have been constantly afflicted with diarrhoea and have been

suffering in consequence from an extraordinary debility...for almost two years I have ceased to attend any social functions, that is because I find it impossible to say to people: I am deaf. If I had any other profession I might be able to cope with my infirmity; but in my profession it is a terrible handicap...it is surprising that some people have never noticed my deafness; but since I have always been liable to fits of absentmindedness, they attribute my hardness of hearing to that.

He went on to write 'you will realise what a sad life I must now lead, seeing that I am cut off from everything that is dear and precious to me'.

Solomon points out that

the gradual closing off of Beethoven's aural contact with the world inevitably led to feelings of painful isolation and encouraged his tendencies towards misanthropy and suspiciousness. But deafness did not impair and indeed may even have heightened his abilities as a composer, perhaps by its exclusion of piano virtuosity as a competing outlet for his creativity, perhaps by permitting a total concentration upon composition within a world of increasing auditory seclusion. In his deaf world, Beethoven could experiment with new forms of experience, free from the intrusive sounds of the external environment; free from the rigidity of the material world; free, like a dreamer, to combine and recombine the stuff of reality, in accordance with his desires, into previously undreamed of forms and structures... Ultimately, Beethoven turned all his defeats into victories. Like Henry James's 'obscure hurt' and Dostoyevsky's 'holy disease', even his loss of hearing was in some indefinable sense necessary (or at least useful) to the fulfilment of his creative quest.

LUDWIG VAN BEETHOVEN meets the criteria for Asperger's syndrome. He also meets the criteria for schizoid personality disorder.

FIFTEEN

Erik Satie
(1866–1925)

ERIK SATIE REMAINS, more than three quarters of a century after his death, one of the most curious figures in contemporary music.

> It is difficult to imagine another twentieth-century composer – of any stripe – whose appeal has cut so deeply across the social and aesthetic boundaries of our time... Satie is one of those relatively rare cultural phenomena, a creative figure embraced both by the Academy and the mass media, a strange, multifaceted personality who continues to delight, confound, bemuse... How is it that a composer of such seemingly limited scope and slender technical resources has become accepted as one of the truly significant precursors of modern aesthetic tendencies? (Gillmor 1988)

Erik Satie's sister Olga stated that 'my brother was always difficult to understand. He doesn't seem to have been quite normal.' While his biographers have tended to ascribe his unusual behaviour to his unstable upbringing or Bohemian milieu, the purpose of this chapter is to present the evidence that Satie's lack of 'normality' may in fact be attributable to Asperger's syndrome.

Life history

Erik Satie was born on 17 May 1866 (christened 'Eric', he changed the spelling to 'Erik'). His mother died when he was six years old, while the family was living in Paris. Satie then went back to Honfleur with his younger brother Conrad, born in 1869, to live with paternal grandparents, Jules and Eulalie Satie. (His sister Olga, born in 1867, stayed in Paris with her father.)

Satie therefore spent some years in 'an elderly household under the care of a religious grandmother and a grandfather of vague eccentricities' (Harding 1975). His grandfather may have had features of an autism spectrum disorder.

At the age of 12, Satie rejoined the household of his father, who had married a young music teacher. Both his father and his stepmother 'suffered from the urge to compose' (Harding 1975). In boarding school (the Collège d'Honfleur), Satie was an undistinguished student. In 1879, at the age of 13, he was sent to the Paris Conservatoire to study music.

Satie disliked the Conservatoire, which he described as 'a vast, uncomfortable, and rather ugly building; a sort of penitentiary with no beauty on the inside – nor on the outside for that matter'. (Albert Einstein made somewhat similar comments about his own school – many people of great genius have had terrible memories of their school experience.) He did poorly at his piano examinations, and 'consistently failed to impress his examiners'. At a piano examination in 1880 he was described as 'gifted but indolent'; the following year he was 'the laziest student in the Conservatoire' (Gillmor 1988). His teacher described his playing of a Mendelssohn prelude as 'worthless'.

Satie left the Conservatoire in early November 1886 with 'unpleasant memories that would haunt him the remainder of his life' (Gillmor 1988). The following year, after a quarrel with his father and stepmother, he left home and moved to Montmartre, where he eked out a living accompanying cabaret singers, and once lost a job because of excessive drinking (his alcohol intake would eventually kill him). Later:

> He lived alone in suburban Acrueil, a dolorous outcrop of Paris. The landscape of family chimneys and grimy workshops pleased him. His home was a room in a working-class tenement. No one else ever penetrated this sanctum while he was alive. He was tenacious in defending his privacy. (Harding 1975)

This room can be seen as an autistic sanctuary. In 1905 he went back to school:

> In his fortieth year Satie made the remarkable and courageous decision to enroll in the Schola Cantorum, that most austere and academic of institutions founded a decade earlier by the august and patrician Vincent d'Indy to uphold the traditions of his revered master, César Frank. (Gillmor 1988)

It was noted that he was diligent and highly musical, although deficient in the craft of musical composition. He graduated with first-class honours in 1908.

Satie was a seminal influence on a variety of vanguard movements, and was interested in art and film. When he died in July 1925, the funeral took place at 'the charming fifteenth-century church in Acrueil, where the composer had lived the last twenty-seven years of his life in poverty' (Gillmor 1988).

Work

> Satie, never lacking in imagination, almost miraculously transformed his alleged technical incapacities into a virtue, thus creating a unique body of music that succeeded in penetrating the lingering mists of Bayreuth and Parnassus like a beacon, clearing the stage for a truly contemporary aesthetic.

> Here we begin to approach the heart of the Satie enigma: by the prevailing canons of classical aesthetic theory Satie emerges quite unequivocally as a seriously flawed composer, one of the second or even the third rank, but one whose effect on the development of contemporary musical thought has been Nonetheless profound. Indeed it is possible to demonstrate that he had a catalytic effect on the emergence of twentieth-century avant-gardism at least the equal of far more celebrated and accomplished contemporaries such as Debussy, Stravinsky, and Schoenberg. (Gillmor 1988)

Satie in his time was, except for a small band of loyal admirers, an obscure and ridiculed musician. He himself stated:

> There's a need to create furnishing music, in other words music that would be a part of the surrounding noises and would take them into account. I imagine it to be melodious; softening the clatter of knives and forks without dominating them, without imposing itself. It would fill up the awkward silence that occasionally descends on guests. It would spare them the usual commonplaces. At the same time it would neutralise the street noises that tactlessly force themselves into the picture. (Harding 1975)

In Satie's vision, 'furnishing music' would play 'the same part as heating and lighting, as comfort in all its forms. It should be supplied in public buildings' (Harding 1975). Art had nothing to do with it.

His major work, *Socrates* (or *Socrate*), was described by Leigh Henry (1921) as follows:

Some may find this – an early Egyptian and Greek sculpture – bald, its reticence unsympathetic, its passionlessness inhuman. But those who realize the psychological tensity of terribly level and resigned speech, of simple gestures, of calm recognition and acceptance of the ordinariness of things portentous to romantic temperaments, will recognise in *Socrate* something of the spirit of its namesake subject, and of that lofty tragic insight which gave the world the drama of Aeschylus and Sophocles.

Igor Stravinsky, while critical of the clumsy orchestration and the boring metrical regularity, felt that the music of Socrates' death was touching and dignifying in a unique way (Stravinsky and Craft 1959). Gillmor (1988) points out that 'it seems reasonable to assume that Satie saw in his own ascetic existence a reflection of the martyred life of the Greek sage'.

> His refusal to commit himself, which in practical matters was a drawback, emerged as one of the great strengths in the artist. He was able to stand back and coolly appraise. Accepted enthusiasms passed him by. Reactions hallowed by unthinking custom were foreign to him. His gaze was cool and fresh. He looked at music anew and put a bomb under it. The incongruous verbal decoration he gave to his derisive piano pieces, the purely musical techniques of parody and satire, were a healthy counterblast to Romantic excess. Having emphasised in this way the absurdities of an outdated style no longer capable of useful exploitation, he evolved an idiom to replace it. (Harding 1975)

John Cage stated that to be interested in Satie 'one must be disinterested to begin with, accept that a sound is a sound and a man is a man, give up illusions about ideas of order, expressions of sentiment, and all the rest of our inherited aesthetic claptrap' (Cage 1958).

Indicators of Asperger's syndrome

Social behaviour

In school, Satie was a loner. According to Harding (1975), 'the picturesque trappings and the mysterious atmosphere of religion had an aesthetic appeal' for him.

In 1892 and again in 1894, Satie presented himself unsuccessfully as a candidate for election to the Académie des Beaux-Arts. In an open letter to Saint-Saens published in *Le Ménestrel*, Satie declared that he had presented himself not through presumptuousness but from a sense of duty. His candidature, he added, had been accepted by God, whence the affliction and surprise felt by Satie at his rejection. 'You can reproach me with only one thing,' he went on, 'that of not knowing me as I know you... By judging me at a distance and making your decision, you have behaved like one cast out by God and you have run the risk of Hell. Your aberration can only spring from poor understanding of the ideas of this century and from your ingratitude towards God, the direct cause of Aesthetic abasement. I forgive You in Jesus Christ and embrace You in the mercy of God. (Harding 1975)

Rather than evidence of lunacy, this communication is fairly typical of a person with high-functioning autism in that it is rather excessive and is outside the bounds of social convention.

According to Harding, Satie 'would not be driven. The slightest threat to his independence made him shy away.' For example, when the proprietress of a café that he liked became over-friendly, he abruptly moved off elsewhere. Gillmor sees in Satie's work 'an aloofness and emotional neutrality all the more poignant in its cool objectivity'. He has been described as intransigent and stubborn.

Satie was a lonely man who defended his shyness with a barrage of sarcasm, held simplicity and bareness to be the highest qualities of style, and remained intransigent to the end. He was capable of extreme rage, was unforgiving with anyone who failed him, and dissociated himself brutally from protégés who didn't do exactly as he wished:

> ...short-tempered and ultra-sensitive, he would flare up into violent rages and exhausted his friends. A slight was never forgotten. His anger burgeoned at trifles and expressed itself in cold, wounding jibes. Yet he could be the most charming of companions. (Harding 1975)

Debussy 'stood towards Satie in the relationship of an uncle, a benevolent elder whose home was always open to him' (Harding 1975). Nevertheless, Satie was 'irascible and fickle with Debussy' (Gillmor 1988).

According to Gillmor, he was interested in community activities and 'spent many hours in the company of ragged street urchins, organizing outings for them to nearby points of interest, listening with great patience to their fascinating chatter, and enthralling them with his own fanciful yarns'.

It is typical for persons with high-functioning autism to be interested in younger people (Fitzgerald 2004). He remained 'on the fringe, buried in virtual anonymity in his remote Parisian suburb. During the twenty-seven years he lived [there] no one, not even his closest friends, ever set foot in his small apartment' (Gillmor 1988).

He had considerable relationship problems. A ballet dancer named Elise (she had been christened Elizabeth Toulemon) was convinced that she alone had understood Satie, 'that exceptional man, so different from all who surrounded him' (Harding 1975). Satie described himself as 'a man whom women do not understand'. He was 'afraid of them, timid, shy, unable to appreciate them. His irony, defensive but penetrating, was not calculated to make him popular with them' (Harding 1975).

According to Harding:

> Satie claimed that he never married for fear of being cuckolded. This is significant. He was afraid of committing himself, afraid of being duped, afraid of attracting derision. He would not dare to take a first step that might reveal him without defence. So he lived alone, choosing to meet friends under circumstances of his own making and at times when he knew his mask was well adjusted. A terrible insecurity haunted him. It drove him to furious rage over trifles. He was ultra-sensitive to imagined slights. He detected insult in the lightest remark and denigration in a passing phrase.

Satie proposed marriage to Suzanne Valadon – an artist and model who had had affairs with Renoir and Degas – the first time that he met her. It appears that they never mentioned the topic again, although they became lovers. 'His bizarre wit amused her' (Harding 1975). The affair lasted two years; Valadon had another lover – a wealthy banker – at the same time. Both men accepted this situation at first.

One evening, Satie 'took Suzanne and the third partner in the odd triangle to the theatre. A pair of black boys, engaged for the purpose, went before them beating on drums.' But when Valadon annoyed Satie, he 'displayed in his window, for all passers-by to see, a trenchant statement about his volatile mistress…this document assailed her virtue with robust language and proclaimed her worthlessness to the universe' (Harding 1975). Satie was very upset when Valadon left him, and pleaded in vain for her to return.

Later in life he formed an affectionate relationship with a beautiful young artist, Valentine Hugo, that was terminated only by his death. She became 'little by little, his child, his friend, his sister' (Gillmor 1988).

Narrow interests and obsessiveness

According to Harding (1975), Satie was

> an original who loved animals, children and his art. He disliked women,
> conventions and accepted ideas. Religious feeling was strong in him. As
> a boy he responded eagerly to the charm of Gothic atmospheres and
> Gregorian modes. The grown man adopted mystical beliefs. The vague
> spell of the Rosicrucians held him for a time. Then he founded his own
> church. It had one member: himself.

Gillmor (1988) describes Satie's obsessive interest in religion:

> Satie began, about 1886, to affect a pseudomystical posture. He spoke a
> great deal at this time of 'his religion' and began to assume an air of
> such great humility that his companions nicknamed him *'Monsieur le
> Pauvre'*. In conjunction with his pietistic behaviour he immersed
> himself in a study of plainsong and Gothic art, spending hours of each
> day – no doubt to the detriment of his studies at the Conservatoire –
> meditating in the gloom of Notre-Dame Cathedral or devouring books
> on medieval subjects at the Bibliotheque Nationale. (Gillmor 1988)

It is interesting that persons with high-functioning autism are very often
interested in animals, children, mysticism and various types of religion.

Satie was 'an inveterate stay-at-home who disliked travelling and preferred the gloomy streets of Acrueil and his favourite Paris café to anything
that abroad could offer' (Harding 1975). Living in near-poverty, he was
fiercely devoted to his art:

> The practice of an art bids us to live in a state of the most complete
> renunciation...music demands much of those who wish to serve it...a
> true musician must be obedient to his art, he must place it above all
> human wretchedness, he must draw his courage from within himself
> and himself alone. (Harding 1975)

As a result of this obsessiveness:

> Imitation of Satie the musician and Satie the writer is doomed to bar-
> renness. This is an indication of his achievement. He stands entirely
> alone, unapproachable. He had always said that an artist should give up
> everything for the sake of his art. Fiercely, despite torments of depres-
> sion and self-questioning, he clung to his idea. There was no compro-
> mise. His failures were the result of the technical inadequacies often
> associated with an original creator. At his best he succeeded in evolving

that true and classic simplicity which can flow only from intense concentration and thorough use of material. (Harding 1975)

When he died of alcoholism and liver cirrhosis, Satie's room was entered.
Nobody else had been there for 27 years.

> The room contained a wretched bed, a table heaped with various
> things, a chair, and a half-empty cupboard on which were piled half a
> dozen unworn and by now unfashionable velvet suits. In every corner
> lay strewn old hats, newspapers, walking sticks. An ancient battered
> piano, its pedals held together with string, was the resting place of a
> postal packet. Wedged behind the piano were the scores of *Jack in the
> Box* and *Geneviève de Brabant* which Satie had long since given up for
> lost. An old cigar box contained thousands of bits of paper on which he
> had inscribed his exquisite calligraphy and inked in with maniacal pre-
> cision fantastic little drawings and plans. A thick pall of dust covered
> everything. The windows were filthy and the curtains faded, rotten
> with age. (Harding 1975)

On the 'thousands of bits of paper' were drawn, in fine detail, imaginary maps,
Gothic houses, incredible machines, and medieval fancies. Satie had a legend-
ary attachment to his umbrellas, hundreds of which are said to have been
found in his room after he died.

Routines and control

In 1886 Satie enlisted in the army, but soon discovered 'that the discipline of
army life was no more to his liking than the oppressive atmosphere of the
Conservatoire' (Gillmor 1988). Control is critical to persons with high-functioning autism.

Gillmor points out that 'Satie never did discover a young composer to
whom he could subordinate himself; it was not in the nature of the man'.

Harding (1975) describes how, towards the end of his life, Satie's compulsive neurosis multiplied.

> The gifts visitors brought him – and they were received with genuine
> pleasure – had to be arranged in a particular formation so that he could
> contemplate them from his bed. The pieces of string, the bric-à-brac he
> hoarded with jealous care, were subject to the most scrupulous rules of
> order. Each item had its place and must be put exactly where habit
> demanded. The money his publisher brought him as an advance
> payment for *Relâche* was stowed away, note by note, inside the pages of
> old newspapers.

Speech, language and humour

The language that Satie used provides evidence of autism:

> Satie's language, though majestic in his early writings, and mischievous in later years, remained constantly throughout his life both clear and simple, which does not exclude occasional rare words, frequently adding a twist to common expressions, or making unexpected combinations of terms one usually thinks of incompatible. (Volta 1996)

Volta also points out that 'no…feeling or introspection is ever allowed to show in his writings, be they memoirs, poems or pamphlets'. Again, this is typical of those with high-functioning autism.

Satie's writings offer many examples of 'autistic' humour and 'autistic' prose, some of it hard to follow, like the writings of Ludwig Wittgenstein. For example:

> It is rumoured that the horse had recently had its first communion in a parish near Vienna. This is the first occurrence of this sort of religious phenomenon in Europe; there are references to a jaguar in Australia which acts as a protestant vicar, and it is said to be managing very well. It is true that there is not much to do.

According to Satie's translator, Anthony Melville:

> Satie knew what he had to say, and he said it. It was sometimes peculiar, frequently absurd, but that was always intended. A large amount of his writing is humorous, often consisting of extended deadpan passages which keep one wondering how much is literal, how much ironic, until he reaches the final twist. He had a great love of puns and double entendres, which do not make life easy for the translator. I have attempted wherever possible to transfer this word play into English. Of course there are cases were I had to come back down and go with only one meaning, but where I have tried, I hope my attempts have not let him down; for Satie may be quizzical and odd, but he is rarely heavy-handed. (quoted in Volta 1996)

Satie showed a typical Asperger-type sense of humour as well as composing Asperger-type music that fits well with 20th-century alienation. ('Asperger-type music' is alienated, utterly original, unrelated to existing conventions; composers with Asperger's syndrome don't necessarily write 'Asperger-type music', although Bartók did.) Igor Stravinsky said that 'he was a knowing old card. He was full of guile and intelligently mischievous. I liked him from the start' (Harding 1975). Stravinsky said that Satie was certainly the oddest person I have ever known, but the most rare and consistently witty person, too. I had a great liking for him and he appreciated my friendliness, I think, and liked me in return. With his pince-nez, umbrella, and galoshes he looked a perfect schoolmaster, but he looked just as much like one without these accoutrements. He spoke very softly, hardly opening his mouth, but he delivered each word in an inimitable, precise way. His handwriting recalls his speech to me: it is exact, drawn. His manuscripts were like him also, which is to say as the French say: '*fin*'. (Harding 1975)

It is arguable that his long, repetitive composition *Vexations* may be 'one of Satie's grandest leg pulls' (Gillmor 1988).

According to Sanders (1917), Satie was

a cynic whose satirical vein is of a peculiarly subtle order. Artistry and wit were his stock in trade, and these, combined with a high degree of intelligence and a well balanced musical technique, provide an equipment sufficiently complete to enable him to lay the world at his feet whenever he chooses to have it there; like all true artists and every recognised wit, he is to the last degree economical and sparing of his ideas. All his productions are short, pithy, and to the point, and there is not a redundant note in a single score of his.

It is typical of persons with high-functioning autism to be economical and brief (allowing for exceptions such as Wittgenstein and Kant).

[Satie] concealed his shyness beneath a façade of elaborate mockery. In his life, as in his work, the deepest feelings were encased by a protective covering of humour and jest. His adoption of the very uniform – bowler, umbrella, dark suit – of those whose conventions he laughed at was the supreme joke. Yet if he sometimes appeared to be a clown, he was a clown with a secret that verged on the tragic. (Harding 1975)

Naïvety and childishness

The child-like quality that is very commonly seen in persons with Asperger's syndrome appears to have been a feature of Satie's personality: 'Satie emerges as a mere clownish eccentric given to mildly amusing puns, whose often child-like (some would say childish) music finds its ideal service as, at best, a superior form of sonic wallpaper' (Gillmor 1988). Harding (1975) states that he had a tendency for 'extreme naïvety', while Gillmor points out that

Satie's music – not unlike the more polished art of Ravel – has infinitely more surface charm than soulful depth, but a charm of such child-like innocence and candour as to disarm criticism. Despite its finality the music is capable of enchanting the listener. Where more ambitious works have failed, Satie's naïve popular tunes and diminutive wooden actors succeed in capturing, with that peculiar brand of ironic detachment he made all his own, something of the mythopoeic essence of the old legend.

Harding also points out that 'In many ways he never grew up. He retained the vision of a child and preserved it wonderfully untainted among the raffish bars and dives where he spent his manhood.'

Satie had an interest in Hans Christian Andersen (one often finds that one genius with high-functioning autism was interested in another). Gillmor notes: 'Like Satie, Andersen was a master of irony and an artist who possessed the rare gift of being able to enter into the mind of the child with such conviction and lack of sentimentality as to appeal to the child in all of us.' Debussy saw in Satie a child-like quality that he also perceived in himself.

Idiosyncrasies

Harding (1975) points out that 'despite his neat appearance he never took baths. It was his habit to clean his person, in little bits at a time, with pumice stone, which, he argued, was more effective than water.'

Gillmor (1988) describes Satie's dress:

> The composer now [1896] entered into what some commentators have described as the period of 'The Velvet Gentleman,' a reference to his rather restricted wardrobe which consisted of a dozen identical gray (or beige) velvet (or corduroy) suits – opinions vary as to the exact color and nature of the fabric.

Harding reports that Satie was regarded as a harmless eccentric, and that by 1910 he had adopted sober garments:

> the black bowler, the black overcoat, the dark suit, the high wing collar whitely starched, the sober tie and waistcoat tightly buttoned. Only the beard, the prim pince-nez and the ironical look remained to link him with the 'velvet gentleman' of his youth. Everywhere he went, and at every time, he carried an umbrella, tautly furled.

Harding writes: 'Impressed by the mystic leanings of his fellow-exile from Honfleur, [Alphonse] Allais nicknamed him "Esoterik Satie", and, on account of his compositions so far, described him as "ogival and gymnopaedic".' The Dadaists quoted with approval the bizarre titles Satie gave to his music, e.g.

Morceaux en forme de poire ('Pear-shaped pieces') and *Embryons desséchés* ('Dried-up embryos').

Sanders (1917) points out Satie's individuality:

> During the whole of his life, also, he has been a revolutionary both in spirit and in practice. Always disdainful of the beaten track, we find him constantly plunging into the unknown, ever speculative, and experimenting with weird, strange, and hitherto unheard-of harmonies. Had he been a philosopher of the Middle Ages, he should most certainly have leagued himself with the powers of darkness, because in the first place, he would thereby have shown his contempt for 'the gods of the things that were', and, in the second place, would have satisfied to some extent his insatiable longing to probe into the great unknown.

These are classic features of the high-functioning person with autism in the genius class. Such persons do not respect handed-down ideas, are not intimidated by authority, and have a truly enormous ability to be creative and to produce original works in whatever field. Sanders also described Satie as being like:

> The artist of the renaissance...so careless of fame...that, but for the generous and disinterested conduct of Debussy and Ravel, who decline to be parties to such culpable secretiveness as he would have them be, he would probably never have been heard of, in his lifetime at all events, beyond the limits of a select and comparatively restricted area.

Persons with high-functioning autism, as they seem 'out of place' or 'out of time', are often said to be like characters from the medieval or renaissance periods. Debussy described Satie as 'a gentle mediaeval musician who has strayed into this century for the joy of Claude Debussy, his friend' (Harding 1975).

There is little doubt that Satie was extremely eccentric, and that his music was highly individual:

> Although he was decidedly removed from the mainstream, his bizarre personality and innovative musical experiments have left their stamp indelibly on the arts of this century. One searches almost in vain for Satie's musical ancestors...his personality was shaped in large part by the motley bohemian contacts of his formative years in Montmartre, then in its heyday as the vibrant center of Parisian artistic life. (Gillmor 1988)

An alternative conjecture is that his personality was shaped by his autistic genes.

Harding points out that 'the hermit of Acrueil lived near to poverty. He despised wealth and material goods. He preached – and practised – an obstinate independence.' Satie wasn't the only person with high-functioning autism to adopt this position – Simone Weil (see Chapter 11) and Ludwig Wittgenstein also despised wealth.

According to Gillmor, 'his attitude toward money was very simple – it was meant, of course, to be spent, and the sooner the better'. His vices were 'great quantities of shirt collars, umbrellas, and handkerchiefs – and one old vice, the one that would eventually kill him – alcohol'. He was contemptuous of money and of bourgeois values, was content with the most trifling sums for his music, and would even feel offended when a publisher offered what, to him, was an immorally high amount.

His brother Conrad said that Satie had chosen poverty, knowing full well that mockery and indifference would be his lot. This 'austere taste for poverty' may have been the reason for his decision to settle in drab, sombre Acrueil – there are parallels here with Wittgenstein's self-imposed exiles in Norway and Ireland, and Spinoza's peripatetic existence in Holland (see Chapter 9).

SATIE'S LIFE AND work show sufficient characteristics of Asperger's syndrome (problems with social interaction; narrow, all-absorbing interests; naïvety; unusual language and humour) to suggest strongly that he did in fact suffer from the disorder. Parallels in terms of life pattern and autistic imagination can be discerned with other geniuses with high-functioning autism, such as Wittgenstein, Spinoza and Lewis Carroll. Common characteristics of Asperger's syndrome that Satie is not known to have exhibited include non-verbal communication problems and motor clumsiness.

SIXTEEN

Béla Bartók
(1881–1945)

Béla Bartók was born on 25 March 1881 in the Austro-Hungarian town of Nagyszentmiklós (now Sînnicolau Mare, Romania). Although he gained little public recognition in his lifetime, he is now regarded as among the most original figures in 20th-century music. His work included 20th-century classics such as *Music for Strings, Percussion and Celesta*, the *Sonata for Two Pianos and Percussion*, the *Violin Concerto*, and the *Concerto for Orchestra*.

Halsey Stevens, in his biography of the pianist and composer, declares Bartók to have been ahead of his contemporaries. His genius rested in his unique approach to composition; he experimented with 'bitonality, dissonant counterpoint, chords in intervals other than thirds' before Stravinsky and Schoenberg did (Stevens 1993). As an innovator he, along with Zoltán Kodály, is credited with having cultivated the Hungarian national musical style, integrating unusual Magyar rhythms. However, Bartók's life is also distinctive for the many features of Asperger's syndrome that he displayed (Fitzgerald 2000).

Family background

Bartók's father, also Béla, was a teacher of considerable ability in the local agricultural training college, and a gifted musician. He died from Addison's disease when Bartók was seven years old. Bartók's mother, Paula Voit, shared her husband's interest in music and taught piano. Throughout his life she helped Bartók enormously, and declared that he was 'always, a good loving son to me' (Chalmers 1995). Chalmers notes that she 'never ceased to be utterly devoted to him'. From accounts of his early life, she clearly was aware of the musical prodigy she had produced:

> At a year and a half he listened intensely to a specific piece, smiling and nodding his head; the next day he brought her to the piano and shook his head until she played the right piece. At three he was given a drum, which he beat in time to his mother's playing; if she changed the rhythm, he would stop momentarily and then begin again in the new rhythm. A year later he was playing from memory – with one finger – as many as forty songs. (Stevens 1993)

Bartók had his first piano lesson from his mother at the age of five. It was discovered he had absolute pitch at the age of seven, and two years later he began 'spontaneously to compose tunes' (Stevens 1993), which his mother notated for him. He made his first public appearance as a pianist at the age of 11, and was well received.

Bartók was a serious and quiet child who did not play with other children, most likely as a result of ill health. Following a smallpox vaccination he developed a recurrent skin rash, possibly eczema, that lasted until the age of five.

Indicators of Asperger's syndrome

Social behaviour

Bartók showed severe impairment in reciprocal social interaction. As a child he found it difficult to form friendships with other children, and 'disliked their noisy games and quarrels' (Stevens 1993). When teaching at the Budapest Academy of Music, he 'kept himself apart from the rest of the staff and administration' (Chalmers 1995).

Bartók also showed a lack of appreciation of social cues. Evidently his ways did not always endear him to people. His Hungarian-American friend, Agatha Fassett, noted his 'lack of social graces and absorption in his own concerns to the point of rudeness'. Similarly, the violinist Jelly Arányi described him in 1922 as 'a little difficult to be with' and (less than a week later) as 'an awfully disgusting character'. Bartók would turn up at the family home of his student, Ferenc Vecsey, in the guise of an 'anarchic folklorist and drop-out', intent on upsetting the 'rigid etiquette' of the Vecsey household. He related his desire for disorder to his aunt Irma: 'As I have a taste for dissonance, I intend to invade this scene of awful orderliness wearing my summer shirt, without collar or cuffs, and my oldest shoes – just to shock them!' (Chalmers 1995).

Bartók was habitually reserved and had few close friends, although he did form lifelong friendships with Kodály (who shared his musical interests and became his confidant) and later with the composer Paul Sacher. Indeed, his reserve was reflected in the impersonality of his music. Bartók commented that Kodály's music was seen as 'much more gentle and humane' than his own (Chalmers 1995).

His lack of desire to interact with his peers, particularly women, made finding a suitable partner difficult. As is often the case in those with Asperger's syndrome, he was pessimistic about relationships. According to Stevens, he searched earnestly for an 'ideal companion', convinced in advance of the futility of the search, certain that disappointment would follow even if it were successful.

Consistent with other geniuses with Asperger's syndrome, such as Wittgenstein and Lewis Carroll, Bartók was attracted to young, innocent, gentle people. Chalmers points out that in all his relationships with women, Bartók 'seems to have reverted to childish behaviour, and yet been attracted to the child-like woman' (Stevens 1993). In 1907 he fell in love with a violin student called Stefi Geyer, who inspired much of the music he began to compose at that time. He wrote frequent letters to her, but, according to Chalmers, she 'may not have given him much encouragement'. The relationship was 'more imagined than real' (Stevens 1993). This bears some similarity to Wittgenstein's relationship with Marguerite Respinger (Fitzgerald 2004).

With persons of genius, it is often the case that their partners are devoted to them; eager to cater for all their needs and wants. This was true in Bartók's case. Being an intensely private man, he initially kept his marriage to his student, Marta Ziegler, secret. She was around 16 years old at the time. Bartók was 'fiercely resentful that his private life should be the subject of comment by his friends, and became angry when Dohnányi sent him a congratulatory note' (Stevens 1993). In 1923 Marta and Bartók divorced, and he married Ditta Pásztory. Ditta was a young student, 'whose pianistic talents were impressive and whose personal charm was irresistible' (Stevens 1993). According to Chalmers (1995), Ditta can be seen in photographs 'observing her husband in rapt devotion that suggests she readily adapted to his needs and desires'. Bartók was evidently attracted to much younger, vivacious women, such as the musically gifted Klára Gombossy and Jelly Arányi.

In common with many geniuses with Asperger's syndrome, Bartók was over-sensitive to criticism and took it badly when there were setbacks and disappointments in his music career, such as failing to win competitions or secure public engagements. He often retreated into isolation. According to Stevens (1993), Bartók weathered 'successive discouragements', but in 1912 he could bring himself to struggle no longer and 'withdrew from all forms of public musical activity'.

Following the break-up of the Austro-Hungarian empire and the ensuing rise to power of the Hungarian communists, Bartók was appointed a member of the Directorate of Music. It was a function to which he was ill-suited. Chalmers (1995) notes that 'it is hard to imagine a man less likely to flourish in a political environment than Bartók; no one ever commented on his tactfulness, and his behaviour in public was never geared to easy social intercourse'.

Throughout his life, Bartók often avoided the social interaction necessary to advance his career. Certainly he suffered financially as a result. In his dealings with the critics, he had 'no interest in or little respect for the profession of music criticism' (Stevens 1993). The Berlin critic, Oscar Bie, accused Bartók of being responsible for his own professional obscurity, of 'bending at the edges' before an important crisis, of withdrawing himself from contact with those who would further his career' (Stevens 1993). In this respect, Bartók, in common with many other geniuses (e.g. Wittgenstein, Einstein, Lewis Carroll), displayed a social naïvety.

Notwithstanding the lack of desire to interact with peers, Bartók, having finished his course at the Budapest Academy of Music, did attempt to gain favour among important people, yet was almost child-like in his approach:

> It is curious to observe Bartók at this period making an effort to play the game of influence – a role which ill suited him, and which he was utterly incapable of maintaining. It is impossible to think of him as devious or scheming; even when he confesses the plot – in his letters – there is something childlike and amiable in it. His inability either to flatter or to arrogate left him at a disadvantage in competition with musicians all too skilful in those accomplishments. (Stevens 1993)

According to Stevens, Bartók, being unprepossessing in appearance and almost painfully shy, could not have assumed a 'mantle of theatricality' even had he wished to. Instead he adopted a twofold approach to satisfy all concerned: 'to present himself to the public through his music, in which the element of personality is of secondary importance, or through his performances as a pianist, in which the personal element assumes a somewhat greater prominence' (Stevens 1993).

Like Einstein, Wittgenstein and Lewis Carroll, Bartók's child-like manner persisted throughout his life. On the death of his mother in 1939, when he was 58, Bartók was so overcome with grief that he failed to attend her funeral (Chalmers 1995). In order to cope, he immersed himself in work, but months later was still berating himself for not having spent more time with her prior to her death.

Bartók, like many geniuses, had questionable teaching skills. Chalmers notes that with his students 'he was unforgiving for the tiniest deviation or sloppiness in rhythm'. In fact, he refused to teach composition to students in the belief that it would impair his own creativity. He resented having to teach less gifted students, and failed to conceal his annoyance with them. During the world wars he refused offers of teaching despite his personally straitened circumstances. That said, like Wittgenstein he was an exceptional teacher where talented students were concerned, and they greatly admired his genius (Stevens 1993).

Narrow interests and obsessiveness

According to Stevens (1993), Bartók's ardent spirit 'enlightened every field to which he turned his attention'. Throughout his life he focused intensely on music. Furthermore, Stevens claims that 'in no other recent composer is there to be observed such an undeviating adherence to the same basic principles throughout an entire career'. While Chalmers (1995) states that music was the only interest of the young Bartók, it is evident that he held passionate interests in ethnology and Hungarian nationalism too.

Occasionally Bartók was so absorbed in his work that current affairs, no matter how threatening, escaped him. His colleague Paul Sacher, on a visit to Bartók shortly before the Second World War, noted: 'I found him completely without misgivings for the future, absorbed in his work. The news of the political events which were so cruelly to interfere in his life had not penetrated to him' (Chalmers 1995).

Bartók was a searching composer, who explored new rhythms and modes of expression not always acceptable to his audiences. Stevens points out that in the 1920s especially, his music was 'so uncompromising, so unyielding, that the general public was left far behind, and only the most adventurous could keep pace with him'.

In his music Bartók moved away from traditional standards of tonality. Particularly in the two sonatas for piano and violin, he avoided anything that could 'indisputably be called a key' (Stevens 1993). Stevens asserts that the 'reaffirmation of fundamental tonality' became a lifelong pursuit for Bartók. The search for fundamental concepts is a striking feature in the work of geniuses with Asperger's syndrome (Wittgenstein's successor at Cambridge, G.H. von Wright, wrote of conversing with him: 'It was terrible. Everything had to be constantly dug up anew, questioned and subjected to the tests of truthfulness. This concerned not only philosophy but the whole of life' (Edmonds and Eidinow 2001)). Very often their work is subject to disapproval. The composer and critic Constant Lambert criticized Bartók's piano concerto and sonata, first performed in 1927, for their 'lack of rapport' between melodic and harmonic elements:

> The melody becoming definitely simpler, squarer, and more 'folky' while the harmonic treatment becomes more cerebral and *outré*. The gap between the two becomes such that in some passages…the composer gives up all attempt to bridge it, merely punctuating each pause in an innocent folksong with a resounding, brutal, and discordant crash, an effect which, did it not remind one of a sadistic schoolmaster chastising some wretched country bumpkin, would verge on the ludicrous. (Stevens 1993)

Simplicity, which is at the heart of many works of genius, is evident in Bartók's too. However, he argued that 'the simpler the melody, the more unusual may be its accompanying harmony' (Stevens 1993). In fact, rhythm became almost more important than melody for Bartók, which is significant given that many geniuses with Asperger's syndrome display a mechanical, logical mindset.

In other areas of his life Bartók displayed an intense focus. Undoubtedly he was a very committed nationalist, who believed that the future of Hungary lay in the 'education of the provinces' (Stevens 1993). To this end he chose to study at Budapest Academy of Music despite being offered a place at the more prestigious Vienna Conservatory. Furthermore, he declared that 'all my life, in every sphere, always and in every way, I shall have one objective: the good of Hungary and the Hungarian nation' (Chalmers 1995). Despite the imminent Nazi occupation of Hungary, Bartók was reluctant to leave his native country, and emigrated to America only upon the death of his mother in 1939.

Bartók's interest in musical ethnology was also politically inspired. He devoted himself to ethnomusicological research after becoming aware in 1904 of an indigenous Magyar music that had its roots in Hungary itself (years earlier Franz Liszt had credited the Bohemian gypsies for originating Hungarian music). He put enormous effort into transcribing and classifying the collection of peasant tunes. In his efforts at collecting, codifying and preserving material he adopted a logical, scientific approach. According to

Stevens, he systematically collected and scientifically classified thousands of melodies from Hungary and other regions such as Romania, Slovakia, Turkey and North Africa. He recorded thousands of peasant tunes on wax cylinders. This collecting was done in periods of enormous intensity, with 'meticulous accuracy' and 'every fluctuation in rhythm or ornamentation painstakingly indicated' (Stevens 1993). He published five important ethnological works in book form, and numerous articles in peridiocals. When he was publicly criticized for a lack of patriotism in his writings on Romanian folk music, 'he gave a painstaking, pedantic response, as if knee-jerk chauvinism could be countered by reasoned, quiet argument' (Chalmers 1995).

Bartók was of a serious disposition, and read widely. Generally his reading matter concerned areas of particular interest to him, namely music and nature. In common with many geniuses with Asperger's syndrome, he was an avid collector. Like Charles Darwin, Bartók had a childhood interest in collecting and mounting insects, which persisted throughout his later life. He was especially fascinated by silkworms. This interest gave rise to certain eccentricities: on tour he always carried a flask of alcohol in which to preserve whatever insects he came across.

Routines and control

In all his undertakings Bartók showed imposition of routines. In this respect his philosophy was simple: 'Work, learn, work, learn, and a third time work and learn: thus we can get somewhere' (Stevens 1993). It meant that he searched and experimented until he felt a piece was complete. Clearly his admission that 'I hate incompleteness' demonstrates the autistic behaviours of needing to finish a task once started and links with desire for order.

His routines endured for an entire lifetime. During the 1930s he spent ten hours per day on his ethnomusicological work at the Academy of Sciences (Chalmers 1995). His output was prolific and larger than that of any of his contemporaries. He was working on an orchestral score shortly before his death. In that sense he never compromised his ideals, or lost his innocence. Chalmers notes his insistence on exactitude. For this reason he imposed great demands on his students and colleagues. Sacher described Bartók as possessing an 'impassioned objectivity' that penetrated everything: 'He was himself clear to the smallest detail and demanded from everyone the utmost in differentiated precision' (Stevens 1993).

From the beginning of his music career at the Academy, Bartók imposed a rigour on his life. In 1902 he wrote to his mother showing his sense of control: 'I have never had any strong drinks in Budapest so far, although I have often had them offered to me' (Chalmers is sure that he was not trying to pull the wool over his mother's eyes).

The American pianist, Storm Bull, recalls Bartók's routine in his house in Budapest. On the second floor Bartók could shut himself away behind two doors, one of which was padded and left him free to concentrate on his composition. There was also a window seat that allowed him to sunbathe as he worked. Bull frequently discovered him writing there, 'naked and tanned from head to foot, with the sun beating down upon him' (Stevens 1993).

Appearance and demeanour

Stevens points out that photographs from 1910 show Bartók as having 'piercing eyes'. He had a profound effect on those that met him. Sacher describes Bartók's impact, reflecting the alien and unique quality common to many geniuses:

> Whoever met Bartók, thinking of the rhythmic strength of his work, was surprised by his slight, delicate figure. He had the outward appearance of a fine-nerved scholar. Possessed of fanatical will and pitiless severity, and propelled by an ardent spirit, he affected inaccessibility and was reservedly polite. His being breathed light and brightness; his eyes burned with a noble fire. In the flash of his searching glance no falseness nor obscurity could endure. If in performance an especially hazardous and refractory passage came off well, he laughed in boyish glee; and when he was pleased with the successful solution of a problem, he actually beamed. That meant more than forced compliments, which I never heard from his mouth. (Stevens 1993)

The quasi-religious awe commonly associated with geniuses is to be found in Bartók's life. A colleague, Balázs, described him as 'a most moving and most marvellous man. His frail, weak delicate body…seemed as if it moved in robes in front of an altar' (Chalmers 1995).

Personality

Clearly Bartók's personality was unique and inspiring. The critic of the *Vossische Zeitung* wrote that 'Bartók is a man who has his own ideas of God and the world; he is a strong personality in himself'. Similarly, the critic Oscar Bie admitted that 'while Bartók played, it was as if all music lived in him, and the listener was impressed with his strong individuality; but when he ceased playing he retired to the remotest depths of some cavern, from which he could be drawn forth only by force' (Stevens 1993).

Bartók displayed a simplicity not unlike that of Wittgenstein throughout his life. Chalmers (1995) notes his 'strain of harsh asceticism'. According to his biogropher Agatha Fasset, he showed a puritanism where material things were concerned. Moreover, there is little evidence to suggest grandiosity or narcissism. On the contrary he displayed 'a genuine modesty', according to his friend Sacher (Stevens 1993). The things that gave him most pleasure were humble and modest. On trips collecting folk songs, it was a delight for him to eat simple peasant food in the open air. Evidently, the political and economic upheavals wrought by two world wars ensured that Bartók did not live comfortably, and despite an international reputation he had constant worries about his income and pension.

Like Wittgenstein, Bartók showed a special affinity for animals. During the First World War he would not allow the chickens kept by his family to be killed for food, and when collecting insects he would smother them so that they would not feel pain.

Lack of empathy

Bartók's marriage in 1909 happened in a bizarre fashion, and was typical of his habitual reserve. Marta was 16 years old at the time and would come to his house for morning lessons. According to Stevens (1993), after lunch on a particular day they left the house for a few hours and returned to continue the lesson. At dinnertime Bartók announced to his mother 'Marta will stay', to which he added 'she is my wife'. Chalmers (1995) remarks that Marta seems to have been the more mature partner in the relationship, and 'her devotion to Bartók is as much remarked on as her sunny straightforward character'.

Speech, language and humour

Bartók was over two years of age before he began to talk. In common with many persons with Asperger's syndrome, he did poorly at school. Stevens (1993) notes that at the gymnasium he attended his progress was unsatisfactory, and he was 'on the verge of failure in arithmetic and geography when his mother withdrew him'. However, Stevens claims it was not lack of ability that hindered his progress, but neglect at the hands of the teachers, who encouraged the more promising students. Certainly he later made better progress at another gymnasium.

In common with Wittgenstein, Lewis Carroll (notwithstanding the cele-brated humour of Carroll's writings) and other geniuses with Asperger's syndrome, Bartók had difficulty with humour. According to his first wife, Marta, 'He rarely laughed – mostly only when a letter arrived from abroad with an error in the address or he received first proofs of one of his works from one of his publishers abroad in which the Hungarian text was littered with misprints' (Chalmers 1995).

Nonetheless, he did show a talent for punning, playing on the meaning of words in various languages. According to Stevens, Bartók referred to his patron, Nat Shilkret, as 'the turtle', a play on the German word *Schildkröte* meaning turtle. Indeed, in the course of his life Bartók mastered many lan-guages – Magyar, German, Latin, French, English, Slovak, Romanian, Turkish – and had a few lessons in Spanish and Italian. Bartók's dedication to learning languages drew many comments from his colleagues, but, according to Chalmers, 'Kodály made the rather sour comment that Bartók had no real gift for languages'. With his excellent memory he had a capacity for remembering vocabulary, but not for the nuances of language.

Motor skills

There is some evidence that Bartók showed clumsy and gauche movement. It appears that when he performed, he was generally well disposed towards his audience but 'unable to demonstrate it'. His acknowledgement of their applause was 'awkward and graceless, and even his absorption in the music was not picturesque' (Chalmers 1995).

He had difficulty with taking photographs, which he described as 'a painful experience…afterwards I am very sorry for every spoiled picture' (Stevens 1993).

Co-morbidity

Throughout his life Bartók suffered from ill-health. In 1899 he began to spit blood and it was suspected that he had tuberculosis. Later he had recurrent bouts of bronchitis and pneumonia. At the outbreak of the First World War, when aged 33, he was turned down for military service because he was under-weight. Setbacks and disappointments brought on bouts of depression. Cer-tainly the events of the war depressed him, leading some of his colleagues to consider his mood 'suicidal'. He died of leukaemia in New York in 1945.

BÉLA BARTÓK MEETS Gillberg's (1991) criteria for Asperger's syndrome except for the uncertainty as to motor clumsiness. Gillberg (1996) has questioned the frequency of this sign in high-IQ persons with Asperger's syndrome. Bartók would also meet the criteria for Asperger's disorder (DSM-IV) except for his delay in language development, a much-criticized (e.g. Gillberg 1991; APA 1994; Twachtman-Cullen 1998; Mesibov et al. 2001) feature of the American Psychiatric Association definition. It would appear that his ability to focus intensively on very narrow interests assisted his creativity. On the negative side, his problems with social relationships inhibited his professional progress in the wider social world.

SEVENTEEN

Glenn Gould
(1932–82)

THE PIANIST AND composer Glenn Gould was born in Toronto on 25 September 1932. He started to play the piano at the age of three, and gave his first public performance as a soloist with orchestra on 8 May 1946. He subsequently toured and recorded extensively, retiring from the former to concentrate on the latter in 1964. He died in Toronto on 4 October 1982, at the age of 50.

Payzant (1997) points out Gould's musical legacy:

> The way we listen to music, or play it, has been permanently transformed by Glenn Gould. Even if sometimes we don't *want* to reveal or

contemplate the 'backbone' of the music, he has added a previously unimaginable degree of lucidity to our musical possibilities; it is there whether we make use of it or not, and it comes from him whether we acknowledge this or not. He achieved it no less by means of his machinery than by means of his pianos.

Payzant also states that Gould 'conformed to no stereotypes, was himself an incongruity, a glorious misfit'. This chapter contends that he does in fact meet a 'stereotype': that of the autistic person.

Family and childhood

Gould was the only child of two musical parents: his mother played the piano and organ; his father played the violin. The Norwegian composer Edvard Grieg was a first cousin of his mother's grandfather. When Gould was three years old it became evident that he possessed exceptional musical abilities, including absolute pitch and some ability to read staff notation. At five, he decided to become a composer, and was playing his own little compositions for family and friends (Payzant 1997).

Gould later said that after he heard his first live musical performance by a celebrated soloist, at the age of six, 'I was in that wonderful state of half-awakeness in which you hear all sorts of incredible sounds going through your mind. They were all *orchestral* sounds, but I was playing them all' (Tovell 1959).

Gould stated that he found going to school a most unhappy experience, and got along miserably with most of his teachers and all of his fellow students (Braithwaite 1959). This is typical of persons with high-functioning autism.

Indicators of Asperger's syndrome

Social behaviour

Gould said that when he was about 10 or 11 years old, he was always bored with the school teacher, and was always 'getting it wrong' with his fellow students (Tovell 1959). He did not complete the requirements for matriculation.

For two or three years after ending his formal lessons with Alberto Guerrero in 1952, Gould 'went into almost complete isolation…with his piano, a tape recorder, and his dog as companions. His intention was to work as hard as he could at the piano to settle for himself the question whether he had the qualities needed to become a ranking concert pianist' (Payzant 1997). This has echoes of Ludwig Wittgenstein trying to work out whether he could become a philosopher (Fitzgerald 2004). Gould believed that he could not survive as an artist without isolation. It is hardly surprising that, in preparing for his debut public performances in the USA, he went about things 'in his own way' (Payzant 1997).

Payzant refers to Gould's 'carefully protected private life', and notes:

> The telephone is Gould's paradigm of action at a distance. In his private life he avoids person-to-person contact as much as possible, and keeps in touch with his friends by telephone. His long-distance telephone bills must be awesome. For him to *see* the person he talks to is to be distracted; he can have a more satisfactory relationship when the visual element is filtered out by distance while the telephone bridges the auditory gap between himself and his interlocutor.

This is the classic autistic style of social relationship.

Gould was a hypochondriac. He spoke about 'his physical disorders, his hypochondria, and his dependence upon tranquilizers and sedatives' (Payzant 1997). He cancelled many concerts because of his hypochondria.

Gould was once asked if he needed people. He replied: 'People are about as important to me as food [he had already said that he ate very little]. As I grow older I find more and more that I can do without them; I separate myself from conflicting and contrasting notions. Monastic seclusion works for me' (Bester 1964). He also said:

> Solitude is the prerequisite for ecstatic experience, especially the experience most valued by the post-Wagnerian artist – the condition of heroism. One can't feel oneself heroic without having first being cast off by the world, or perhaps by having done the casting-off oneself... To such men [Arnold Schoenberg, for example] isolation fashioned a heroic life and heroism was the patron of creativity. (Gould 1974)

Narrow interests and obsessiveness

The author and editor Robert Fulford wrote:

> Glenn was a remarkable kid. I met him in the third grade when we were nine years old. We lived next door to each other in the east end of Toronto. Even as a child Glenn was isolated because he was working like hell to be a great man. He had a tremendous feeling and loving affection for music... It was an utter, complete feeling. He knew who he was and where he was going. (Fulford 1976)

According to Payzant (1997), 'by the time he was ten he could play all of Book I of J.S. Bach's *The Well-Tempered Clavier,* at twelve and thirteen he was learning the Partitas (among other things)'. A local critic described him as playing 'like a young Mozart classic' at the age of 12.

Like many geniuses, Gould could speak with authority on his subject. The journalist Edward W. Wodson (1947) wrote: 'He sat at the piano a child among professors, and he talked with them as one with authority.'

Payzant notes that for Gould there was a conflict 'between the physical characteristics of specific musical instruments or types of instruments (such as the piano) on the one hand, and purely cerebral music, as it might exist in the imagination, or in unspecified open score, on the other'. For Gould, 'music was more mental than physical, more a form of cognition than of sensation'. The critic John Briggs wrote that 'Gould's complete enthralment with the abstract, abstruse beauties of these contrasting works seems to result in a sense of almost other-worldly dedication' (Briggs 1955). Payzant further states that:

> Glenn Gould the person has thoroughly merged with the works of Glenn Gould. His life is no longer separate from his works because the major events of his life are embodied in those works. He has continued to live in Toronto a solitary and incredibly productive life, ecstatically committed to the exploration of audio technology and its applications to 'music' in his own wide sense of that word, which includes the manipulation of all kinds of sounds, including speech.

Gould was obsessed with getting to the core or backbone of a piece of music. This is suggestive of the fundamental essence that persons with high-functioning autism and genius often wish to achieve. Payzant notes:

> On mike or on camera he works with an almost unimaginable intensity, indeed almost frightening to people who are not accustomed to it. And he still wants the air conditioning turned off, no matter how hot the lights, although he says he has moderated his stand on this in recent years.

Like many persons with high-functioning autism, he did develop. Paul Myers, a producer who worked with him, stated that 'I have…found the greatest enjoyment from listening to a Gould performance of a work I believe I already "know" for, as he pulls it apart and reconstructs it in this unique manner, he reveals new facets of the music which I, for one, may never have considered' (Myers 1973).

Like Ludwig Wittgenstein, Gould had an interest in landscape. With reference to the area north of Toronto, he wrote that:

> Something really does happen to most people who go into the north – they become at least aware of the creativity opportunity which the physical fact of the country represents and, quite often I think, come to measure their work and life against that rather staggering creative possibility – they become, in effect, philosophers. (Gould 1971)

According to Payzant (1997), Gould was attracted to 'Ibsenesque gloom... which he associates with wild terrain and dull, low skies'. Payzant remarks on Gould's 'individualistic stand in moral and aesthetical matters; he seldom deviates when pursuing these connections' (i.e. 'between North, solitude, the music he prefers, and the moral conduct he esteems').

Routines and control

Payzant (1997) notes that 'Creative genius works in solitude, seeks to control the self and the environment and in seeking tries to impose inward order upon outward disorder.' Gould had an obsessional artistic personality, to which control was always central and critical.

Anthony Storr (1972) wrote that 'creative activity may represent an attempt on the part of an obsessional character to transcend the limitations and restrictions of his own personality, or even to escape altogether from the body'. Storr stated that 'a ritual may actually serve a valuable purpose by putting a person in touch with his own inner life, or by inducing in him a state of mind conducive to health and progress'. This applies to autistic persons, although Storr wasn't specifically referring to them.

Payzant (1997) describes Gould as 'ritualistic', with 'his famous folding chair; his arms and hands require massage before a recording session and at intervals during it; he requires a piano technician on standby duty in the studio or within easy reach. He prefers to record at night, all night if necessary.' For Gould, 'the ritual objects included a small carpet under his feet, a bottle of Poland water at his side, numerous medications, and his battered, squeaky chair. This chair can be heard in most Gould recordings, and is as much a secondary trademark of his performance as his vocal noise' (Payzant 1997).

Gould made some very interesting comments on teaching:

> I'm afraid of teaching. I find it extremely stimulating when I'm in the mood to sit down and talk with people and analyze music, but I'm

subject to periods of noncommunication, so it would be very draining
to have to do it at prerequisite hours. Also, I need spinal resilience when
I am confronted with opinions not my own. (Bester 1964)

This is classically autistic. Again there is the autistic non-communication and
the resistance to opinions of others. Indeed, Gould referred to himself as 'a
hermit' (Gould 1970a).

Between the ages of 11 and 13, Gould would play the same records of
Beethoven's Fourth Piano Concerto over and over again: 'Almost every
day...some or all of the eight 78-rpm sides served as accompaniment for
practice-sessions in which I faithfully traced every inflective nuance' (Gould
1970a).

Gould gave up concert performance in 1964, basically so that he could
have more control, or almost complete control. He wanted to spend his time
'composing, writing, and experimenting with applications of technology to
music-making' (Payzant 1997). He had an autistic approach to listening to
music, and stated that he almost never went to concerts because 'I'm extremely
uncomfortable about concerts and, for me, the real approach to music is sitting
at home...listening to recordings' (Tovell 1959). 'Coherence and control'
were lost in concert halls, notwithstanding 'the old saying that a performer
needs an audience for support, for excitement, for spiritual nourishment'
(Payzant 1997). Of course this is not what a person with autism, like Gould,
required. He felt suffocated by audiences, and spoke of them as 'people sitting
there with the perspiration of two thousand, two hundred and ninety-nine
others penetrating their nostrils' (Gould 1966a). If he couldn't avoid attending a concert, he would stand in the wings rather than sitting in the best seat in
the house.

According to Payzant, when Gould was performing he would pretend to
himself 'that what he was doing up there on the platform he would be doing
anyway for his own pleasure, whether or not anyone wanted to hang around
and listen'. Gould 'also wishes we could abolish the custom of applauding at
concerts', because 'applauding gives the audience a false sense of active partic-
ipation in the occasion'. It could be said that Gould required music to be a
completely autistic activity.

Payzant points out that Gould was preoccupied with the structure of
music, and preferred 'coherence of structure to luscious tone, control of detail
to emotional impulse'. This again is an autistic approach to music.

Like many people with autism, Gould was interested in mechanical things
and technology. Indeed, he preferred them to human beings. He had, in a way,

a mechanical musical mind. Gould's philosophy of recording was to admit 'the futility of emulating concert hall sonorities' (Gould 1966b). He liked the autistic sensation of having a vacuum cleaner on beside the piano while playing Mozart: this happened one day when he was 12 or 13 and 'having a feud with the housekeeper'. Gould said:

> I began to feel what I was doing – the tactile presence of that fugue as represented by finger positions, and as represented also by the kind of sound you might get if you stood in the shower and shook your head with water coming out both ears... And I suddenly realized that the particular screen through which I was viewing this, and which I had erected between myself and Mozart and his fugue, was exactly what I needed – exactly why, as I later understood, a certain mechanical process could indeed come between myself and the work of art that I was involved in. (Gould 1970b)

This was a tremendous experience for Gould. Here 'Music is represented by Glenn Gould playing the Mozart C Major Fugue; technology is represented by the housekeeper with the vacuum cleaner' (Payzant 1997). Payzant points out that

> The mechanical noise came between him and the work all right, but not as an obstruction. Instead it was taken up by him into a higher aesthetical unity, of which he was then the author, and which consisted of Mozart's music, Gould's piano sounds, and the noise of the machine.

For Gould, 'machinery might be a complement to music rather than an impediment' (Payzant 1997).

Gould was quite sensitive to criticism and, like Ludwig Wittgenstein, he was very interested in morality. He stated that 'I believe in the intrusion of technology because, essentially, that intrusion imposes upon art a notion of morality which transcends the idea of art itself' (Gould 1974–75).

Payzant goes on to discuss Gould's 'love affair with the microphone'. In December 1950, Gould discovered that

> in the privacy, the solitude and...the womb-like security of the studio, it was possible to make music in a more direct, more personal manner than any concert hall would ever permit. I fell in love with broadcasting that day, and I have not since then been able to think of the potential of music...without some reference to the limitless possibilities of the broadcasting and/or recording medium. For me, the microphone has never been that hostile, clinical, inspiration-sapping analyst some critics, fearing it, complain about. That day in 1950 became, and has

remained, a friend... The microphone does encourage you to develop attitudes to performance which are entirely out of place in the diffuse acoustic of the concert hall. It permits you to cultivate a degree of textural clarity which simply doesn't pay dividends in the concert hall. (Gould 1967)

The question is: Was the microphone a kind of autistic object for Gould? As Payzant (1997) points out, technology was not dehumanizing for him.

When Gould was recording Bach's *Goldberg Variations*, he stated that he utilized 'the first twenty takes to erase all superfluous expression from my reading of it, and there is nothing more difficult to do' (Gould 1967). The journalist Joseph Roddy stated that 'the young Canadian relates each part of the piece to the whole work in a way that leaves Bach scholars convinced that he knew in the most precise detail how he would play the last variation before he intoned the first one' (Roddy 1960). Payzant (1997) points out that what Gould actually knew 'in the most precise detail' was what he already had on tape. Gould had a phenomenal memory for the characteristics of each take of a piece, as well as carrying an immense amount of music in his head. The question arises whether he had weak central coherence. It appears that he was good at disembedding pieces of music from the whole because of his autism. He called some of the recordings he made 'montage': they were recorded in bits and put together at the end.

According to Payzant (1997), Gould explained how 'technological progress would make it possible for musical recording to advance from its early archival stage to a higher stage in which technology and technicians would participate in the creative process actively and in their own right'. Payzant also points out that 'since Gould is a solitary, and wants to be in complete control of all that he does, he is not in [the Socratic] tradition; he has no taste for dialectics'.

Payzant observes that 'Gould displays astonishing control...in his piano playing (just as he does, incidentally, in his speech). This is why his extremely slow performances do not fall apart, and his extremely fast ones do not become muddled.'

Speech, language and humour

As we have seen, Payzant (1997) commented on the astonishing control that Gould displayed in his speech. By 1964, 'The ratio of talking to playing in his life was...much in favour of talking.' Evidently, then, he did not have a problem with speech, although he did use some idiosyncratic phrases: for example, 'non-take-twoness' was his term for the 'no second chance' nature of concert performance, which he disliked as it implied a lack of control.

Regarding humour, Payzant notes that Gould 'has difficulty letting go or terminating a joke, particularly when he is doing a skit in dialect'. This is possibly an autistic trait.

Lack of empathy

Gould was the first pianist from North America, and the first musician from Canada, to perform in the Soviet Union. He showed tactlessness and a lack of empathy by 'giving lectures…on the music of the twentieth century Viennese School, music which was proscribed in the Soviet Union' (Payzant 1997).

'Ecstasy' was very important for Gould; it meant 'a condition in which an individual has some sense of standing outside himself. Gould uses it with heavy emphasis upon the solitary aspect. It is not a condition attainable collectively by…an audience at a concert' (Payzant 1997). Gould was uneasy with the rare 'moments of powerful magic in which performer and audience seem to merge in oneness, in total sympathy', because he could not control these moments.

In one of Gould's lectures:

> most of the audience did not find his statements…illuminating because these statements – representing his knowledge of the music they referred to – did not connect in the minds of his hearers with the similar knowledge of the music needed to make the statements meaningful to them, and because Gould did not sufficiently provide them with this knowledge by playing the music on the piano. (Haggin 1964)

Persons with autism are very poor teachers: they don't take account of the audience.

In 1962 Gould performed the Brahms D Minor Concerto with Leonard Bernstein and the New York Philharmonic:

> Just before the performance Bernstein read a statement to the audience in which he disassociated himself and the orchestra from the interpretation proposed by Gould, who intended to experiment with the work, to see what would happen if it were treated in an understated manner with the solo exhibition reduced to a minimum by means of restrained dynamics and consistent tempos. (Payzant 1997)

Motor clumsiness

Clearly, as a pianist of genius, Gould was not deficient in motor skills. However, he did display some peculiarities. At the piano he was known for 'extravagant gestures and...singing' (Payzant 1997). Edward W. Wodson described him as 'loose-jointed...his feet were as agile as his hands' (Wodson 1945).

Gould sometimes felt that audiences and critics 'were more interested in his stage mannerisms than in the music' (Payzant 1997).

Eccentricity

Payzant (1997) refers to Gould's 'sometimes crackpot' ideas, and goes on to point out that 'People who know Glenn Gould only by his reputation for clowning, or from his more eccentric interpretations on disc, dismiss him as completely mad'. Gould was interested in psychoanalysis and psychiatry, like Ludwig Wittgenstein, possibly unconsciously wanting to try to understand himself better.

Gould said of himself:

> Crazy as it sounds, I always write with at least two competing audio sources – usually one TV program and one radio program in – I was going to say – the background, but I think the middle-ground might be more accurate. And if I go to a restaurant, I automatically find myself disentangling three or four conversations from tables nearby. (Gould 1975)

There are descriptions of physical eccentricities such as arriving for a recording session on a 'balmy June day...in a coat, beret, muffler and gloves' (press release, Columbia Records). Another account tells of an encounter where Gould:

> was wearing woollen gloves, though the day was warm; and he politely declined to shake hands with me, evidently fearing that my grip might put his hand out of action. Frequently, I understand, he wears two pairs of gloves and...he is no lover of fresh air...his manner was unorthodox; not to say eccentric... But...as soon as the music started his absorption was complete. (Rutland 1959)

Gould went on his first and only fishing trip at the age of six; when a fish was caught, he 'suddenly saw this thing entirely from the fish's point of view' (Braithwaite 1959). It took him ten years to convince his father to abandon fishing: 'this is probably the greatest thing I have ever done', he later said. In later life, Gould's anti-fishing views developed into an active campaign:

> ...at Gould's summer home at Lake Simcoe, Glenn goes out in his power boat every morning and evening and roars about the lake, weaving among the fishermen to spook the fish and save them from their doom...it's quite a sight to watch the fishermen in bathing suits hollering at Gould, and Gould in overcoat and cap yelling back. (Bester 1964)

NEITHER ABNORMALITIES OF speech and language nor motor clumsiness are necessary for a diagnosis of Asperger's disorder under the American Psychiatric Association (1994) classification (DSM-IV), therefore Gould meets the criteria for Asperger's disorder.

PART IV

Asperger's Syndrome and Painters

ACCORDING TO WEST (1991), the right cerebral hemisphere of the brain 'thinks visually in pictures and images in three-dimensional space'. Nevertheless, Sigman and Capps (1997) have shown 'reversed or absent lateralisation of brain activity in autism'. Persons with autism have strengths in the visuo-spatial area. Clearly right-hemisphere functions are important in painters, e.g. 'processing visual images, spatial relationships...pattern recognition and proportion' (West 1991).

Steven Pinker (2002) believes that 'art (other than narrative) is a by-product of three other adaptations: the hunger for status, the aesthetic pleasure of experiencing adaptive objects and environments and the ability to design artefacts to achieve desired ends'. He points out that 'vision researchers...have suggested that the pleasing visual motifs used in art and decoration exaggerate...patterns, which tell the brain that the visual system is functioning properly and analysing the world accurately'.

According to Frith (1989), it is of interest that Laurent Mottron noted that the drawings of a draughtsman savant 'always started from a single, unimportant detail' rather than the usual method of making a rough outline. Hermelin (2001) points out that the 'superior memory for visual detail was only evident in the drawings rather than the mere observations of savant artists'. She notes that according to J.C. Gibson, a psychologist, 'seeing the world as a picture was an alternative to normal perception'. Persons with autism and savantism can achieve this.

Richard Rothe (quoted in Weeks and James 1997) discusses various techniques of art production. The first approach he cites could be seen as an

Asperger type of approach – the artist 'builds up his drawings or sculpture out of separate parts, as one would build bricks'. The second approach could be seen as the neurotypical (non-autistic) approach, or the 'seeing type', to use Weeks and James's (1997) phrase. Weeks and James note that this artist 'proceeds quite differently by moulding the form he is aiming at out of a single piece'.

Hermelin also notes that 'artistically gifted savants' performance on drawing tasks was not determined by their intelligence but by their specific ability to draw. This indicates that savant capability was confined to the execution of that activity for which they were gifted', and that 'the degree of accuracy in drawings proved to be independent of intelligence'. She showed that 'pictorial rules were employed with equal efficiency by savant artists and by those of higher intelligence who had a gift for drawing', and that the former can, perhaps surprisingly, draw 'a scene not only as they themselves see it, but also how it might appear from somebody else's perspective'.

Nevertheless, the issue of enhanced perceptual functioning in visual artists with high-functioning autism has to be considered. Mottron and Burack (2001) state that there is only one area of 'over-functioning' in an individual. This may be one of the factors associated with a visual artist of genius.

EIGHTEEN

Vincent van Gogh
(1853–90)

THE DUTCH PAINTER Vincent Willem van Gogh was one of the great artists of the 19th century, and an unusual and tormented man. He was born on 30 March 1853 in Groot-Zundert, the first surviving child of Théodorus van Gogh, a minister of the Dutch Reformed Church, and Anna (née Carbentus). From the age of 16 onwards he dabbled in a number of occupations: assistant to a firm of art dealers in London, French teacher, trainee Methodist preacher, evangelist to Belgian miners.

In 1879 van Gogh decided to become an artist, and dissociated himself from the family name – his adult paintings and drawings are all signed 'Vincent'. In 1886 he went to Paris, where he studied art and lived with his brother Théo, an art dealer. In 1888 he moved to Provence, attracted by its intense colours and bright

© Keith Levit/Alamy

sunlight. The painter Paul Gauguin joined him there; the two quarrelled and, after threatening Gauguin with a razor, van Gogh cut off part of his own ear. He then spent a year in an asylum, where he continued to paint between bouts of insanity. He shot himself on 27 July 1890, and died two days later.

Van Gogh's psychiatric condition has been a matter of debate for many years (Jamison 1993). The possibility of Asperger's syndrome has not been considered.

This chapter presents evidence that van Gogh had Asperger's syndrome. He showed severe impairment in social interaction, imposed routines on himself and others, had all-absorbing narrow interests, and showed unusual non-verbal communication. Persons with Asperger's syndrome are fascinated by landscape and colour; clearly van Gogh showed this characteristic to an unusual degree, as well as an extraordinary talent for expressing it. Unless otherwise indicated, all of the biographical details and quoted extracts in this chapter come from Lubin (1972).

Family and childhood

Vincent's parents were 'conscientious, austere, middle-class Dutch'. Vincent, who had five younger siblings, described his father as 'obstinate, unintelligent, icy cold and narrow-minded'. The sermons of Théodorus van Gogh were uninspired, and his speech was halting; all five of his brothers (Vincent's uncles) 'surpassed Théodorus in terms of prominence and prosperity'.

Anna van Gogh-Carbentus was 'a strong woman with a plain face... industrious and talented, proficient in writing, drawing, painting watercolours, and sewing'. Vincent recalled his youth as 'gloomy and cold and sterile'. Even then, as his sister Elizabeth noted, he was a stranger to his family (as he was later a stranger to the world). He was often 'singled out by his parents for "unruly behaviour", and the discipline in his moralistic environment was strict'. Nonetheless, a family story tells: 'As a child he was of a difficult temper, often troublesome and self-willed; his upbringing was not fitted to counterbalance these faults, as the parents were very tender-hearted, especially towards their eldest.'

Lubin notes that in adult life Vincent was critical of his mother, especially after his widowed cousin Kee Vos-Stricker, with whom he had fallen in love in 1881, rejected him. He protested that his mother 'cut off every opportunity for him to discuss the unhappy situation with her; like his father, she did not understand him'.

Vincent's formal education at public school began three months before his eighth birthday. His parents, fearing that 'intercourse with the peasant boys made him too rough', soon withdrew him and tutored him at home; after a time he went to boarding school. He later claimed to have learned 'absolutely nothing' at school.

Indicators of Asperger's syndrome

Social behaviour

In 1876, at the age of 23, Vincent gave a sermon in a small Methodist church in Richmond, England, that suggested his sense of aloneness. It was based on Psalm 119:19: 'I am a stranger on the earth, hide not Thy commandments from me'. He said: 'It is an old faith and it is a good faith, that our life is a pilgrim's progress – that we are strangers on the earth, but that though this be so yet we are not alone for our Father is with us.'

Lubin notes: 'Plagued by loneliness, Vincent never ceased to yearn for closeness with another human being... To be united with a woman in love was the most pressing desire of Vincent's adult life, even though this desire was doomed to frustration.' He wrote that 'a man and wife can be one'. According to Lubin, 'when he was criticised for living with the prostitute Sien, he replied that he preferred "certain death" to separation'.

Throughout Vincent's adult life, there appears to have been a tension between the solitude that he embraced and the loneliness that plagued him. He valued his self-isolation, quoting Zola: 'If at present I am worth something, it is because I am alone, and I hate fools, the impotent, cynics, idiotic and stupid scoffers.' After deciding to become an artist, he 'stressed the importance of his self-isolating proclivities' and 'praised his alienation as a necessary part of his creative life'. In his paintings, he often used walls to portray a feeling of isolation. He wrote: 'We are at present sailing the high seas in our wretched little boats, all alone on the great waves of our time.'

Lubin points out: 'Although he inevitably became an outcast wherever he went, he continued his search for an accepting environment: during his ten years as an artist he lived in eleven different places...his self-alienating behaviour, however, made it inevitable that his relations with people would be short-lasting, and that he would never be so thoroughly attached to anyone or anyone's ideas as to become an imitator rather than an innovator.' His plans for an artists' cooperative were never consummated, and involvement in a community of artists failed to bring him the satisfaction he sought.

Vincent wrote: 'The worse I get on with people, the more I learn to have faith in nature and concentrate on her.' Lubin points out that 'he equated a lone tree with a lonely person, and he paired trees in the same way that he paired humans'. Furthermore, during the last year of his life he 'conceived of many of his paintings in terms of pairs. Those of round, golden sunflowers and of tall, dark, flame-shaped cypresses are examples.' 'This pairing, repeated over and over again, expressed Vincent's wish that the Yellow House [in Arles, where he was renting a room] would end his isolation and become "a home of my own, which frees the mind from melancholy of being out on the streets".'

It is clear that Vincent's relations with women generally ended in disaster. In London, when he was 20 years old, he fell in love with his landlady's daughter, Ursula Loyer; she was already engaged, and he tried in vain to get her to break off the engagement. Her rejection caused him many years of humiliation: he lost interest in his job, argued with his employers, and became increasingly eccentric. In 1887 Vincent wrote that he went on having 'the most impossible, and not very seemly, love affairs, from which I emerge as a rule damaged and shamed and little else'.

On Christmas Day 1881 he provoked a violent argument with his father, who demanded that he leave. He then undertook tuition in The Hague with the Dutch artist Anton Mauve. He couldn't maintain his relationship with Mauve, who soon refused to see him. It is likely that Vincent's irascible behaviour brought about the termination. (Lubin points out that Vincent 'resented having his creative self disrupted by conventional teachers just as he resented having his personality influenced by conventional parents'.) He then formed a relationship with Clasina Maria Hoornik (whom he called Christine or Sien), a prostitute; later he wrote: 'I hated being alone so much that I preferred being with a bad whore to being alone.' He looked after her and her two children – the only prolonged period of intimacy that he had with a woman.

Rachel, the prostitute to whom Vincent brought part of his ear as a gift, was 'the last in a series of women with whom he had miserably unhappy relationships'. It is possible that his relations with prostitutes were simpler than other relationships, since they were based to some extent on finance and generally were time-limited. Like Vincent, the prostitute was an outsider in the world.

As Lubin observes, Vincent was 'a colourful man who clashed rather than harmonized with other people, and he could not find satisfaction in the smooth harmonies of tonal effects'. This made him difficult to get on with. For example, he was very unsympathetic to his brother Théo, who continually gave him money although he was himself in debt. On receiving a late payment, Vincent was indignant: 'Am I less than your creditors? – who must wait, *they* or *I*???' This shows an enormous lack of gratitude.

Théo complained to their sister Wil about Vincent when the two brothers lived together in Paris: 'My home life is almost unbearable. No one wants to come and see me any more because it always ends in quarrels, and besides, he is so untidy that the room looks far from attractive. I wish he would go and live by himself.' A friend of Théo, Andries Bonger, wrote that Vincent 'hasn't the slightest notion of social behaviour. He is always quarrelling with everybody.' An art dealer named Alexander Reid shared the apartment with them for a time, and when Reid became depressed, Vincent allegedly responded by suggesting *suicide à deux*, which scared Reid off. In Paris, 'the models would not pose for him; he was forbidden to work in the streets, and because of his violent temper there were continual scenes…he became completely unapproachable and in the end he became heartily sick of Paris'. There is evidence that Toulouse-Lautrec 'praised Arles and encouraged Vincent to go there, hoping to be rid of a nuisance'.

Vincent's 'inability to remain part of a closely knit group, like his fear of intimacy in general, did not allow him to adhere to one school of art any more than remain committed to one woman or one church; it also facilitated his fight against self-satisfied orthodoxies'. It appears that he was happy to be a member of the Impressionists, because as a group it did not hem him in. This suggests that he had a fear of entrapment in a group.

Narrow interests and obsessiveness

Vincent was obsessed with painting, and produced a very large number of paintings in a short artistic life. He said: 'Life means painting to me and not so much preserving my constitution.' At the Antwerp Academy of Art he painted 'feverishly, furiously, with a repetition that stupefied his fellow students'. He worked from morning until midnight, saying that 'times are not cheerful *unless one finds satisfaction in one's work*'. In Arles he turned out an astonishing body of work. His confidence in his talent was high there. There was 'no budging him' once he started to paint.

He had an irresistible desire for books. He read certain books over and over: the Bible, Dickens's Christmas stories, etc.

Routines and control

Vincent imposed an intense routine of work on himself in relation to his main interest – art – and was also very controlling of his brother Théo and others. Lubin notes that 'feeling unloved and deprived, he was convinced that his parents and their psychological successors owed him his due, and did not hesitate to demand help that ordinarily is only given to a child'. This also shows his failure to appreciate the imperatives of the 'real world'.

As Lubin points out, art was Vincent's burden, and it wore him out. He said that 'the pains of producing pictures will have taken my whole life from me, and it will seem to me then that I have not lived'.

Speech, language and humour

An artist who met Vincent in Paris said that he 'had an extraordinary way of pouring out sentences in Dutch, English and French, then glancing back over his shoulder and hissing through his teeth. Vincent, like his father, was described as having 'halting speech' – a serious handicap for a preacher. The language that came easiest to him was 'the pictorial language of nature'. It has been said that one can recognize Vincent's paintings in his 'queer and angular sentence structure'. Dr Mendes da Costa, who taught Vincent Latin and Greek in Amsterdam, mentioned that he spoke with a deep melancholic voice.

He was 'vehement in speech, interminable in explaining and developing his ideas, but not very ready to argue'. He does not appear to have been a humorous man.

Lack of empathy

As we have seen, Vincent fell in love with Kee Vos-Stricker, a cousin on his mother's side who had recently been widowed. He proposed marriage, apparently not realizing that this was an inappropriate advance to a woman who had just lost her husband. She refused him and left Amsterdam, saying that she could not return his feelings. He refused to accept the rejection, preferring to believe that she was ill and would change her mind when she recovered. He quarrelled with both her family and his own.

The figures in many of Vincent's early paintings embody a 'rigidity and remoteness' that reminds one of L.S. Lowry's work: a woman holds her child at a distance; a stiff waiter, 'like a standing corpse', is 'entombed by the narrow wall behind and the lamppost beside him'; an estranged man and woman gaze towards some people who are interacting.

Naïvety and childishness

In the period of his religious ministry he was accused of displaying 'an excessive zeal bordering on the scandalous' because 'in caring for these mistreated men and women, he gave away his possessions, his money, and his clothes and became sick and emaciated himself'. In Vincent's attitude to the poor, one might discern a parallel with Simone Weil's 'naïve idealization – if not canonization – of the proletariat, which she saw as a form of contemporary sainthood' (Gray 2001).

Appearance and demeanour

Early in Vincent's working life, a colleague stated that 'he led an absolutely solitary life. He took many walks on the island but always alone... In the shop he hardly spoke a word. In short, he was a recluse.' His unkempt appearance may have contributed to his dismissal from this job.

Dr Mendes da Costa described his forlorn pupil as follows: he pulled his mouth down at the corners, producing an 'indescribable haze of sad despair'. According to Lubin,

> Vincent was an eccentric character, mentally and physically distorted by inner strains. People said for example, that he made a 'queer impression', and described him as 'an ugly creature', and 'a rare specimen out of a collection of freaks'. He himself recognised his bizarre aspects, but hoped that his pictures would help others perceive that there was more to him than the impression he gave.

Lubin points out that in the Borinage area of Belgium, Vincent 'lived in poverty, dressed in rags, and ate only the simplest fare'. According to his sister-in-law,

> religion gave way more and more to practical work – such as nursing the sick and the wounded; he gave away all his possessions, clothes, money, even his bed. He no longer lived in a boarding house, but in a small miner's hut where even the barest necessities were wanting. In this way he tried to follow Jesus's teachings literally.

He made shirts out of sacking, and a local baker later reported: 'My kind-hearted mother said to him: Monsieur Vincent, why do you deprive yourself of all your clothes like this – you who are descended from such a noble family of Dutch pastors? He answered: I am a friend of the poor like Jesus was.'

In 1886 he entered the Antwerp Academy of Art. A fellow student described him as a strange fellow, dressed in a blue blouse similar to those worn by Flemish cattle dealers, wearing a fur cap on his head, and using a crude board for a palette – 'an unpolished, nervous, restless man who crashed like a bombshell into the Antwerp Academy'.

Emile Bernard described him as 'Red-haired with a goatee, rough moustache, shaven skull, eagle eye and incisive mouth as if he were about to speak; medium height, stocky without being in the least fat, lively gestures, jerky step…with his everlasting pipe, canvas, engraving or sketch.' His sister Elizabeth said that as a child 'he kept his eyes half-closed when eating with his family'. It was also noted that he stared straight ahead while walking, refusing to recognize anyone in the street. Later, an acquaintance commented on his 'small, narrowed peering eyes'.

Gauguin described him walking in Paris during the winter of 1886–7: 'a fantastically dressed, shivering man who is hurrying along to reach the outer boulevards. He is wrapped in a sheepskin coat with a cap that is undoubtedly of rabbit-fur and he has a bristling red beard. He looks like a cattle drover.'

In Arles, Vincent added to his unhappiness and isolation

> by continuing to dress and behave in a way that excited the ridicule of the townspeople. The children, being franker than most, openly poked fun at him. 'His appearance made a highly comical impression on us', one of them wrote later on. 'His long smock, his gigantic hat, the man himself, continually stopping and peering at things excited our ridicule.'

His eccentric appearance was exaggerated by frenzied behaviour. He was described there as 'an odd fellow', and he stated: 'I am thinking of frankly accepting my role of madman.'

Affective disorder

There is no doubt that Vincent suffered from affective disorder (manic-depressive psychosis) throughout his life (Jamison 1993), and that this played a role in his ultimate suicide. He tended to embrace his recurring depression: 'Why should he give it up? After all, he explained, "the history of great men is tragic… For a long time during their lives they are under a kind of depression because of the opposition and difficulties of struggling through life".'

Self-mutilation and self-abuse

This was very much a feature of his adult life. Lubin notes that 'Vincent was overtly masochistic. This can be seen in the humiliation and physical abuse that he brought on himself, his ascetic habits of eating and dressing, his fear of success, and his self-mutilation.' Vincent wrote: 'I consciously choose the dog's path.'

According to Dr da Costa,

> whenever Vincent felt that his thoughts strayed further than they should, he took a cudgel to bed with him and belaboured his back with it; and whenever he was convinced that he had forfeited the privilege of passing the night in his bed, he slunk out of the house unobserved at night, and then, when he came back and found the door double-locked, was forced to go and lie on the floor of a little wooden shed, without bed or blanket. He preferred to do this in winter, so that the punishment, which I am disposed to think arose from mental masochism, might be more severe.

Lubin notes: 'Vincent's lifelong tendency to starve himself and to restrict his diet to the simplest of foods was another means of torturing his body. Similarly, he exposed it to the elements by divesting himself of adequate clothing.'

Vincent identified himself closely with Christ: it seems that in beating himself, he was reenacting the beatings suffered by Christ on the way to Calvary. He emphasized the necessity for self-sacrifice.

The mutilation of his ear, and his ultimate suicide, fit the same pattern.

Self-mutilation has not been documented in Vincent's childhood, but there was evidence of destruction of his own creative products. His sister-in-law recorded that 'at the age of eight he once modelled a little clay elephant that drew his parents' attention, but he destroyed it at once when, according to his notion, such a fuss was made about it'.

VINCENT VAN GOGH meets the Gillberg criteria for Asperger's syndrome, with the exception of speech and language problems, and there is uncertainty as to whether he showed motor clumsiness.

He meets the DSM-IV criteria for Asperger's disorder, which does not require abnormalities in language or motor problems. While it is also correct to state that he had an affective disorder, this is quite common in association with autism spectrum disorders, of which Asperger's disorder is one (Smalley, McCracken and Tanguay 1995).

It appears that his psychopathology was more complex than has generally been realized. Alternative (or additional) diagnoses of Meniere's disease and acute intermittent porphyria are unsupported at present (Jamison 1991; Loftus and Arnold 1991).

NINETEEN

Jack B. Yeats
(1871–1957)

T HE IRISH PAINTER and writer Jack Butler Yeats was born in London on 29 August 1871; his father was the well-known painter John Butler Yeats and his brother was the poet William Butler Yeats. At the age of eight he moved to Sligo, in the west of Ireland, where he lived with his maternal grandparents; he later studied art in London.

Yeats worked as an illustrator from 1890 to 1910; in 1894 he married Mary Cottenham White (known as 'Cottie') and they lived in Devon from 1897; they had no children. Yeats produced watercolours and drawings during this time, and held one-man shows. In 1910 they moved to Ireland. Yeats took up oil painting and gradually became a successful and established artist, known for his vivid and extravagant use of colour. He was also a serious writer, and published several books. He died in Dublin on 28 March 1957.

Yeats was a tremendous observer, as persons with Asperger's syndrome often are. He vividly painted the scenes that were all around him, capturing them in a 'pared down' fashion like the American artist Edward Hopper, who also had Asperger's syndrome. Samuel Beckett wrote that Yeats 'is with the great of our time because he brings light, as only the great dare to bring light, to the issueless predicament of existence, reduces the dark where there might have been mathematically at least a door' (Pyle 1970).

This chapter presents evidence that Jack B. Yeats, like his more famous brother, may have had Asperger's syndrome. All of the biographical details and quoted extracts in this chapter come from Pyle (1970).

Family and childhood

Jack was the fifth and final child in his family. His mother was Susan Pollexfen, a member of a prominent Sligo family.

Pyle (1970) describes Jack Yeats's ancestors as 'unconventional, characterful men, accomplished in action, in curiosity and imagination, sometimes mystical in thought'. William Pollexfen, Yeats's maternal grandfather and a prosperous ship owner, was a strange man with whom 'no one, not even his wife, became intimate'. He had a violent temper, and kept a hatchet beside his bed in readiness for burglars. He 'made no friends in Sligo' and 'kept himself to himself, always silent and reserved'. An uncle of Jack's, who designed the Sligo quays, 'gradually went mad, seeking to invent a warship that could not be sunk because of its hull of solid wood. There was a mystical trait, too, coming out in Uncle George's interest in the occult.' W.B. Yeats wrote of the 'silent grandfather, inspiring fear and deference, of the quiet religious grandmother interested in nature cures, of the visits of the strange melancholic uncles, and of nearly wild dogs roaming the spacious lands about Merville'. It is possible that there were quite a few relatives with autistic-like traits.

His father painted a portrait of Jack as a boy which, according to Pyle, shows 'a complete understanding of the shy, fair-haired boy, his head bent at a typical angle; he is carried away in a dream on his own, and yet alert at the same time to what is going on before him, inquiring, without giving anything away'. According to his father, two things were to be noticed about the drawings he did as a child:

> he never showed them to anyone. Also, his drawings were never of one object, one person, or one animal, but of groups engaged in some kind of drama. For instance, one day I picked up one of his drawings and made out that there was a cab and two men and a telescope; one man looking through the small end and the other man looking through the large end. The telescope itself, which was of monstrous size, lying on the ground – and I asked what it meant and was told that the man at the larger end was the cab man and that he was trying to find out what the other was looking at. At this time Jack's education had not gone beyond learning his letters.

At school Jack Yeats was at the bottom of the class academically, and 'preferred to live the life of Sligo and to "learn" the characters and the skies and the hills, rather than the lessons. He had begun to amuse everyone with his drawings.

He walked about the country roads, studying the country people, attending fairs, sports, circuses and races.' According to his father, Jack

> spent many hours leaning over that bridge [in the town of Sligo] looking into that pool and he regrets that he did not spend many more hours in that apparently unprofitable pastime. My son's affection for Sligo comes out in one small detail. He is ever careful to preserve a certain roll and lurch in his gait, that being the mark of the Sligo man.

This is probably more likely to be an autistic type of gait. According to Pyle, 'his manner of walking, and his intimate knowledge of the sea gave rise to a legend, current still, that he spent seven years of his life as a sailor'.

Many traits of his mother's side of the family were evident in Jack: 'the silence, the independence, the reserve, the calm elusiveness and puckish humour, the absence of irritability, the love of ceremony, the upright nature'. His father wrote that 'He has the habits of a man who knows his own mind.' Pyle notes that Jack 'was mainly a listener, absorbing all, but he remembered'; he 'kept his views to himself, mulled over them and reproduced definite and mildly quizzical statements which no one could parry'. In early life, on returning from Sligo to London he used to shout Sligo nonsense rhymes. His father said he was 'a comical boy and I can't convey the serious way in which he delivers...remarks'.

When his mother died in January 1900 he made no comment but appears to have stopped sketching for a period.

Indicators of Asperger's syndrome

Social behaviour

Yeats was a shy man – taciturn, elusive and retiring. He was a loner in his work and was particularly interested in horses and horse buses. He was very much an independent person, and had an individual style of drawing, which in the early days comprised angular movement, economy, and an absence of cross-hatching. In his early career he painted almost exclusively in the watercolour medium, 'a descriptive artist, adapting what he observed to his artistic idiom, but preserving details faithfully and relishing in [sic] the idiosyncrasies of man and the poetry to which man reaches'. He 'never attempted to form a school of painting, or to join any group of artists' (unlike his father, who had tried to form a new Pre-Raphaelite Brotherhood): this reminds one of Erik Satie (see Chapter 15). Like Satie (and many other people with Asperger's syndrome), Yeats got on very well with children: he liked to put on shows for them.

According to Pyle, the Irish short-story writer Sean O'Faolain found Yeats 'odd', 'difficult' and 'wilful' both in writing and in painting.

Narrow interests and obsessiveness

Pyle notes that 'his work is curiously out of context with its time. Yeats was born into a changing art world, but he took little notice of what the upheaval brought about. He…did not meet young artists.' This is all rather autistic. Until late in life he was not a popular painter. He was 'a familiar, unostentatious figure in a crowd, screening the sketch book within the flap of his great coat, and noting down pictorially and verbally the idiosyncrasies of the human race'.

Jack said little: he 'preferred to put what he thought into practice'. He took an interest in miniature theatre, and made 'toy ships…photographs and drawings exist of objects made from matchboxes, corks, straw, even a banana skin, and so on, up until about 1928'. Many persons with high-functioning autism have been model builders (including Isaac Newton, James Clerk Maxwell and Ludwig Wittgenstein).

Yeats was 'an active member of the Dublin United Arts Club, sometimes keeping aloof, reading in a corner quietly, gliding out of the door silently'. According to Pyle, 'when he was "incubating" a picture he became silent, his mind withdrawn, and after a while, as the scheming ceased, he became more talkative and returned to his normal manner'. This was not unlike, in my view, the way that W.B. Yeats would incubate a poem.

Pyle notes that Yeats denounced old masters as painters of 'brown pictures', they were 'journalists' – except for Goya; and English painters as a race were dismissed summarily. This lack of respect for the past was very similar to that of Wittgenstein.

Routines and control

Terence de Vere White wrote of Yeats: 'He accords to all things their proper dignity. And this is apparent in his manner which, though kind and easy, is not without a certain ceremoniousness.' According to Pyle,

> He allowed no one to see him painting, but shut himself away in his studio within regular hours to work… Any interruption would break his concentration for the rest of the day; and since Cottie, feeding the birds, would rush in unwittingly to tell him about the latest visitant, he used to remind her of his wish to remain undisturbed by tying a pipe cleaner around the door handle whilst he was at work.

Pyle quotes a letter that he wrote to Joseph Hone: 'No one creates...the artist assembles memories.' Memory interested him a great deal.

He did his drawings for *Punch* under the pseudonym W. Bird, and tried to conceal his creation of them even from his family. He unburdened himself to nobody, and would not even allow his date of birth to be published in a catalogue: 'Jack's heart was always in his own custody and he clung to it possessively'.

Speech, language and humour

Pyle points out: 'The artist's strong sense of humour could be whimsical or macabre, almost appearing cruel, were it not for his deep sense of humanity. It blended with a child-like love of slapstick comedy.' Indeed, slapstick humour is very much what persons with Asperger's syndrome like. Once when he stayed with Bishop Harvey at Lissadel, Yeats said:

> I know I haven't the same sense of humour that other people have. Listen to this story. Two men were walking along a road and beside them lay a fence. One looked at the fence and said 'Oh there's a hen.' 'That's not a hen,' said the other, 'That's an owl.' 'Oh,' rejoined the other, 'I don't care how owld it is.'

This is rather autistic humour.

According to Pyle, in the 1920s 'his humour was yet perverse'. She notes that 'Yeats's metaphysical irony anticipates Beckett by some twenty years, though with an enigmatic humour and a calm forbearance that hindered his popularity'.

Pyle states that Yeats 'abhorred unkindness or coercion, and hated pomposity. His humour was paramount, gay and simple with a quick patter – Would you like to be a twin? – No, I'd only be half a person.'

According to Pyle, he had 'a nautical neatness' and 'a slow way of speech'. Like Wittgenstein, he was fascinated with 'colloquial idiom'.

Naïvety and childishness

We have seen that Yeats showed a child-like love of slapstick comedy. He lived in a Dublin nursing home in old age, where he 'impressed the nurses with his simplicity'. In 1922 he spoke of painting as 'the fairest and the finest means of communication humanity has yet found because it is the most simple'.

Appearance and demeanour

In his early thirties, Yeats was described as 'a tall untidy figure, dressed in loose clothes, and wearing a nonchalantly-fastened tie, a rough frieze coat, a broad-brimmed hat and a Claddagh ring. He walked with a rolling gait, and proceeded along the street always with a picture or drawing pad in his hand, sometimes passing his friends by without noticing them, because his mind was on other things' (this is reminiscent of a cartoon in *Dublin Opinion* in 1925 in which W.B. Yeats has his head in the air, oblivious to his old friend Æ [George Russell] passing him by on the street).

An early studio photograph shows him in a loose tall collar smoking a cigar and ruminating; another has caught 'a typically wistful look'. When he was 85 years of age – the last time he was seen in public – 'the artist was walking alone with his unmistakable sailor's gait down the south quays of the Liffey, completely absorbed in the river and the ships that he loved' ('Irishman's Diary', *Irish Times*, 30 March 1957).

JACK B. YEATS meets the criteria for Asperger's syndrome.

TWENTY

L.S. Lowry
(1887–1976)

THE ENGLISH ARTIST Laurence Stephen Lowry was born in Manchester on 1 November 1887, the only child of Robert, a clerk, and Elizabeth (née Hobson). On leaving school he failed to get into art college, and became a clerk. He took art lessons in his spare time for many years (there are parallels with Erik Satie and Ludwig Wittgenstein attending classes), and painted at night in his attic. In 1910 he was made redundant, and gained employment as a rent collector – a job he would do for the next 42 years. He was exempted from service in the First World War because of his flat feet.

In 1918 Lowry was accepted as a student member of the Manchester Academy of Fine Arts, and he submitted three paintings to its 1919 annual exhibition, none of which sold at the time. He made his first sale the same year, but his paintings were derided in many quarters. Nevertheless, he persisted with his art, managing to keep it almost entirely separate from his working life, which he contrived to keep a secret from the general public even as he gained a reputation as an artist. The style of his paintings was wholly original; the subjects consisted mainly of industrial or urban scenes from the north of England. There is absolutely no doubt that he was an original painter and a genius.

Lowry continued to exhibit through the following decades, with moderate success. After his father died in 1932 he looked after his mother, who was totally dependent on him up to her death in 1939. He began to make a profit on his art in the 1940s, gained popular acceptance in the 1950s, and sold his work for high prices in the 1960s. He declined numerous honours, including the OBE and CBE.

Although he had friendships with a succession of young women, he remained single and celibate. He was still living alone at the time of his death, at the age of 88, on 23 February 1976. His work later changed hands for huge sums of money (*Piccadilly Circus* sold for £510,000 at Sotheby's in 1998).

Lowry was an enigma. He was completely devoted to his painting, and regarded as unusual and eccentric by his peers. His friend Hugh Maitland noted the 'baffling oddities that emerge from Lowry's personality' (Rohde 1999). The evidence presented in this chapter suggests that those 'oddities' were attributable to Asperger's syndrome: certainly he appears to have shown many Asperger-style traits. Unless otherwise indicated, all of the biographical details and quoted extracts come from Rohde (1999).

Family and childhood

Lowry's life was in many ways dominated by his mother, who was never interested in his work and always managed to convey the impression that he had disappointed her. A brilliant pianist with hypochondriac tendencies, she had aspirations beyond her lower-middle-class situation; a cousin of Lowry's described her as 'a fearful snob'. His father – described by Lowry as 'a very sober, punctual man' and 'a cold fish' – was rather obsessional; he had financial difficulties and bequeathed considerable debts to his family.

Lowry was a sickly, uncoordinated and timid child, 'desperately shy with strangers, awkward in company and difficult with his peers'. A friend commented that 'if the term autistic had been in use then, it would have been applied to Lowry'. He had an unhappy school experience: his mother insisted on sending him to a school for the children of the rich, and he hated it. He had to endure 'teasing and ragging' from the boys and sarcasm from the teachers. He never seemed to have any friends.

Indicators of Asperger's syndrome

Social behaviour

The powerful impact of persons with autism on other people is often remarked upon, and is very important. Shelley Rohde states that when she met Lowry she 'almost immediately fell under the spell of his personality'. She also describes his impact on many other people: 'he affected their thinking, their attitudes to life...the younger ones speak of the broadening of their personalities under his tutelage, and artists mentioned the faith he gave them in themselves'.

In his adult life, although Lowry was often mistaken for a recluse, he did have friends and they were important to him, yet Rohde notes that 'he was never truly sociable; despite all his friends he was close to no one'. He once said to a friend 'don't ask me to socialise; that I cannot do'. He 'habitually compartmentalised his relationships; he rarely spoke of one friend to another, nor did he introduce them. He actively disliked chance meetings that exposed one to the other.'

Lowry stated that 'my temperament made me very unsociable although that was not my wish'. He was a very silent man, and avoided any friendships that would have impinged upon his personal solitude. Rohde points out that 'Lowry's loneliness was the loneliness of the crowd, the solitude of a man alone in company, a personal isolation of spirit and of the mind… No one *knew* him and he *knew* no one.' This is an autistic position. Sir John Betjeman described Lowry as 'a loner'. Because of his autism, it is not surprising that he never involved himself with the art establishment. He seemed barely to notice matters of great public moment, such as the First World War and the Depression.

According to Rohde, 'he could not communicate as he wanted to communicate; he could not give fully of himself, as to have done so would have allowed a glimpse behind his mask, a knowledge of the secret of his most private emotions'. Again, this is an autistic position.

The artist Harold Riley stated that 'he shut himself quite firmly into his own box… It was as if he felt that, if he was open, people would climb into him and see what he was – and he really didn't think he was very much.' Rohde observes that he had a

> damaged ego; he was self-absorbed almost to the point of self-hate. But when the full flowering of respect and repute came at last he could not accept it… All too often he felt their praise excessive or insincere, motivated perhaps by greed; and he turned away from it; fearing that they were, in truth, laughing at him behind his back, as they had done to his face not so very long ago.

Lowry had the integrity that is often found in persons with high-functioning autism: it is perhaps part of the autistic superego.

He was fascinated by Luigi Pirandello's play *Six Characters in Search of an Author*, and went to see it many times. He was himself a man in search of an identity; this is possibly why it fascinated him. The composer and pianist Frederick May described the play as

an ironic tragedy, the tragedy of man tormented by the enigma of personality, perplexed by the impossibility of arriving at truth, and forever
questioning the nature and the purpose of existence…he achieves intelligence only to recognise that he can communicate with no one, not
even with himself, and that no one can communicate with him – that he
is, in the fullest sense, alone.

Of course this is also a description of autism, and of Lowry.

Rohde describes Lowry's interest in girls:

Throughout his life, Lowry continued to develop a sequence of relationships with young girls, almost one a decade, all of whom bore a
striking resemblance to each other. So great were their similarities,
according to his reminiscences, that in the minds of those who heard
him speak of them they merged into one being called Ann.

This interest in young girls has echoes of Lewis Carroll, who also had autism
(see Chapter 4). People with autism tend to relate better to younger people.

He had a significant relationship with a girl called Carol Ann Lowry (no
relation), whom he met in 1957. She was 13 years old at the time. She said
that he became to her

more than my mother, or my father, or anyone. He made me. He
moulded me. He fashioned me in his image of Ann and in so doing
made me to a great extent like him. I was sufficiently young for him to
be able to do it; and sufficiently malleable. I think he recognised that,
right from the beginning.

What is critical here again is the enormous impact that a person with
high-functioning autism can have on other people. (We see this also with
Wittgenstein, for example: an entire generation of younger philosophers not
only replicated his ideas but also, as Will Self (2001b) noted, 'dressed like the
great man, spoke like the great man, and wrote like him…[Wittgenstein
showed] effortless dominance.'). This interest in young girls, 'with one
notable exception, ceased or at least waned when the protégées in question
married'.

Narrow interests and obsessiveness

Lowry began drawing at an early age, and gradually became obsessed with it:
a cousin recalled: 'He was always sketching and doing little books of
drawings and had his pockets crammed with bits of paper with scrawly things

on them.' Rohde describes painting as 'the driving compulsion that obsessed him', and refers to his 'lust for work'.

Lowry was able to 'withdraw at will from the world around him, seemingly oblivious to all outside distractions: the compulsive observer'. This is one of the secrets of success of persons with high-functioning autism. A friend who chanced upon him in an art gallery wrote:

> I found Lowry standing alone in the centre of the room, leaning slightly sideways and backwards upon his walking-stick, his isolation immediate and total. There was no one present for him. There was only himself and his work. When he wished, he always had this ability to put a wall around himself.

He had a great capacity for accurate visual observation: 'He was enormously interested in everybody, in everything; one wouldn't have known it – he didn't sit and stare at people, he just soaked it all in.'

According to Rohde, he was addicted to his art and was 'doomed to paint on compulsively'. Once, asked what he was doing when not painting, he replied, 'Thinking about painting.' Nonetheless, he was never a commercial painter. Persons with high-functioning autism often show little interest in accumulating wealth or earthly possessions.

Sir John Rothenstein, former director of the Tate Gallery, stated that once Lowry had developed his vision, he became 'almost enslaved' and 'to an extraordinary degree, dependent' on it. Rohde points out that 'he painted on without recognition or understanding. Despite the derision of his peers and the apathy of his friends, he never compromised; he continued to work in his own way, "sustained only by his vision and the conviction that what he was doing was worthwhile".' He was a workaholic.

As a classic autistic creative artist, his philosophy (as urged upon a protégée) was 'never, never to get my ideas from art books or other paintings'. This is like Wittgenstein, who 'hated theories impartially' (Fodor 2001). With regard to public funding, he maintained that 'only if you were totally independent and free from grants would your work be truthful – because you would be doing it out of your own heart, you would be doing it for the right reasons'.

Referring to his early art, Professor Millard stated that 'they all look like marionettes, and if you pulled the strings they would all cock their legs up'. Lowry said 'I tried to get them to look like human beings and I couldn't'; later he stated that:

> I look upon human beings as automatons: to see them eating, to see
> them running to catch a train, is funny beyond belief...*because they all
> think they can do what they want*...and they can't, you know. They are not
> free. No one is.

This sounds like an autistic view of the world.

It is hardly surprising that he wasn't interested in symbolism; indeed,
Rohde states that 'he habitually avoided any conversation that hinted at an
inner meaning in art, or one that looked as if it might lead to such conclusions;
he was not above teasing even his own friends, in order to deflate pomposity
or pretension'. He was 'a chronicler of industrial reality'.

The portraits that his young friend Kathleen Leatherbarrow called 'his
horrible heads' show faces in a state of autistic terror and panic.

Later in life he developed 'a new obsession':

> his single figures, his grotesques. The struggling, surging, misshapen
> homunculi who had lived for so long in the shadow of the mills
> emerged at last from their background to stand alone, as he stood alone.
> If he saw them as odd, it was because he felt himself to be odd.

In a way they were representations of his autistic self.

Routines and control

As we have seen, Lowry tended to compartmentalize his relationships, and to
keep his artistic life and his 'ordinary' work entirely separate. In his relationship with Pat Cooke, one of his young female protégées, 'he was even more
possessive than was usual; as if he wanted nothing or no-one to impinge on
their friendship. He was to repeat this pattern, for a brief period, usually no
more than a year, with each of his young protégées.'

Like with Wittgenstein, 'it was quite a difficult thing to please
him...because he wanted a hundred per cent attention, a hundred per cent of
the time. He was very demanding and a very powerful personality.' He was
extraordinarily controlling and independent: 'he did tire of people; he tired of
everyone sooner or later. Each friend had his or her allotted span in Mr
Lowry's life and when it was done, he moved on.'

Rohde notes that 'all his life he had been an original, unique in his vision,
in his approach to his art, in his attitudes to the Battle of Life. He resisted all
blandishments designed to bring him to a conventional and conformist old
age and remained steadfastly, obstinately, his own man.' Rohde also points out
the similarity of subject matter between Lowry and Pieter Brueghel.

Although Lowry admired Brueghel's work greatly, he bridled at the idea that he was influenced by anyone: control, independence and originality are critical to a person with autism.

Lowry was meticulous in keeping records, and a stickler for punctuality.

Speech, language and humour

It appears that Lowry, unlike most people with Asperger's syndrome, did display a somewhat developed sense of humour. The artist Sheila Fell thought that he had a zany sense of humour, and that 'as a companion he was marvellously humorous, inquisitive, mischievous as a child and gentle, but he was more than that: he had great shrewdness and understanding. In short, he was unique.' Lowry's friend David Carr was 'possibly the most attuned to his quirky sense of humour'. As Carr's wife put it: 'They saw the odd side of life together.'

According to Rohde, Lowry's speech was 'a blend of Dickensian rhetoric, de la Rochefoucauld cynicism, and dry Lancastrian humour'.

Lack of empathy

Referring to a drawing of a courting couple, Rohde notes that they 'are not touching, or sitting close, or even relating to one another'. In a way they have taken up autistic positions. More generally, it has often been noted that the figures in Lowry's paintings show little connection with each other. This is a possible autistic feature.

Lowry described himself as a 'cold fish', and stated that 'I usually prefer to be by myself'. In a paper prepared for publication in the *Journal of Mental Science*, Norman Colquhoun and Harold Palmer stated that Lowry

> reveals himself as a spectator in a world in miniature and moreover that the position he assumes is that of looking down on this world from a height. He is not making a social comment on man or his environment, but revealing a type of mental organisation which sees the world from the heightened standpoint of a watcher or spectator. Moreover, the spectator himself becomes identified with the scene he is watching; he is not only spectator, but is himself aware of being under observation.

Rohde notes that when Lowry announced his retirement from painting soon after his eightieth birthday, 'he was not so much laying down his brushes as retreating from the world in which he now found himself, a world he neither understood nor sought to understand'. When he retired from his rent-collector job after 42 years, 'he gave his colleagues no opportunity for an emotional send-off. "I'll not be in tomorrow", he announced casually.' He also showed a 'lack of emotion or interest when someone dear…had died. On at least two occasions he neither sent condolences nor attended the funerals of men with whom he had been especially friendly.' He was referred to as 'the Lowry automaton'.

On the other hand, Lowry did appear to show empathy at times. Sheila Fell said of him when he died:

> I miss his wit; I miss his humour; I miss him. He was a great humanist and no one ever seems to mention that. To be a humanist one has first to love human beings, and to be a great humanist one has to be slightly detached from human beings after having had great love for them; which is exactly what he was.

This again shows the problems with international classifications of autism and the criteria used. None of the criteria exactly describes every individual with autism. Autism presents in a myriad ways; every individual with autism is different and unique, and has features that would lead a person superficially examining them to say that this person can't have autism.

Naïvety and childishness

Lowry was 'politically naïve'. He was variously called 'primitive', 'almost childish', 'self-taught'. According to Pat Cooke, 'he had no real understanding of sexuality because, I believe, he had no experience of it'. At 34 years of age, he was said to be 'quite unmotivated by ambition'.

Motor clumsiness

As a child, Lowry was clumsy. Rohde states that he had a large nose, 'his hands and feet were disproportionately large on his tiny body, and he had difficulty in coordinating his limbs'.

Rohde remarks that in his capacity as rent collector he was 'something of a strange figure, and barefoot children followed him on his way, mimicking his lolloping gait and calling rude names from a safe distance'. She also describes him as 'a lurching, uncoordinated man'.

Appearance and demeanour

Maurice Collis (1951) described Lowry as a 'tallish man, rather thin, with a big nose and white hair, a haggard face which, nevertheless, is youthful. His mouth is sensitive, his gestures agitated, and his eyes shrink and yet are piercing.' Rohde notes that, as a young man, Lowry

> had a large oval head and a tache of sandy hair which, no matter how often he tried to smooth it, invariably stuck straight up from his head like a well-cropped field of hay, and which prompted one contemporary to describe him as looking like 'a boiled egg with pepper on top'.

He was a poor dresser.

Depression

Rohde notes: 'When in rare moments of despair he thought of ending it all, he dismissed such thoughts with the assertion that "it would have been an awful messy business for whoever found me".' Lowry also said: 'I know what it is to want to commit suicide. I can understand how people do. Life can get too much and you feel "Why not? It is only hastening the end."' Nonetheless, his depression did evaporate. Music partly saved him from suicide, as it did Ludwig Wittgenstein. Of course the major thing that saved him from suicide was his painting.

Harold Palmer, a doctor, stated that Lowry was

> a severely depressed man; sometimes he would wake in the morning, engulfed in a feeling of awful desolation, and, not knowing how he was going to get through the day, would find himself, somehow, before his easel with perhaps a brush in each hand and no recollection of having painted what he now saw before him.

Sexuality

James Fitton, who knew Lowry at art school, described him as 'an asexual being; a kind of neuter'.

Rohde refers to rather dark aspects of Lowry's 'repressed sexuality' as expressed in some unsigned drawings discovered long after his death, and points out that 'the more perceptive of the critics' had been aware of these aspects for some time:

> Richard Dorment, writing in the *Daily Telegraph* after visiting the Arts Council Centenary Exhibition at the Barbican in 1988, observed: 'The section of the exhibition I found most revealing of Lowry's troubled inner life was that devoted to the late pencil drawings of the 1970s. A grotesque young girl with clawlike fingernails encased in a mini-skirt that looks like an instrument of torture, or a phallus-shaped cartoon

man, devoured by a grinning shark, seems to me to reveal a sexual anxiety which is never so much as hinted at in the work of the previous 60 years.

Ian Stephenson, in discussing Lowry's portraits of 'Ann', stated:

> I never regarded them as portraits of a real person. While I am prepared to believe that a girl called Ann quite probably existed, and Lowry quite probably knew her well, I do not believe that his image of Ann was of one individual person alone. If she was, I would not have liked to tangle with her – there was something terrifying about her: a Lucrezia Borgia or Clytemnestra.

Becoming less autistic as he grew older

There was evidence of a reduction in the compartmentalization of Lowry's relationships as he got older. This is a clear sign of some improvement in his autism. There is little doubt that Lowry's art was what kept him alive and stabilized his mental state. Rohde says:

> Films were to be made of him, much was to be written about him and more said; but the effect upon him was of rain upon granite. He changed a few of his ways, adjusted a few attitudes, bought a few things, but his lifestyle remained the same – the frugality and abstention from indulgence as seen in the non-smoking, non-drinking, non-womanising habits of a lifetime. His modesty and humility remained, and his determination to go his own way as an artist. The enjoyment he derived from his observation of what he liked to call the great Battle of Life was enough to bring him contentment, if not actual or lasting joy.

Indeed, this is a good summary of a person with high-functioning autism. The changes that can be made, and are made, are rather small. Life is a very difficult battle for a person with high-functioning autism.

L.S. LOWRY CERTAINLY had Asperger's syndrome. He displayed enough of the traits associated with Asperger's syndrome to meet the criteria for this condition.

TWENTY ONE

Andy Warhol

(1928–87)

IT HAS BEEN said that Andy Warhol is now famous chiefly for one much-quoted saying: 'In the future, everyone will be famous for 15 minutes.' Nonetheless, he was one of the most famous artists of the 20th century, and is possibly more famous now than ever.

Warhol was the pioneer and leading exponent of pop art, and an influen-

tial avant-garde filmmaker, as well as being involved in other fields. He is heavily associated with cultural upheavals of the 1960s, the New York drug and homosexual scenes and the later punk rock movement, and has been described as the inventor of the lifestyle of the 1960s.

Many aspects of Warhol's life are indicative of Asperger's syndrome, as this chapter will attempt to show. Unless otherwise indicated, the biographical details and quoted extracts in this chapter come from Bockris (1997).

© Martin Bobrovsky/Alamy

Life history

Andy Warhol was born on 6 August 1928 in Pittsburgh, the third son of emigrants from Eastern Europe named Ondrej (Andrew) and Julia Warhola. (He later said that being born was a mistake, that it was like 'being kidnapped and sold into slavery'.) His father was a dour, strongly built roadworker; his mother, who had more difficulty adjusting to American life, was strong and resilient but 'wildly superstitious and eccentric'.

Warhol later described himself as an aggressive and pushy child, although his demeanour at school has been described as 'so shy he could hardly speak'. Others said that he was an intelligent loner, in a world of his own (many Asperger's syndrome subjects show very high intelligence). John Warhol, his brother, remembers Andy drawing on the porch a lot (this mirrors Ramanujan doing mathematics on the porch in India: (Fitzgerald 2004). He was bullied at school.

His mother was like him in many respects. She was a loner and hardly ever went out, except to the grocery store. She has been variously described as complex, mad, manipulative, powerful, weird and a myth-maker – all of this under a 'naïve peasant exterior'. She was chaotic in terms of the organization of her home, and is reported as having said on one occasion 'I am Andy Warhol'. It is quite possible that she also had Asperger's syndrome. She was described as a pack rat, with the habit of never discarding anything – this, as we shall see, also describes Andy.

Warhol studied at Carnegie Institute of Technology, and then became a successful commercial artist in New York before finding fame with colourful and repetitive reproductions, especially screenprints, of everyday objects and celebrities. He gathered a coterie of strange, creative acolytes at his Greenwich Village 'Factory'.

Warhol was described as having 'the kind of strength people who are leaders have' (several well-known leaders have in fact had Asperger's syndrome). However, he had a fear of death and of hospitals, and delayed a routine operation to remove gallstones to the point where the condition became life-threatening. He died in a New York hospital on 22 February 1987, at the age of 58.

Work

A student called Lelia Davies said: 'His work stood out, because he seemed to have a different approach. His development of a project would always be a little more unique than anybody else's.' (Persons with autism/Asperger's syndrome are frequently described as 'unique'.)

A friend, Charles Lisanby, stated:

> Andy didn't really know what he wanted to do with art at all. He was totally unfocussed. Except he had this overwhelming creative drive to do something and never stopped going. It would have helped if he could have been a little more specific but he didn't know what it was he should be doing, or could be doing, or ought to be doing. It was very strange.

It appears that he was going through a period of autistic identity diffusion.

Bockris notes that Warhol

> called upon everything he had learned from advertising and television, where the dollar sign and the gun were the predominant symbols and the common denominator was to arouse sexual desires without satisfying them and to shock. He decided to paint a series of big black and white pictures of what artists were suppose to hate most, advertisements for wigs, nose jobs, television sets and cans of food... The paintings were ugly and banal but reverberated with anger and contempt.

One observer said 'basically it was an act of compulsion, he had to do it'. A second series of paintings depicted his childhood heroes Dick Tracy, Popeye, Little Nancy. He painted pictures of Coke bottles.

The critic Robert Hughes described Warhol as 'the shallow painter whose entire sense of reality was shaped, like Reagan's sense of power, by the television tube' (Hughes 1982). He was fascinated by television. The screenwriter Robert Heidie said that Warhol told him that, even though he had learned to draw the required bowl of fruit on the dining-table at art school, what he really wanted to paint was that can of Campbell's tomato soup (his favourite) from his mother's pantry.

With the Campbell soup cans, Warhol decided to do one portrait of each of the 32 cans as exactly as possible, alone against a white background – showing his autistic repetitiveness. He came to symbolize the time in America, and what is extraordinary is that it was being symbolized by an artist with autism. He convinced the art world, with some exceptions, that this 'autistic' view was one to be reckoned with. *Time* magazine ridiculed him, but he didn't care. It was advertising. It gave him publicity. Warhol captured the imagination of the media and the public as no other artist of his generation. 'Andy was pop and pop was Andy'.

Warhol said: 'I just paint things I always thought were beautiful, things you use every day and never think about' (*Time*, 11 May 1962). His autistic eye for art was what made his paintings so dramatic. They were from a completely new angle, and of subjects that artists had not previously considered. A person with Asperger's syndrome typically sees possibilities from a totally new angle. This approach undermined standard patterns of art.

Warhol was very pleased to be told about screenprinting – a quick and easy means of indulging his penchant for repetition.

Indicators of Asperger's syndrome

Social behaviour

In art class as a child, Andy, rather than playing with the other children, went straight to his desk, got out his materials and began to draw. He 'drew and drew and drew', never looking up to discuss his work (as an adult he would behave very similarly in company, drawing 'like a robot' while the talk flowed around him). One of the other youngsters recalled that 'he wasn't part of any of the cliques, he was sort of left out'. He always had huge difficulties in interpersonal relationships.

Later, a teacher described him as

> [P]ersonally not attractive, and a little bit obnoxious. He had no consideration for other people. He lacked all the amenities. He was socially inept...and showed little or no appreciation for anything. He was not pleasant with the members of his class or with any of the people with whom he associated.

He always tended to isolate himself at parties. He was confused in the sense of 'wanting to have a romantic involvement with another man and his almost insurmountable incapacity to do so'. He once said that he was from another planet, and didn't know how he got here: persons with Asperger's syndrome often describe themselves as aliens. He was also described as 'a fragile night creature who discovered himself living in the blaze of an alien but fascinating world'. An onlooker at an art show described him as 'like a white witch, looking at America from an alien and obtuse angle' (i.e. an autistic angle).

Andy Warhol behaved towards Truman Capote as a stalker would behave. He sent Capote letters every day, and would hang around outside the building where Capote lived, waiting to see him go in and out. To Capote, Warhol appeared to be 'just a hopeless born loser, the loneliest, most friendless person I had ever seen in my life'. Warhol was also a foot fetishist – later on he found kissing his lover's shoes particularly erotic. He made drawings of many feet as well as of male genitalia.

He often appeared not to know how to behave in social situations: for example, on one occasion he returned to the USA with a friend and immediately left the friend at the airport with all his bags and packages, getting into a cab and going home without saying a word. When Andy was confronted with this, he said he thought he was supposed to go home alone. This is very similar to an incident in Dublin when Ludwig Wittgenstein, while waiting in a queue in O'Connell Street, took off without saying goodbye or giving any explanation (Fitzgerald 2004). Another friend described Warhol as 'the Cheshire cat. Just when you're sure he'll be somewhere, he vanishes' (Carrol 1969).

Warhol did not adopt the customary social postures in relation to death and bereavement, and hence was often seen as unfeeling. He did not attend his mother's funeral. When his friend Freddie Herko danced out of a fifth-floor window while high on LSD, Andy's reaction was: 'Why didn't he tell me he was going to do it? We could have gone down there and filmed it.' According to Bockris, 'when Ralph Ward's long-term friend Dougie died, Andy presented no condolences but eagerly asked if his Tchelitchev paintings were for sale, earning Ralph's lasting contempt'. When the fashion photographer Dick Rutledge said that he was going to kill himself, Andy asked if he could have his watch. Rutledge took it off and threw it at him. Andy kept the watch for the rest of his life.

It seemed to be easy for him to wipe people out of his life and to erase them from his mind. He admitted to having no very close friendships. The underground film actor Taylor Mead stated that 'Andy didn't give a shit about people. He was out of it as a human. His word meant nothing.' The art critic Otto Hahn wrote that Warhol found his only exaltation

> in this frigidity and anonymity which kills the good and the bad, which sadistically degrades the world where emotion proliferates, which kills human warmth, childhood. He needs to kill any sentiment within and without himself in order to achieve a clean, mechanical world. And when everything is sparse and emotionless, the world becomes pure…and the frozen universe, where Andy Warhol finds refuge to protect himself from the world, then becomes livable. (Hahn 1965)

Bockris states that 'Andy became more humanised in the 80s'. Persons with Asperger's syndrome can become less autistic; this was seen with Spinoza (Chapter 9), Lowry (Chapter 20) and Wittgenstein (Fitzgerald 2004).

Narrow interests and obsessiveness

Warhol had a collecting mania and also tended to be obsessive, for example about work, publicity and his health. When his apartment was entered after his death, his dining room was described as the room of a shopper, an accumulator, a pack rat with all the money in the world – a hoarder rather than a collector in the sense of a connoisseur. Much of what he collected and bought was never unpacked. The rooms had 'the air of a never-visited but exceedingly well-kept provincial museum'. Bockris quotes a friend who said that Andy 'found a lot of absurdity in the auction rooms. He loved the absurdity of the art world just as he loved the absurdity of life in general.' Of course, from an autistic perspective life does appear absurd. Persons with Asperger's syndrome are often attracted to nonsense.

Robert Hughes wrote that Warhol 'went after publicity with the voracious singlemindedness of a feeding bluefish' (Hughes 1982). He was also described as the most single-minded and most spectacular artist. He was obsessed with his health and, like many people with Asperger's syndrome, everything he did was related to his work. He rarely went anywhere for fun. He even went to movies in an obsessive way.

Routines and control

One reason for Warhol's success may have been that he represented the machine age. Romanticism was meaningless to him; the machine age was everything.

> Andy loved all sorts of machines and gadgets, embracing new techniques and technologies, working with tape recorders, cassettes, Polaroid, Thermofax, but the heart of all this experimentation had as its central focus photography and silkscreen for making a painting. This was by extension his love for the machine because the screen process was very machinelike. (Malanga and Giulano 1988)

Warhol told *Time* magazine in May 1963: 'The things I want to show you are mechanical. Machines have less problems. I would like to be a machine, wouldn't you?' Much of his work relied heavily on machine-like repetition. He had the autistic mechanical mind.

Speech, language and humour

When Barbara Deisroth of Sotheby's visited Warhol's rooms after his death, she thought that 'there was no life, no laughter'. According to Bockris, a childhood friend said that he couldn't remember Andy laughing – 'He always had a kind of sad face'.

The critic Peter York wrote that 'the absolute flatness [of his voice], the affectlessness meant you couldn't see behind it all' (York 1984). He was also reported to have 'a high-pitched voice', and to use 'ungrammatical speech patterns'. The Bob Dylan song 'Like a Rolling Stone' contains the lines 'You used to be so amused/At Napoleon in rags, and the language that he used'. 'Napoleon in rags' is said to be Warhol, although this may not be significant!

Bockris refers to Warhol's 'peculiar way of communicating his ideas, often by a single word'. His spelling was said to be 'atrocious', and his reading skills were poor.

Naïvety and childishness

As a young adult, Warhol was described as 'the damnedest mixture of a six-year-old child' and a well-trained artist; it was also said that he was 'very naïve and left himself open... He was like an angel in the sky at the beginning of his college times', and became the class baby. There was something fragile and unprotected about him.

The critic John Richardson said that Andy was 'a throwback to that Russian phenomenon the *yurodivyi* (the holy fool): the simpleton whose quasi-divine naïveté protects him against an inimical world' (Richardson 1987). Historically, persons with autism have often been described in this way.

Motor clumsiness

Warhol was a clumsy dancer: after he took modern-dance lessons as a young man, the teacher described him as 'a nut'. He had little natural rhythm and 'found it agonising to do his pliés'.

According to Bockris, 'often he would leave his shoes untied. One friend maintained that Andy never knew how to knot a tie.'

Anxiety and depression

According to Bockris, in 1959 and half of 1960 Warhol had what he called a nervous breakdown: 'a period when he was hurting very much inside, was very confused, and did not know what to do about it'. He blamed the problem on 'picking up problems from the people I knew. I had never felt that I had problems, because I had never specifically defined any...but now I felt that these problems of friends were spreading themselves on to me like germs.'

He tended to panic: sometimes he had death anxiety during the night and would telephone and arrange to meet a friend such as Henry Geldzahler, a museum curator, who saw 'a man who had detached himself from his emotions and got stuck on the way between heaven and hell in a kind of metaphysical twilight zone where he was alone with his work' (Geldzahler 1987). He was 'very much a night creature and literally afraid to go to sleep at night. He wouldn't fall asleep until dawn cracked because sleep equals death and night is fearsome.' Also, as we have seen, he was very fearful of hospitals and doctors.

Idiosyncrasies

Warhol was certainly narcissistic, and fed his narcissism with his publicity and his control of other people. He was often described as a voyeur, for example by Mick Jagger. He was voyeuristic both in the specifically sexual sense and in the wider sense of a person who truly enjoyed vicariously the experiences of others. He got enormous satisfaction from seeing people abusing drugs and alcohol and behaving in eccentric ways.

Henry Geldzahler said:

> Andy was a voyeur-sadist and he needed exhibitionist-masochists in order to fulfil both halves of his destiny. And it's obvious that an exhibitionist-masochist is not going to last very long. And then the voyeur-sadist needs another exhibitionist-masochist. There are always more people around than Andy could use in any one situation. Therefore there was constant fighting to get into the royal enclave. (Geldzahler 1987)

FROM THE ABOVE, it is apparent that a very strong case can be made for the contention that Andy Warhol had Asperger's syndrome. He had major social relationship problems and showed a lack of empathy with people. He was a workaholic with very narrowly focused interests. He showed motor clumsiness and spoke in a monotonous voice. His thinking style was mechanical; he was extremely controlling and immature in personality. He was also an artistic genius.

Conclusion

What features of Asperger's syndrome might foster artistic success?

PERSONS WITH THE syndrome are often workaholics, highly persistent, content with their own company and solitary artistic occupations; they focus on detail with massive curiosity and total immersion; they are novelty-seekers in terms of their art, with massive imagination in their specialized spheres. They are also far less influenced by previous or contemporary artists in their work than are 'neurotypicals'. It appears that the autistic artist, because of his or her rather diffuse identity and diffuse psychological boundaries, has the capacity to do what the artist George Bruce described as being necessary for art: 'one must not just depict the objects, one must penetrate them, and one must oneself become the object' (quoted in Weeks and James 1997).

It appears to me that conflict also plays a role – their artistic work is an effort to sort out their confused identities, which are associated with their subtle language difficulties. The work is a focus of self-help or self-therapy (autotherapy). It can be an effort to sort out the perceptual puzzlement that they experience, and to make sense of their autistic worlds. They are driven by a desire for 'immortality', and they 'achieve' this with their works of art.

They often have a fascination with words and language, which would clearly be helpful in literary and philosophical work. Persons with Asperger's syndrome often suffer from depression, and artistic work can have an antide-pressant effect. They are probably more likely to get depressed when they suffer artistic blocks. Their artistic work boosts their often low self-esteem.

Literary works by persons with Asperger's syndrome often have strong autobiographical elements (e.g. Conan Doyle and Sherlock Holmes). They are thus a form of self-expression for persons with Asperger's syndrome, who find other forms of expression difficult.

The striking paradox is that living in an autistic world, persons with Asperger's syndrome have a great capacity to describe and illustrate the neurotypical (non-autistic) world. This is because they have a different perspective on account of their weak central coherence and focus on detail, and are able to show neurotypicals part of the world that they miss because of their normal global processing of the world for gist.

Persons with Asperger's syndrome generally have immature personalities and retain a child-like capacity. The retention of this child-like view helps their artistic work. They are also non-conformist, which creates novelty and interest.

Of course the writings of Asperger philosophers are often very difficult to understand because of their language and communication abnormalities. Weeks and James (1997) point out that while

> eccentrics may be more prone to express their thoughts in strange and aberrant ways, they are not less eloquent for that. If there were such a thing as speech that was purely logical and completely devoid of communication disorders, it would suffer from the worst linguistic defect of all: dullness. And while eccentrics may at times be infuriating, absurd or puzzling, they are never, never dull.

This applies in part to autistic artists, although we must be cautious in discussing eccentrics in the present context, as only some eccentrics have Asperger's syndrome.

Evolution, art and autism

Asperger's syndrome and high-functioning autism are highly genetic disorders. There appears to be an overlap between the constellation of genes for Asperger's syndrome/high-functioning autism and artistic creativity. The elaboration of this at a molecular genetic level is in the future. We are dealing with complex multigenetic traits.

Gardner (1997) is correct when he states that 'all forms of giftedness have some biological basis'. Nevertheless, creativity of genius proportions is rare. The coming together of a particular constellation of genes predisposing to creativity of genius happens only rarely. This book brings together a number of individuals in whom genius and Asperger's syndrome coincided. Clearly an artistically nurturing environment was partly necessary for their expression of these talents.

The development of the arts parallels the evolutionary development of the brain. The art of the great caves of Lascaux, Altamira, etc. was done about 30,000 years ago, and the 'Abbé Breuil viewed the paintings functionally as a form of hunting magic' ('if you draw them properly they will come') (Gould 2002).

Pinker (2002) points out that 'the study of evolutionary aesthetics is also documenting the features that make a face or body beautiful. The prized lineaments are those that signal health, vigour and fertility.' The possession of artistic ability and the capacity to produce great art makes the artist more attractive to potential mates, and therefore facilitates the reproduction of the artist's talent. This might be a partial explanation for the reproductive success of persons with Asperger's syndrome and artistic genius.

THE CREATIVE TALENTS of genius in this book have ranged over music, painting, literature, poetry and philosophy. This will surprise those that equate Asperger's syndrome with engineering and mathematics. The book is a celebration of persons with artistic genius and Asperger's syndrome. Of course the vast majority of persons with Asperger's syndrome do not have talent of genius proportions, but then neither do the vast majority of so-called normal people – the 'neurotypicals'.

References

Alldritt, K. (1997) *W.B. Yeats – The Man and the Milieu*. London: John Murray.

American Psychiatric Association (APA) (1994) *Diagnostic and Statistical Manual of Mental Disorders* (revised 4th edition). Washington, DC: American Psychiatric Association.

Andersen, H.C. (1975) *The Fairy Tale of My Life* (first published 1855). London: Paddington Press.

Asperger, H. (1944) 'Die "Autistischen Psychopathen" im Kindesalter.' *Archiv für Psychiatrie und Nervenkrankheiten 117*, 76–136. Translated in U. Frith (ed.) (1991) *Autism and Asperger's Syndrome*. Cambridge: Cambridge University Press.

Asperger, H. (1974) 'Formen des Autismus bei Kindern.' *Deutsches Ärzteblatt 14*, 4.

Attwood, T. (1991) *Asperger's Syndrome*. London: Jessica Kingsley Publishers.

Ayer, A.J. (1977) *Part of My Life*. London: Collins.

Ayer, A.J. (1980) 'The identity of indiscernibles.' In *Philosophical Essays*. London: Greenwood Press.

Ayer, A.J. (1984) *More of My Life*. London: Collins.

Barlow, F. (1952) *Mental Prodigies*. London: Hutchinson.

Baron-Cohen, S. (2003) *The Essential Difference*. London: Penguin.

Bartley, W.W. (1973) 'Lewis Carroll as a logician.' *Times Literary Supplement*, 15 June, p.665.

Bester, A. (1964) 'The zany genius of Glenn Gould.' *Holiday 35*, no. 4, April, p.156.

Biederman, J. (1998) 'Resolved: Mania is mistaken for ADHD in prepubertal children.' *Journal of the American Academy of Child and Adolescent Psychiatry 37* 10, 1091–1093.

Blakemore, C. (1988) *The Mind Machine*. London: BBC Books.

Bloch, W. (1975) *Paa Rejse med H.C. Andersen*, Copenhagen, 1942. Translated by Reginald Spink in Danish Ministry of Foreign Affairs, *Danish Journal*, Copenhagen, p.13.

Bockris, V. (1997) *Warhol*. New York: Da Capo Press.

Braithwaite, D. (1959) 'Glenn Gould.' *Toronto Daily Star*, 28 March.

Brandes, G. (1886) *Eminent Authors of the Nineteenth Century*. New York: Crowell.

Bredsdorff, E. (1954) *H.C. Andersen og England*. Copenhagen: Rosenkilde og Bagger.

Briggs, J. (1955) *Musical Courier 153*, 3, 1 February, p.86.

Brown, T. (1999) *The Life of W.B. Yeats – A Critical Biography*. Dublin: Gill and Macmillan.

Cage, J. (1958) *Art News Annual 27*, 81.

Carey, J. (1999) 'Collected poems by Yeats.' *Sunday Times*, 18 June 1999, p.7.

Carrol, P. (1969) 'What's a Warhol?' *Playboy 16*, no.9.

Carter, R. (1998) *Mapping the Mind*. London: Weidenfeld and Nicolson.

Chalmers, K. (1995) *Béla Bartók*. London: Phaidon Press.

Cohen, M.N. (1995) *Lewis Carroll: A Biography*. London: Papermac.

Collin, E. (1882) *H.C. Andersen og det Collinske Huus*. Copenhagen: C.A. Reitzels Forlag.

Collin, J. (1945–8) *H.C. Andersens Brevveksling med Jonas Collin den Ældre og andre Medlemmer af det Collinske hus* (3 vols, ed. H. Topsøe-Jensen). Vol. 1, Letters of Hans Christian Andersen to Jonas Collin. Copenhagen: Det danske Sprog og, Litteraturselskab.

Collis, M. (1951) *The Discovery of LS Lowry*. London: Alex Reid and Lefevre.

Colum, M. (1939) 'Memories of Yeats.' *The Saturday Review of Literature XIX*, 25 February, p.4.

Cox, C.M. (1926) *Genetic Studies of Genius. Vol. II: The Early Mental Traits of Three Hundred Geniuses*. Stanford, CA: Stanford University Press.

Cronin, A. (1999) 'Down from Olympus.' *Sunday Independent*, 29 August, p.9.

Davies, P. (1987) 'Mozart's manic depressive tendencies.' *Musical Times*, 123–126.

Davies, P. (1989) *Mozart in Person: His Character and Health*. Westport, CT: Greenwood Press.

Deglar, C.N. (1991) *In Search of Human Nature*. Oxford: Oxford University Press.

de Villiers, J. (2000) 'Language and theory of mind: What are the developmental relationships?' In S. Baron-Cohen, H. Tager-Flusberg and D.J. Cohen (eds) *Understanding Other Minds*. Oxford: Oxford University Press.

Edmonds, D. and Eidinow, J. (2001) *Wittgenstein's Poker*. London: Faber and Faber.

Elias, A.C. (ed) (1997) *Memoirs of Laetitia Pilkington*, 2 vols. Athens, GA: University of Georgia Press. First published as *Memoirs of Mrs Laetitia Pilkington, Written by Herself*, 3 vols., 1749–54.

Ellmann, R. (1979) *Yeats: The Man and the Masks*. London: Penguin.

Fitzgerald, M. (1999) 'Did Isaac Newton have Asperger's syndrome?' *European Child and Adolescent Psychiatry Journal 8*, 24.

Fitzgerald, M. (2000) 'Did Bartók have High Functioning Autism/Asperger's Syndrome?' *Autism – European Link 29*, 21.

Fitzgerald, M. (2004) *Autism and Creativity: Is There a Link Between Autism in Men and Exceptional Ability?* Hove: Brunner-Routledge.

Fedor, J. (2001) 'Dicing with shadows.' *Times Literary Supplement*, 6 July, p.6.

Foster, J. (1985) *Ayer*. London: Routledge.

Freeman, D. (1983) *Margaret Mead and Samoa: the Making and Unmaking of an Anthropological Myth*. Cambridge, MA: Harvard University Press.

Frith, U. (1989) *Autism: Explaining the Enigma*. Oxford: Blackwell.

Frith, U. and Houston, R. (2000) *Autism in History*. Oxford: Blackwell.

Fulford, R. (1976) 'Beach boy.' In W. Kilbourn (ed) *The Toronto Book* (pp.89–98). Toronto: Macmillan of Canada.

Gagne, F. (1998) 'A biased survey and interpretation of the nature–nurture literature.' *Behavioral and Brain Sciences 21*, 3, 415–416.

Gardner, H. (1993) *Frames of Mind: The Theory of Multiple Intelligences*. London: Fontana.

Gardner, H. (1997) *Extraordinary Minds: Portraits of Exceptional Individuals and an Examination of Our Extraordinariness*. London: Weidenfeld and Nicolson.

Geldzahler, H. (1987) 'Andy Warhol – A tribute.' *Vogue* (UK) *144*, no. 5.

Gillberg, C. (1991) 'Clinical and neurobiological aspects in six family studies of Asperger's syndrome.' In U. Frith (ed) *Autism and Asperger's Syndrome*. Cambridge: Cambridge University Press.

Gillberg, C. (1996) 'Asperger's syndrome and high functioning autism.' Blake Marsh Lecture, *Quarterly Meeting of Royal College of Psychiatrists*, Stratford-upon-Avon.

Gillberg, C. (2002) *A Guide to Asperger's Syndrome.* Cambridge: Cambridge University Press.

Gillberg, C. and Coleman, M. (2000) *The Biological Basis of Autism.* Cambridge: MacKeith Press.

Gillmor, A.M. (1988) *Erik Satie.* Basingstoke: Macmillan.

Glendinning, V. (1998) *Jonathan Swift.* London: Hutchinson.

Gould, G. (1966a) *Conversations with Glenn Gould: Bach* (film). BBC.

Gould, G. (1966b) 'The prospects of recording.' *High Fidelity Magazine 16,* no. 4, April, p.49.

Gould, G. (1967) Broadcast. CBC, 30 April.

Gould, G. (1970a) 'His country's "most experienced hermit" chooses a desert-island discography.' *High Fidelity Magazine 20,* no. 6, 29–32.

Gould, G. (1970b) 'The well-tempered listener' (telecast). CBC, 22 March.

Gould, G. (1971) Liner notes to *The Idea of North* (disc). CBC, PR-8.

Gould, G. (1974) *The Age of Ecstasy* (telecast). CBC, 20 February.

Gould, G. (1974–5) 'An epistle to the Parisians: Music and technology, Part I.' *Piano Quarterly 23,* no. 88, Winter, p.18.

Gould, G. (1975) *Radio as Music* (film). CBC.

Gould, S.J. (2002) *The Structure of Evolutionary Theory.* Cambridge, MA: Harvard University Press.

Grandin, T. (1995) *Thinking in Pictures – And Other Reports from My Life with Autism.* New York: Doubleday.

Gray, F. du P. (2001) *Simone Weil.* London: Weidenfeld and Nicolson.

Gregory, R. (1987) *Oxford Companion to the Mind.* Oxford: Oxford University Press.

Gullan-Whur, M. (1998) *Within Reason: A Life of Spinoza.* London: Jonathan Cape.

Haggin, B.H. (1964) 'Music and ballet chronicle.' *Hudson Review 17,* no. 3, Autumn, pp.441–442.

Hahn, O. (1965) Ileana Sonnabend Flowers catalogue, Paris.

Hallowell, E. and Ratey, J. (1994) *Answers to Distraction.* New York: Bantam Books.

Hamann, J.G. (1776) *Briefwechsel,* Vols. 5, 6.

Happé, F. (1994) *Autism: An Introduction to Psychological Theory.* London: University College London Press.

Happé, F. (1999) 'Autism: cognitive deficit or cognitive style?' *Trends in Cognitive Sciences 3,* 6, 216–222.

Happé, F. (2001) 'Why success is more interesting than failure.' In J. Richer and S. Coates (eds) *Autism – The Search for Coherence.* London: Jessica Kingsley Publishers.

Harding, J. (1975) *Erik Satie.* London: Secker & Warburg.

Heine, H. (1955) *Adam International Review,* nos. 248–249, p.3.

Heine, H. (1962) 'Religion und Philosophie in Deutschland.' *Lyrik und Prosa.* 2 vols (ed. M. Greiner). Frankfurt am Main: Büchergilde Gutenberg.

Heller, K.A. and Ziegler, A. (1998) 'Experience is no improvement over talent.' *Behavioral and Brain Sciences 21,* 3, 417–418.

Henry, L. (1921) 'Socrate and the new asceticism.' *Musical Standard,* 23 April, p. 146.

Hermelin, B. (2001) *Bright Splinters of the Mind.* London: Jessica Kingsley Publishers.

Hoffman, P. (1998) *The Man Who Loved Only Numbers.* London: Fourth Estate.

Howe, M.A. (1999) *Genius Explained.* Cambridge: Cambridge University Press.

Hughes, R. (1982) 'The rise of Andy Warhol.' *New York Review of Books 29,* 2.

Iles, G. (1906) *Inventors at Work*. New York: Doubleday.

Jamison, K.R. (1991) 'Van Gogh: Meniere's disease?' *Journal of the American Medical Association 265*, 723–724.

Jamison, K.R. (1993) *Touched with Fire*. New York: Free Press.

Jardine, L. (1999) 'Female muse.' *New Statesman*, 21 June, p.48.

Jordan, R. and Powell, S. (1995) *Understanding and Teaching Children with Autism*. Chichester: Wiley.

Kanner, L. (1943) 'Autistic disturbances of affective contact.' *The Nervous Child 2*, 217.

Kant, I. (1967) *Philosophical Correspondence, 1759–1799* (ed. and trans. A. Zweig). Chicago: University of Chicago Press.

Kant, I. (1990) *Gesammelte Schriften*, published by Preussische Akademie der Wissenschaften. Vols. 1, 6, 7, 10, 20. Berlin: Walter de Gruyter.

Kennedy, D.M. (2002) *The ADHD Autism Connection: A Step Toward More Accurate Diagnosis and Effective Treatment*. Colorado Springs, CO: Waterbrook Press.

Kolb, A. (1937) *Mozart*. Vienna: Bermann-Fisher Verlag (also published in 1998 by Prion Books, London).

Kuehn, M. (2001) *Kant*. Cambridge: Cambridge University Press.

Larsen, S. (1941–6) 'H.C. Andersens Brevveksling med Henriette Hanck 1830–46.' In *Anderseniana IX-XIII*, Hans Christian Andersen to Henriette Hanck, Odense, November 1834.

Loftus, L.S. and Arnold, W.N. (1991) 'Vincent van Gogh's illness: Acute intermittent porphyria?' *British Medical Journal 303*, 1589–91.

Longe, J. (ed.) (1911) *Martha, Lady Giffard, Her Life and Correspondence, 1664–1722*. London: Allen.

Lubin, A.J. (1972) *Stranger on the Earth: A Psychological Biography of Vincent van Gogh*. New York: Holt, Rinehart and Winston.

Lykken, D.T. (1998) 'The genetics of genius.' In A. Steptoe (ed) *Genius and the Mind*. Oxford: Oxford University Press.

Lykken, D., Gue, M., Tellegen, A. and Bouchard, T. (1992) 'Emergenesis: Genetic traits that may not run in families.' *American Psychologist 47*, 12, 1072.

McGahern, J. (1999) 'Introduction.' In J. Hone (ed) *John Butler Yeats: Letters to his Son W.B. Yeats and Others, 1869–1922*. London: Faber and Faber.

McGee, H. (1999) 'Romantic Yeats is dead and gone.' *Sunday Tribune*, 30 May, p.8.

Maddox, B. (1999) *George's Ghosts: A New Life of W.B. Yeats*. London: Picador.

Malanga, G. and Giulano, C. (1988) 'Working with Warhol'. *Art New England*.

Malter, R. (1990) *Kant in Rede und Gespräch*. Hamburg: Felix Meiner Verlag.

Mead, M. (1949) *Male and Female*. New York: William Morrow.

Mesibov, G., Shea, V. and Adam, L. (2001) *Understanding Asperger's Syndrome and High Functioning Autism*. Lancaster: Kluwer Academic/Plenum Press.

Meyers, J. (2000) *Orwell: Wintry Conscience of a Generation*. New York: Norton.

Mikhail, E.H. (1977) *W.B. Yeats: Interviews and Recollections* (Vol. 1). London: Macmillan.

Miller, B.L., Cummings, J., Mishkin, F., Boone, K., Prince, F., Ponton, M. and Cotman, C. (1998) 'Emergence of artistic talent in fronto-temporal dementia.' *Neurology 51*, 978–982.

Monk, R. (1990) *Ludwig Wittgenstein – The Duty of Genius*. London: Jonathan Cape.

Morrisroe, P. (1997) *Mapplethorpe: A Biography*. New York: Da Capo Press.

Mottron, L. and Burack, J. (2001) 'Enhanced perceptual functioning.' in J. Burack, T. Charman, N. Yirmiya and P. Zelazo (eds) *The Development of Autism.* Mahwah, NJ: Lawrence Erlbaum.

Murray, P. (ed) (1989) *Genius: The History of an Idea.* Oxford: Basil Blackwell.

Myers, P. (1973) 'Glenn Gould.' *Gramophone 50,* no. 597, February, p.1478.

O'Connor, N. and Hermelin, B. (1987) 'Visual and graphic abilities of the idiot savant artist.' *Psychological Medicine 17,* 79–90.

O'Connor, N. and Hermelin, B. (1989) 'Visual memory and motor programmes: Their use by idiot-savant artists and controls.' *British Journal of Psychology 78,* 3, 307–323.

Ollard, R. (1999) *A Man of Contradictions – A Life of A.L. Rowse.* London: Allen Lane.

Payzant, G. (1997) *Glenn Gould: Music and Mind* (6th edn). Toronto: Key Porter Books.

Pinker, S. (2002) *The Blank Slate.* London: Allen Lane.

Plomin, R. (1998) 'Genetic influence and cognitive abilities.' *Behavioural and Brain Sciences 21,* 3, 420–421.

Prior, M. and Ozonoff, S. (1998) 'Psychological factors in autism.' In F. Volkmar (ed) *Autism and Pervasive Developmental Disorders.* Cambridge: Cambridge University Press.

Pyle, H. (1970) *Jack B. Yeats: A Biography* (rev. edn). London: Andre Deutsch.

Quigley, J. (2000) *The Grammar of Autobiography: A Developmental Account.* Hillsdale, NJ: Lawrence Erlbaum.

Radford, J. (1990) *Child Prodigies and Exceptional Early Achievers.* Hemel Hempstead: Harvester Wheatsheaf.

Richardson, J. (1987) 'The secret Warhol.' *Vanity Fair 50,* no. 7.

Rimland, B. (1978) 'Inside the mind of the autistic savant.' *Psychology Today 12,* 3, 69–80.

Rink, F.T. (1805) *Ansichten aus Immanuel Kants Leben.* Königsberg: Göbbels & Unzer.

Robertson-Lorant, L. (1998) *Melville: A Biography.* Amherst: University of Massachusetts Press.

Roddy, J. (1960) 'Apollonian.' *The New Yorker 36,* no. 13, 14 May, p.52.

Rogers, B. (1999) *AJ Ayer: A Life.* New York: Grove Press.

Rohde, S. (1999) *L.S. Lowry: A Biography* (3rd edn). Salford: The Lowry Press.

Rutland, H. (1959) 'Impressions of Glenn Gould.' *Musical Times 100,* no. 1397, July, p.388.

Sacks, O. (1995) *An Anthropologist on Mars.* London: Picador.

Sanders, W. (1917) *Musical News 53,* 8 Sept., 147–148.

Scar, S. and McCartney, K. (1983) 'How people make their own environments: A theory of genotype–environment effects.' *Child Development 54,* 424–435.

Schultz, R.T., Klin, A. and Volkmar, F.R. (2000) 'Abnormal ventral temporal cortical activity during face discrimination among individuals with autism and Asperger's syndrome.' *Archives of General Psychiatry 57,* 4, 331–340.

Self, W. (2001a) 'Weekend Review.' *The Independent,* 11 August, p.1.

Self, W. (2001b) 'Oh no, not another silly title.' *New Statesman,* 9 April, pp.5–52.

Shakespeare, N. (2000) *Bruce Chatwin: A Biography.* London: Vintage.

Shattock, P. and Savery, P. (1997) *Autism as a Metabolic Disorder.* Sunderland: Autism Research Unit.

Sigman, M. and Capps, L. (1997) *Children with Autism.* Cambridge, MA: Harvard University Press.

Simonton, D.K. (1991) 'Emergence and realization of genius: The lives and works of 120 classical composers.' *Journal of Personality and Social Psychology 61*, 829–840.

Simonton, D.K. (1994) *Greatness: Who Makes History and Why*. New York: Guilford Press.

Simonton, D.K. (1998) 'Defining and finding talent: Data and a multiplicative model?' *Behavioral and Brain Sciences 21*, 3, 424.

Slater, E. and Meyer, A. (1960) 'Contributions to pathography of the musicians. Organic and psychotic disorders.' *Confinia Psychiatrica 3*, 129–145.

Smalley, S.L., McCracken, J. and Tanguay, P. (1995) 'Autism, affective disorders, and social phobia.' *American Journal of Medical Genetics 60*, 19–26.

Solomon, M. (1998) *Beethoven*. New York: Schirmer Trade Books.

Stanley, J.C. (1993) *The Origins and Development of High Ability*. Ciba Foundation Symposium 178. Chichester: Wiley.

Stashower, D. (1999) *Teller of Tales: The Life of Arthur Conan Doyle*. London: Allen Lane.

Steptoe, A. (ed) (1998) *Genius and the Mind*. Oxford: Oxford University Press.

Stevens, H. (1993) *The Life and Music of Béla Bartók* (3rd edn, prepared by M. Gillies). Oxford: Oxford University Press.

Storey, M.G. (1939) *Dickens and Daughter*. London: Muller.

Storr, A. (1972) *The Dynamics of Creation*. London: Secker and Warburg.

Storr, A. (1988) *Solitude*. New York: The Free Press.

Stravinsky, I. and Craft, R. (1959) *Conversations with Igor Stravinsky*. London: Faber and Faber.

Tantam, D. (1991) 'Asperger's syndrome in adulthood.' In U. Frith (ed) *Autism and Asperger's Syndrome*. Cambridge: Cambridge University Press.

Thiele, J.M. (1873) *Af mit Livs Aarbøger 1795–1825*. Copenhagen: H. Hagerup.

Topsøe-Jensen, H. (ed) (1962) *H.C. Andersens Levnedsbøg*. Copenhagen: Schønberg.

Tovell, V. (1959) *At Home with Glenn Gould* (disc). Radio Canada Transcription E-156, CBC.

Twachtman-Cullen, D. (1998) *A Passion to Believe: Autism and the Facilitated Communication Phenomenon*. Boulder, CO: Westview Press.

van Krevelen, A. and Kuipers, C. (1962) 'The psychopathology of autistic psychopathy.' *Acta Paedopsychiatrica 29*, 22–31.

Volta, O. (ed) (1996) *Collected Writings of Erik Satie*. London: Atlas Press.

Vorländer, K. (1911) *Immanuel Kants Leben*. Leipzig: Felix Meiner.

Waterhouse, S. (2000) *A Positive Approach to Autism*. London: Jessica Kingsley Publishers.

Watson, J.B. (1924) *Behaviorism*. Chicago: University of Chicago Press.

Weeks, D. and James, J. (1997) *Eccentrics*. London: Phoenix.

West, T. (1991) *In the Mind's Eye*. Buffalo, NY: Prometheus Books.

Wetherby, A.M., Schuler, A. and Prizant, B. (1997) 'Enhancing language and communication development: Theoretical foundations.' In D.J. Cohen and F. Volkmar (eds) *Handbook of Autism and Pervasive Developmental Disorders* (2nd edn.). New York: Wiley.

Wilens, T., Prince, J., Biederman, J., Spencer, T. and Francis, R. (1995) 'Attention-deficit hyperactivity disorder and comorbid substance use disorders in adults.' *Psychiatric Services 46*, 8, 761–763.

Williams, D. (1998) *Autism and Sensing: The Unlost Instinct*. London: Jessica Kingsley Publishers.

Wilson, I. (1989) *Super Self.* London: Sidgwick & Jackson.

Wing, L. (1981) 'Asperger's syndrome – A clinical account.' *Psychological Medicine 11,* 115–129.

Wing, L. (1996) *The Autistic Spectrum.* London: Constable.

Winner, E. (1996) *Gifted Children: Myths and Realities.* New York: Basic Books.

Wodson, E.W. (1945) *Toronto Telegram,* 13 December.

Wodson, E.W. (1947) *Toronto Telegram,* 15 January.

Wolff, S. (1995) *Loners: The Life Path of Unusual Children.* London: Routledge.

Wollheim, R. (1992) 'Ayer: The man, the philosopher, the teacher.' in A.P. Griffiths (ed), *A.J. Ayer: Memorial Essays.* Cambridge: Cambridge University Press.

Wullschlager, J. (2000) *Hans Christian Andersen: The Life of a Storyteller.* London: Allen Lane.

Yeats, M.B. (1999) *Cast a Cold Eye – Memories of a Poet's Son and Politician.* Dublin: Blackwater Press.

York, P. (1984) 'The voice.' *Vanity Fair,* April.

Subject index

Author index